THE HOUSE & GARDEN BOOK OF
LIVING-ROOMS

(Opposite) An interior in Baltimore, decorated by Anthony Browne, skilfully combines the two most covetable of qualities for a drawing-room: comfort and sophistication. A country casualness, interwoven with refined furniture and decorative objects, produces a cheerful, colourful setting. Enlarged by the incorporation of the adjoining staircase-hall, the room has painted panelling on the chimneypiece wall and dado. Above the dado, chevron fabric is outlined with red-and-white braid.

THE HOUSE & GARDEN BOOK OF
LIVING-ROOMS

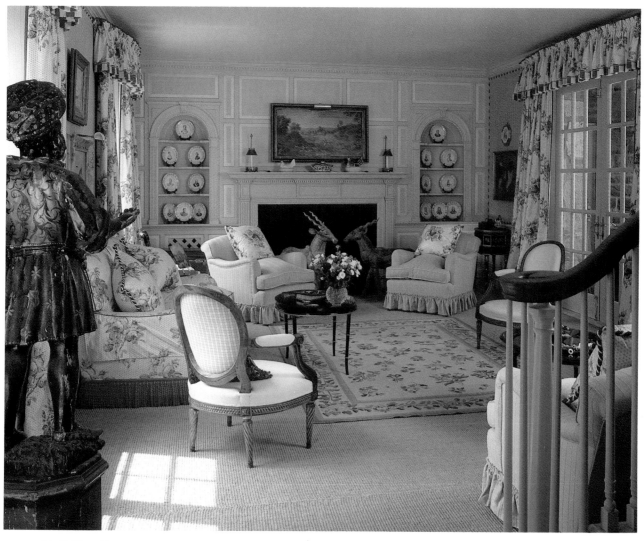

ROBERT HARLING · LEONIE HIGHTON · JOHN BRIDGES

The Vendome Press
New York

Acknowledgements

PHOTOGRAPHS

Ari Ashley and Peter Warner 95

Simon Brown 20, 21, 22, 23, 24, 25, 28, 36, 37, 54, 55, 64, 65, 68, 69, 84 (bottom right), 98 (top left), 101, 114, 115, 125 (top right, bottom right), 186 (bottom right), 187 (top left, bottom right), 196, 197, 207 (top right, bottom left), 209, 212, 213, 220, 221, 223 (bottom right)

Andreas von Einsiedel 12, 13, 14, 15, 16, 17, 29 (bottom left, bottom right), 31, 34, 35, 46, 47, 48, 49, 50, 51, 56, 57, 60, 61, 62, 63, 80, 81, 82, 83, 84 (top left), 88, 89, 94, 95, 98 (bottom left, bottom right), 99 (top right, bottom left), 102, 103, 110, 111, 116, 117, 118, 119, 120, 121, 122 (top left, bottom left, bottom right), 123 (top right, bottom right), 124, 128, 129, 130, 131, 132, 133, 148, 149, 158 (bottom), 164, 165, 168, 169, 174, 175, 176, 177, 187, (bottom left), 204, 205, 206 (bottom left), 207 (top left), 210, 211, 214, 215, 216, 217, 222 (top left), 223 (bottom left)

John Hollingshead 84 (top right), 206 (top left)

David Massey 144, 145, 159 (top left)

James Mortimer 52, 53, 87, 99 (bottom right), 123 (bottom left), 142, 143, 186 (top left), 222 (bottom left)

Keith Scott Morton 3, 11, 18, 19, 29 (top left), 74, 75, 84 (bottom left), 99 (top left), 106, 107, 108, 109, 139, 152, 153, 154, 155, 158 (top right), 159 (bottom left), 170, 171, 222 (top right, bottom right)

Antoine Rozes 38, 39, 40, 41, 70, 71

Ianthe Ruthven 44, 45

Fritz von der Schulenburg 26, 27, 29 (top right), 32, 33, 42, 43, 58, 59, 67, 72, 73, 78, 79, 85, 90, 91, 92, 93, 98 (top right), 104, 105, 112, 113, 122 (top right), 123 (top left), 125 (top left, bottom left), 127, 146, 147, 150, 151, 158 (bottom left), 166, 167, 172, 173, 178, 179, 182, 183, 184, 185, 186 (top right, bottom left), 187 (top right), 189, 190, 191, 192, 193, 194, 195, 200, 201, 202, 203, 206 (top right, bottom right), 207 (bottom right), 223 (top left, top right), 224

Rene Stoltie 76, 77, 96, 97

Jeremy Whitaker 159 (bottom right)

Many of the rooms illustrated in this book were researched
by Lavinia Bolton and Sally Griffiths

Published in the United States and Canada
by The Vendome Press
515 Madison Avenue
New York City 10022

Distributed by Rizzoli International Publications
300 Park Avenue South
New York City 10010

First published in 1991 by
Random Century Group Ltd
20 Vauxhall Bridge Road
London SW1V 2SA

© The Condé Nast Publications Ltd 1991

Library of Congress Cataloging-in-Publication Data

Harling, Robert.
    The House & garden book of living-rooms/by Robert Harling,
Leonie Highton, and John Bridges.
        p.   cm.
    ISBN 0-86565-125-6
        1. Living rooms.   2. Interior decoration.   I. Highton, Leonie.
II. Bridges, John.   III. House & garden.   IV. Title.   V. Title:
House & garden book of living-rooms.   VI. Title: Book of living-rooms.
NK2117.L5H37   1991   91–12815
747.7′5–dc20   CIP

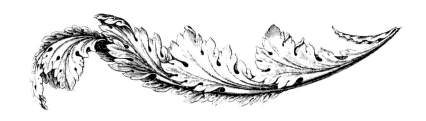

Contents

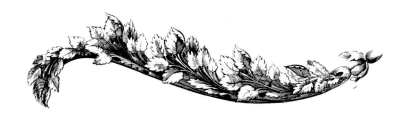

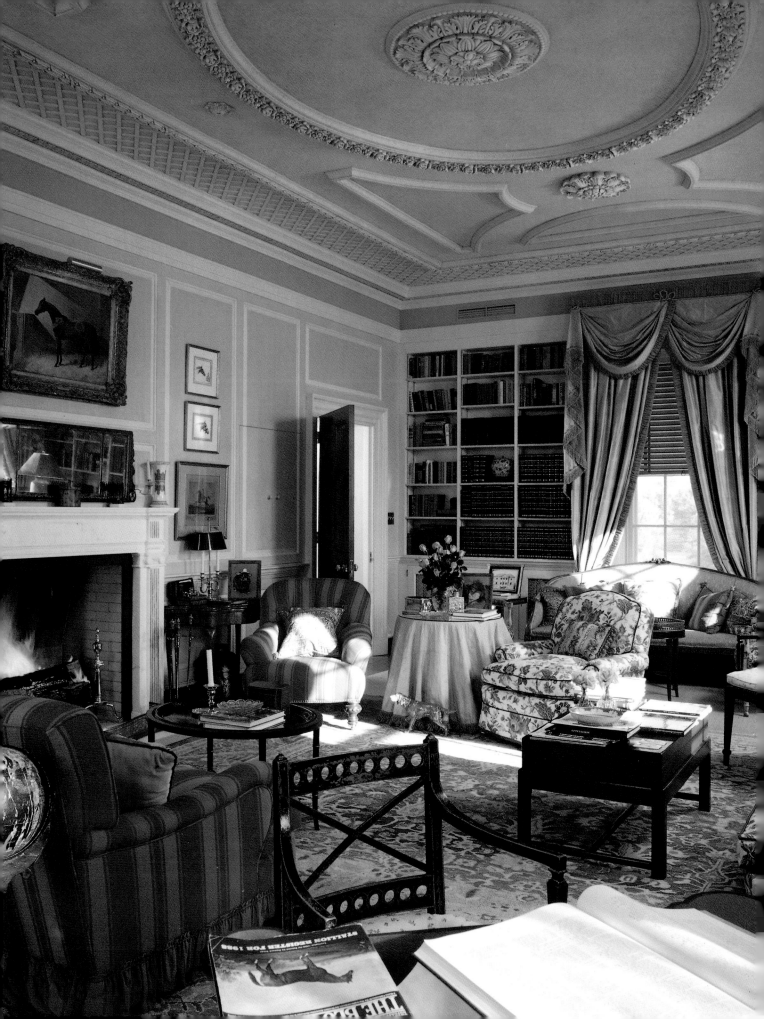

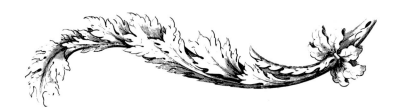

Heart of the home

Whether you call it a drawing-room, sitting-room or living-room, this room is now receiving wider decorative attention than ever. And that attention shows a marked interest in a return to traditional themes

The architects and cabinet-makers of the eighteenth and early nineteenth centuries – those notable characters who established the British and North American classical tradition – were men of positive views, outspoken comment and not a few quirks of character and outlook. Perhaps the most entertaining of these features was a supreme confidence in their own omnipotence. Not only in technical and aesthetic accomplishment, but in matters far more elusive of definition. Social behaviour, for example.

Most of these men had been reared in humble circumstance, usually followed by apprenticeship at a tender age to a stonemason's yard or a cabinet-maker's workshop. These modest beginnings did not, however, deter them from becoming, by the time they were forty or so, fully-fledged arbiters upon social as well as artistic matters. They knew what would be best for their patrons and expressed those views in handsome, authoritative pattern-books.

Consider, for example, the opinings of Thomas Sheraton, that legendary figure amongst furniture designers. Although no pieces made by Sheraton have been authenticated, he was a born authoritarian where matters of interior design and decoration were concerned. In his book, *The Cabinet Dictionary*, published in 1803, he is at his best on those interests clearly most near and dear to him: drawing-rooms and drawing-room furniture. The drawing-room was, he opined, 'the chief apartment of a noble or genteel house, to which it is usual for company to draw after dinner and in which formal visits are made.' (Sheraton's use of the term 'drawing-room' had, of course, derived from the earlier usage, 'withdrawing room'. Hence his reference to 'draw after dinner'.)

For such apartments, he continued: 'the most elegant furniture is requisite, as they are for the reception of persons of the highest rank.' After all, 'the drawing-room is to concentrate the elegance of the whole house, and is the highest display of the richness of furniture.'

In common with other arbiters upon these matters, Sheraton also had his own clear-cut, even eccentric, views upon the social proceedings he would prefer to have conducted within his ideal drawing-room. 'Nothing of a scientific nature should be introduced to take up the attention of any individual from the general conversation that takes place on such occasions,' he declared. Our current pseudo-scientific chitter-chat concerning global warming, computer-calculating, traffic control and so on would clearly be socially unacceptable to Sheraton. He then goes on to give an opinion which would invalidate virtually every room in this book: 'the walls should be free

(Opposite) The drawing-room of Josephine Abercrombie's neo-Palladian house in Kentucky achieves a perfect balance between grandeur and informality. The free arrangement of the furniture, enriched with beautiful textiles and patterns, complements the decorated ceiling and walls. Classic and comfortable, the room epitomizes the late-twentieth-century revival of traditionally-based interior decoration, with ornamentation being a key component. The house was designed by Quinlan Terry; the interior decoration was by Anthony Browne.

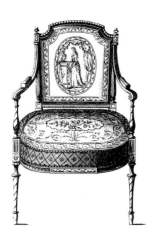
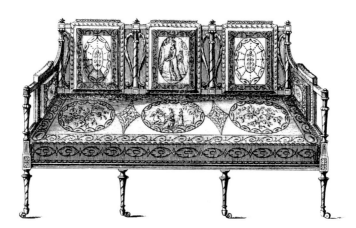
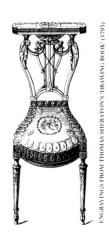

of pictures, the tables not lined with books.'

Today's arbiters on interior design may be less dictatorial than Sheraton, but since the 1960s and 1970s, when open-plan modernism was all the vogue, there has been a noticeable return to a more traditional way of using domestic living-space. Many people have now gone back to the idea of separate rooms for sitting and dining, and this reversion has, in part, sponsored a revival of interest in traditional comforts and aesthetics in interior decoration. In Britain, the change in the way the home is organized has also led to changes in terminology. Twenty years ago, every house or flat had a 'living-area', but in the 1990s, the main reception room is once again being designated the 'drawing-room' or 'sitting-room', thus subtly reflecting the current preference for established aesthetics. In the United States and in France, however, things are much simpler: 'living-room' and 'salon', respectively, continue to serve very well, thank you, whatever the style of decoration.

One of the most popular genres in present-day traditional interior decoration is the 'English country-house style'. The fashion has no doubt come about partly in reaction to the earlier, more austere forms of contemporary design and partly because it seems to represent a more reassuring, sympathetic way of life. Home-owners who had happily lived with the basic modern furniture and geometric patterns of the 1960s gradually began to appreciate the cosier, bucolic patterns offered by Laura Ashley, and to discover – or rediscover – the elegance and richer vein of traditionalism by Colefax and Fowler, Sister Parish and others. These nostalgic influences, which have become increasingly widespread, are shown in many variants throughout this book.

More or less inevitably, interest in the country-house style has generated a greater interest in antique and decorative furniture, paintings, *objets d'art* and so on. The world has returned to the pleasures of yesteryear but, happily, without paying overmuch attention to rigid diktats concerning what is socially and aesthetically OK.

As people have become more and more interested in traditional comforts in their homes, so the passion for an interesting and elegant reception room has grown. Today, this room is once again what it was in earlier, less frenetic times: a well-considered, well-loved retreat where family and friends may meet, relax and entertain. And, above all, the room in which cultural preferences and individuality of taste can be indulged to the full.

Against such decorative and personal interests, Sheraton's rather constricting philosophy on interior design doesn't stand a chance. We don't have to be full-time collectors, dilettantes and aesthetes to wish to have and to show our favourite possessions, whether antique or modern as the minute, in our personal retreats. More to the point, perhaps, are speculations on what might be the particular features that go to the making of an elegant drawing-room, sitting-room or living-room for today.

Is size important? Can a room be made elegant if it measures less than, say, twenty feet by fifteen? 'Not possibly, my dear,' a latterday Lady Bracknell might murmur, but other, more imaginative souls press on and make wondrous rooms no more spatial than twelve by twelve with a ceiling eight-foot high.

Must such a room have more than a fair share of expensive furniture, fabrics and ornaments? 'Absolutely not,' a contemporary interior decorator would answer with the utmost conviction. Some highly sophisticated rooms are spare and restrained in their furnishing and decoration; others opulent, colourful and theatrical. The truly adventurous decorators mix old and new, expensive and fairground finds. The main requirements are taste and flair.

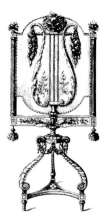
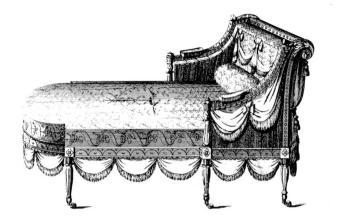
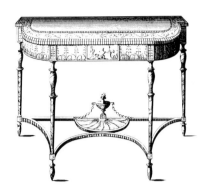

And who would now follow that Sheraton edict concerning no pictures on the walls? After all, where else to let the eyes wander when Uncle Richard is boring us to death with his reminiscences? And why are books not permitted on the tables? Aren't books also a subject for both meditation and conversation? And what about all those splendid *objets d'art et d'artifice* which gladden our own eyes, hearts and memories? That kilim we found in Istanbul. That ormolu clock in Carcassonne. That glass bowl in Murano. And so on. Don't these decorative finds also entertain the eyes of our friends? These are surely the truly individual elements in any *mise en scène*.

Page after page in this book illustrates the highly personal aspects of the art of arrangement practised by enthusiastic amateurs in decoration and zestful professionals alike. Here are demonstrations of flair, taste, waywardness and upending of conventional notions.

But such visions will inevitably sponsor the query. 'That's all very well and exciting, but could I do anything of the same kind?' The first thing is to believe that you can. Confidence is all-important in interior decoration. The next is to follow your inclinations. That will ensure that your sitting-room will be different and your own.

'But surely all of these rooms were designed and decorated by professionals,' the faint-hearted may protest. Not a bit of it. Many of the rooms shown in these pages were either entirely, or in large part, designed, furnished and decorated by amateurs. They knew what kind of interiors they wanted and then went ahead to get them. They had ideas and they made those ideas work to achieve colourful, comfortable, warm and welcoming homes.

Although there is a strong element of traditionalism throughout this book, the rooms are certainly not staid. Today's approach to interior decoration is highly eclectic, picking and choosing from the best of the past, incorporating new forms, calling on different cultures and using modern technology, especially lighting, to create interesting effects. There is a preference for a more ornamental style of decoration, with texture and textiles sponsoring a visual stimulation and warmth, but even in those rooms where simplicity is the theme, there is a perceptible eclecticism, breaking away from the uncompromising nature of harsh modernism.

Interior decoration is now so diffuse that it would be impossible to categorize it into definitive styles or influences but there are trends which can be pointed out. Some of the chapters in this book reflect those trends, concentrating, for example, on the greater emphasis on elegance and symmetry, on ceiling decoration, on the increasing use of gilding, and on displaying favourite objects and pictures. Then, too, there is the unmistakable cross-fertilization between rural and metropolitan design. Other chapters are less specific about styles of decoration but show rooms which have a particular character – split level with galleries, for example, or double-rooms where two spaces have been turned into one.

All the rooms reproduced in this book have been selected from the best that have appeared in *House & Garden* magazine in the recent past. Making the selection has been highly enjoyable, but one thing has become clear: the rich variety of the illustrations shows how hopeless a task it would be to essay a *guide book* to would-be designer-decorators. Far better to see what others have done, distil the results of their decorative impulses, let your own imagination take over and then go to it.

After all, for most of us, this is the second most entertaining pastime in the world and one which occupies, in the most wonderful way, all those caught by the countless enchantments of designing, furnishing and decorating their favourite room □

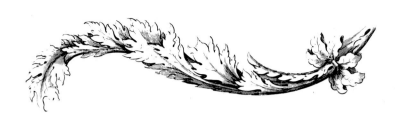

Elegance and symmetry

Symmetry may seem an obvious means of achieving an elegant effect in interior decoration, but it is no less pleasing for that. By comparison, many essays in asymmetry strike a jarring note, looking unconvincing and contrived. This can prove especially true in the display of objects. Place a clock in the centre of a mantelshelf, then challenge someone to position a pair of vases or candlesticks on the same shelf, and almost certainly he or she would put one to either side of, and equidistant from, the clock. That seems the natural thing to do, and anything else might be perilously close to a self-conscious attempt to be 'different'.

But why? Maybe it is because human beings are apt to think of themselves as being fairly symmetrical, and thus feel more at ease when dealing with what they see as balanced structures. There is a harmony in symmetry that Western cultures tend to find easier to appreciate than asymmetry.

All the rooms in this chapter have a strong element of symmetry, both in the placing of the furniture and in the presentation of decorative objects and pictures. They have a poised, serene ambience rarely possessed by a room which has a deliberate asymmetrical trait. Sometimes, the symmetry is not so much an end in itself as a means of pulling together a scheme which involves many disparate components.

There are limits, however, and symmetry can pall if it is taken too far or if a room does not include the odd quirk. Even the most classic of milieus benefits from an injection of the unexpected.

(Right) Everything in this drawing-room, decorated by Hethea Nye and Ralph Harvard, is in total, elegant accord. The colour scheme is a symphonic composition of ivory and creamy-beiges against butter-yellow walls and pale yellow silk taffeta curtains. The setting-out of the furniture is highly symmetrical, with facing sofas each backed by a table and pair of chairs. The chimneypiece and oval mirror are at the centre of a balanced arrangement of lacquer commodes, candelabra lamps, pole firescreens, urns and wall-sconces.

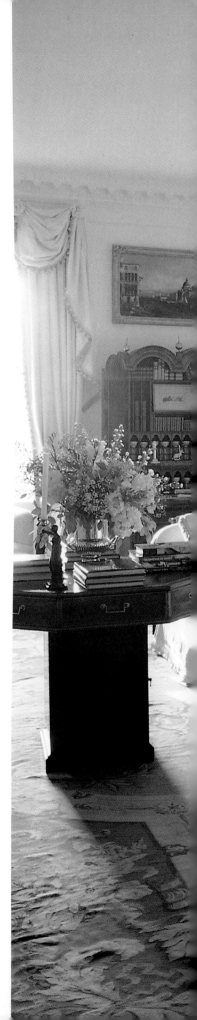

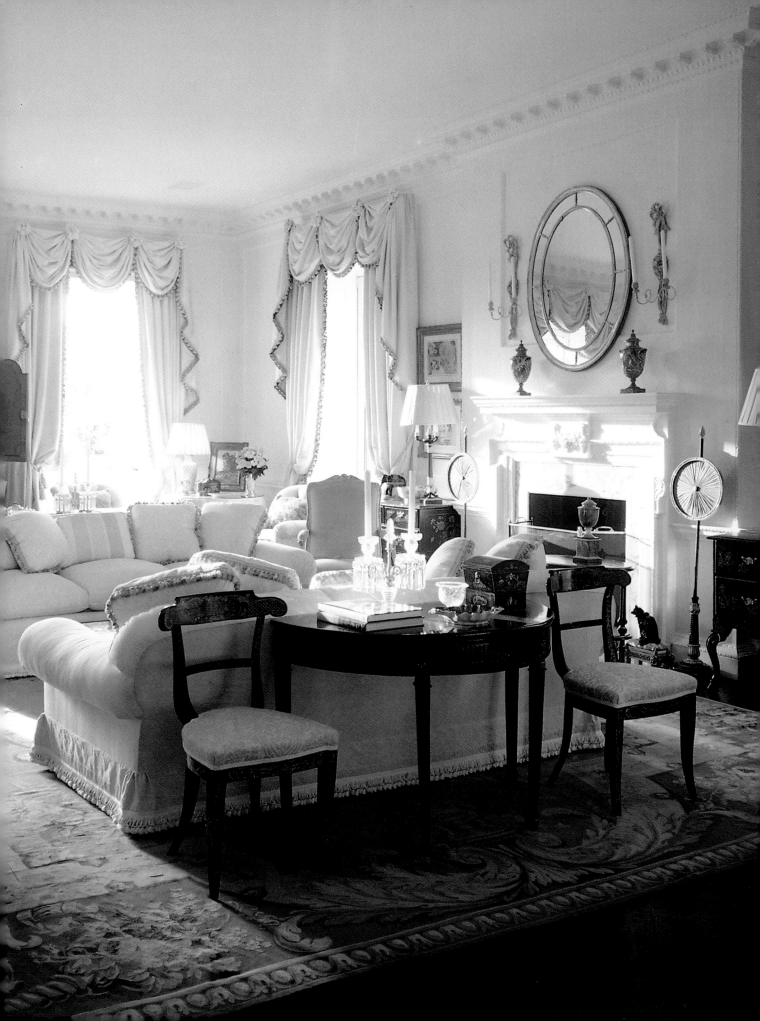

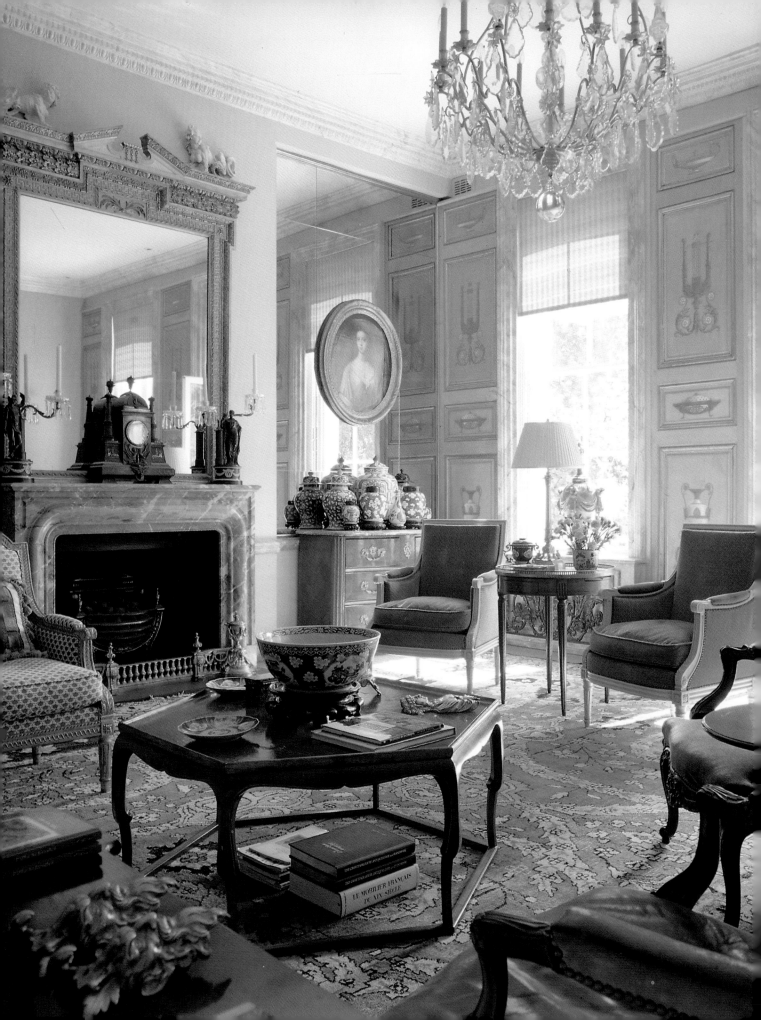

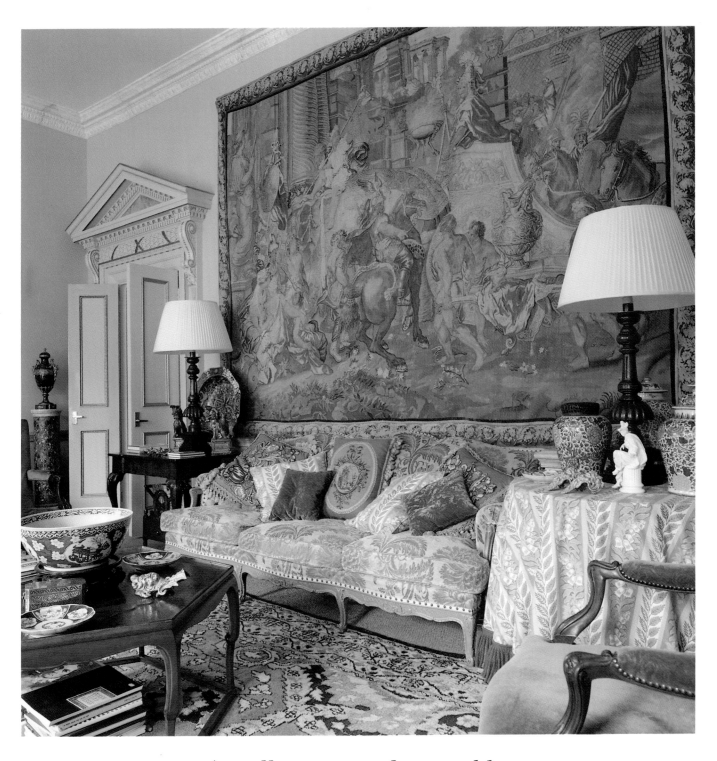

A well-mannered assembly

The elegance of Peter Hurford's London sitting-room emanates not only from the intrinsically elegant style of the furnishing, which is mainly continental, but also from the way in which the individual elements are juxtaposed. An underlying symmetry and pairing hold the scheme together: table lamps are positioned to either end of the French Régence sofa; the chimneypiece has twin candelabra to either side of the clock; the marble-topped console has a seventeenth-century Japanese Imari vase centred between >

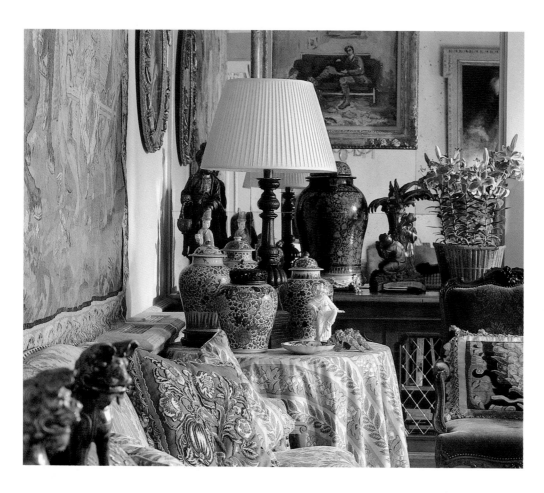

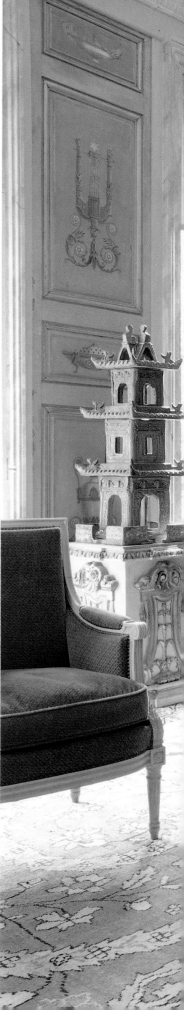

< marbled urns. The good proportions of the full-length windows and French doors are not obscured by curtains; instead, blinds are set within the reveals. Alternating with the windows are four late-eighteenth-century French panels, exquisitely painted with neo-classical motifs. On the opposite wall hangs an eighteenth-century Gobelins tapestry.

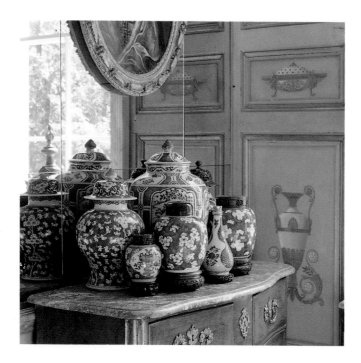

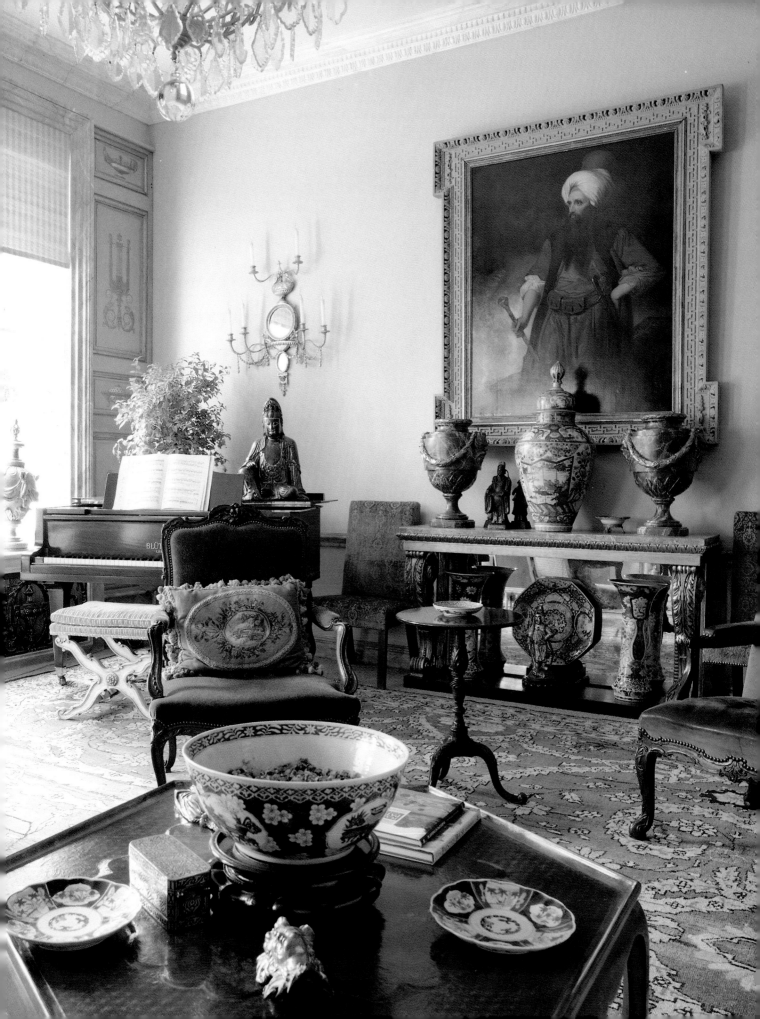

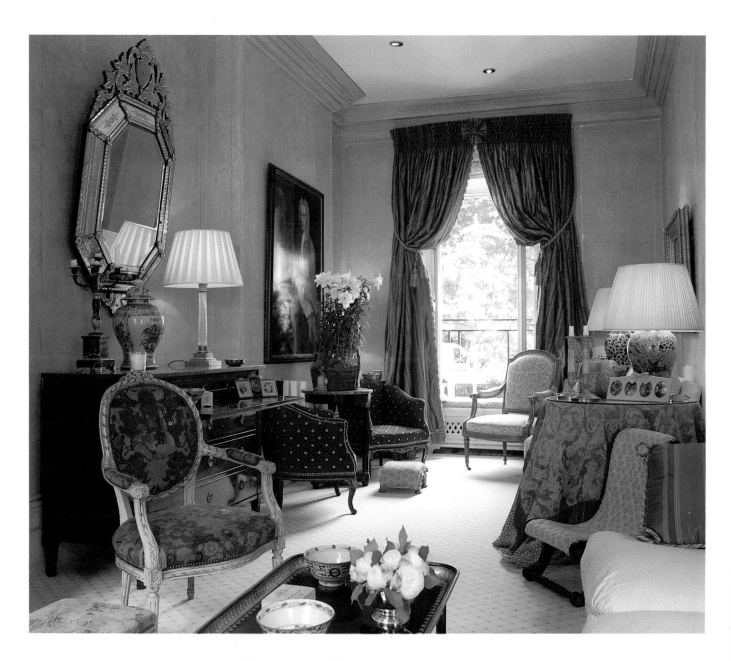

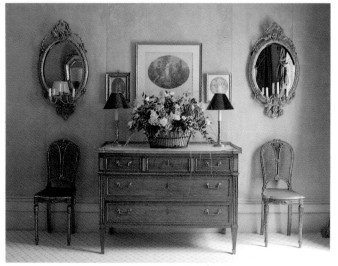

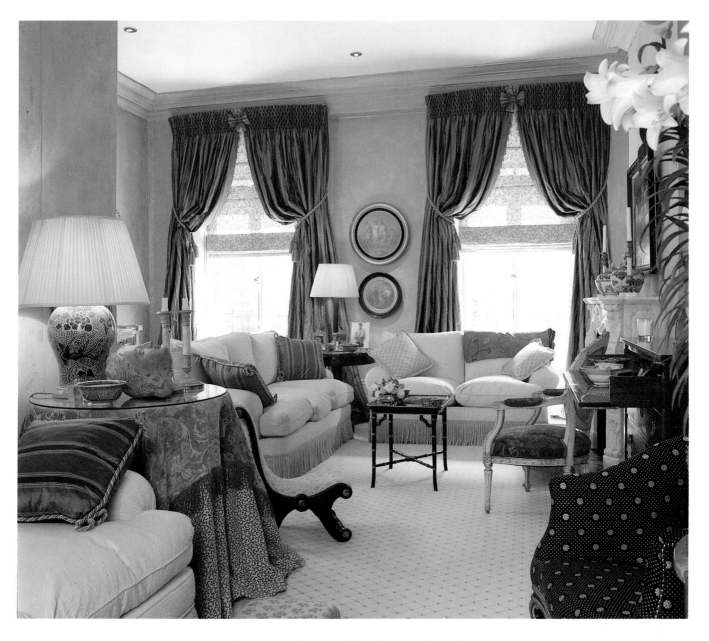

A timeless Italian look

Everything about this L-shaped room in London, decorated by Monika Apponyi, is refined and well balanced. The weight and tones of the colours are beautifully harmonized, and there is a pleasing interplay of complementary patterns. The walls have a splendid yet subtle finish resembling verdigris, skilfully rendered by Geoffrey Lamb. First, he applied a base colour of orange, then gold, then green. The gold appears in arbitrary glints, 'lifting' the paintwork without being unduly prominent or gaudy. The windows have striped curtains, reefed back at a fairly high level, and

contrasting Roman blinds. Between the windows in the front half of the room are two eighteenth-century stipple engravings similar in style and subject to the three engravings above the French marble-topped commode. In an exercise in pure symmetry, the trio of prints is flanked by a pair of mirrored sconces, and the commode is flanked by a pair of canework chairs. Even the candlelamps are paired. Monika Apponyi aimed at creating an interior with an antique 'Italian look' – timeless yet comfortable and practical for a family whose lives are active and involve frequent entertaining.

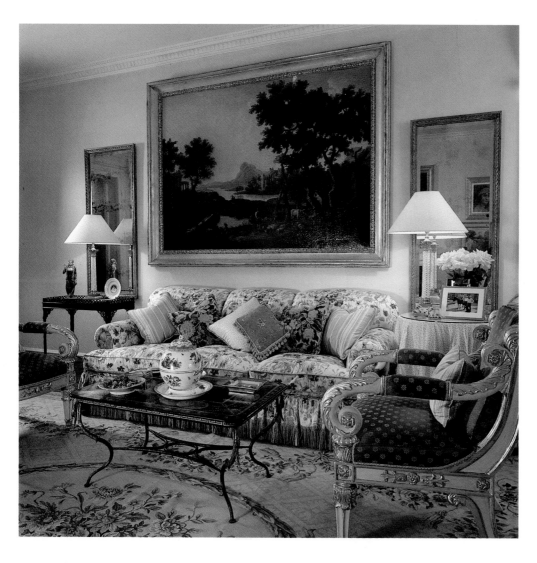

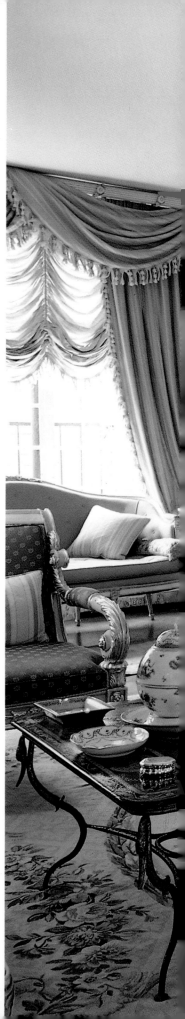

Inner-city tranquillity

Nancy Kirwan Taylor's scheme for her drawing-room in New York exudes tranquillity. Decorated around the soft colours of the eighteenth-century Aubusson rug, the room has a gentleness and restraint which belie its urban surroundings. The main seating-area has a formal layout, with a pair of magnificent gilt and painted-wood Russian chairs flanking the sofa beneath an eighteenth-century Irish landscape. Paired to either side of the marble chimneypiece are two Swedish chairs, restored and re-covered with a Napoleonic bee-motif fabric. The centre of the floor area has been kept free of solid, heavy furniture so that the beauty of the rug can be appreciated to the full.

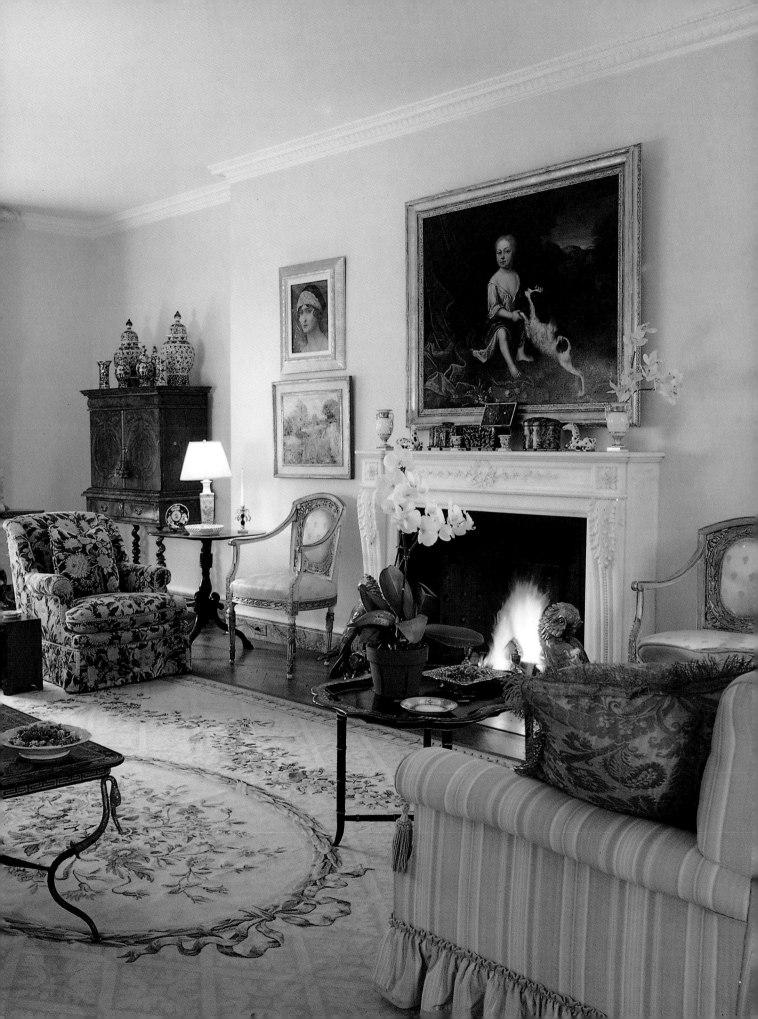

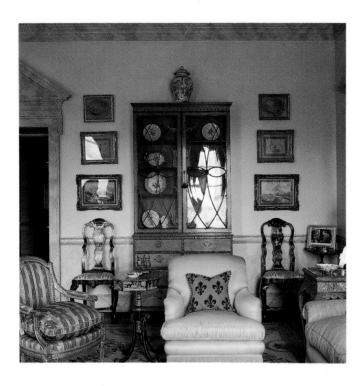

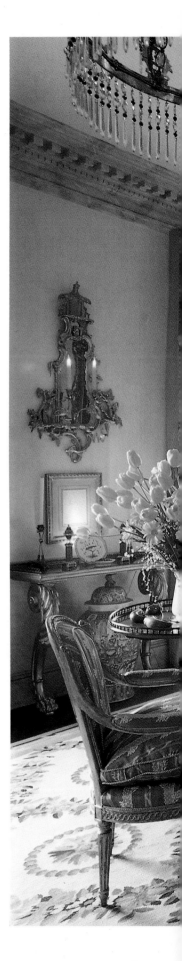

Pastel colours in a formal setting

Overlooking New York's Central Park, Carroll and Milton Petrie's drawing-room is formal and slightly French, a consummately refined setting devised by David Easton. As the room previously lacked architectural interest, David Easton and his assistant, John Christensen, installed a dado rail, cornice and pediments above the doors, thus establishing a fitting period milieu for the Petries' exceptional furniture, paintings and objects. There are two main seating-areas in the room: one is centred on the marble chimneypiece; the other, at the opposite end, is between paired doorways. The formality of the room derives >

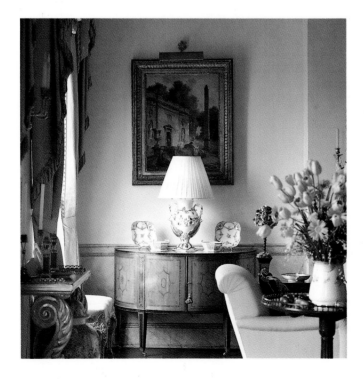

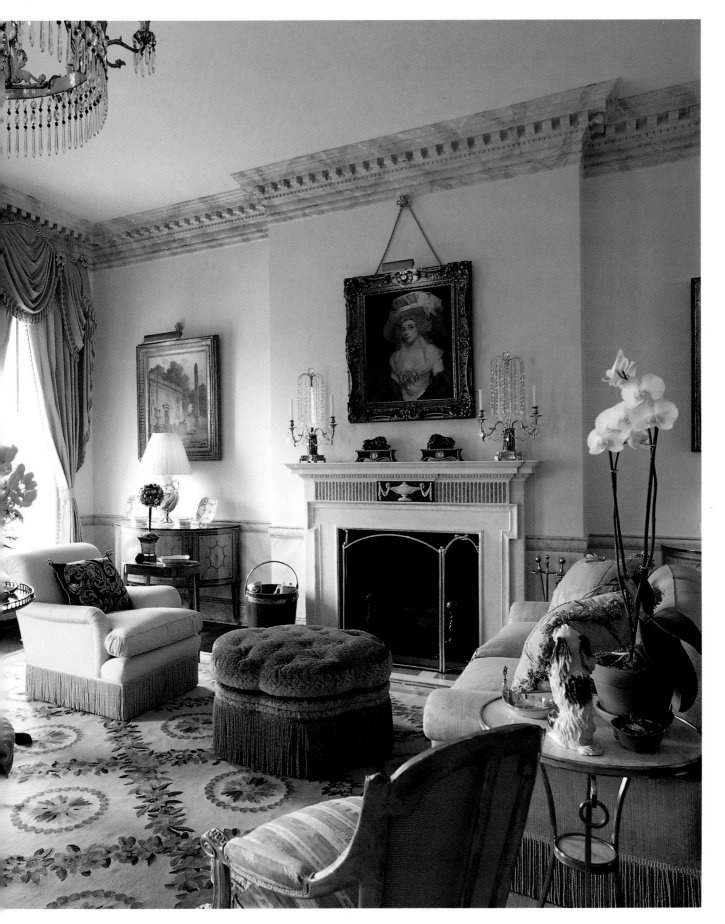

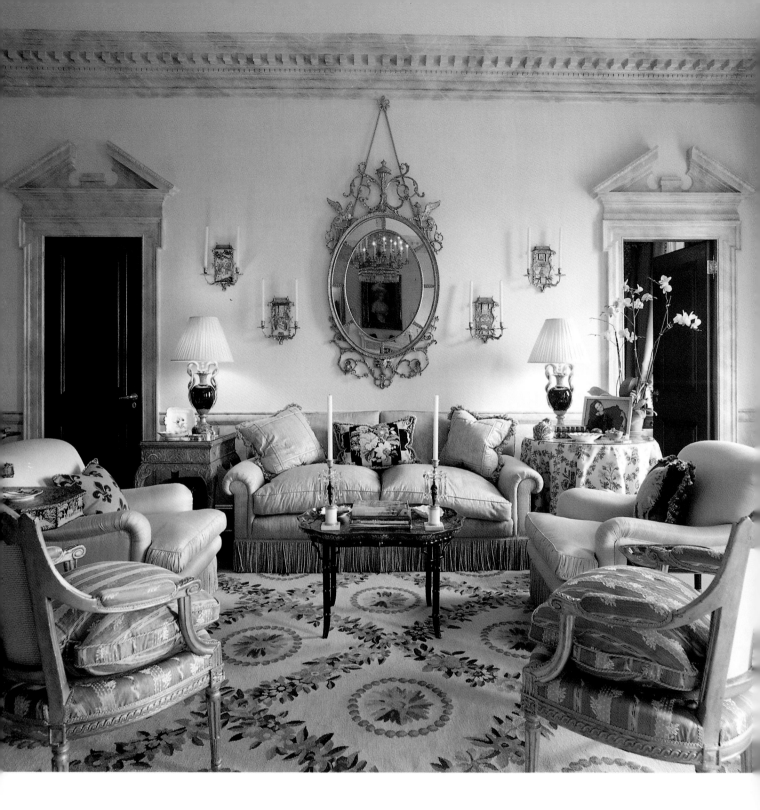

< partly from the nature of the furniture and partly from the controlled and symmetrical placement. This symmetry is carried through at all levels: two glass-fronted bookcases containing similar displays of porcelain are bordered by identical chairs beneath carefully aligned pictures. Against another wall, a quartet of Chinese porcelain wall sconces is hung to either side of the Adam mirror, while half-moon commodes are matched to either side of the fireplace. The pattern of the French carpet, reproduced from an Empire original, and handworked in petit point, brings together the colours of the walls – which have a pink *strié* finish above a beige marbled dado – and those of the textiles.

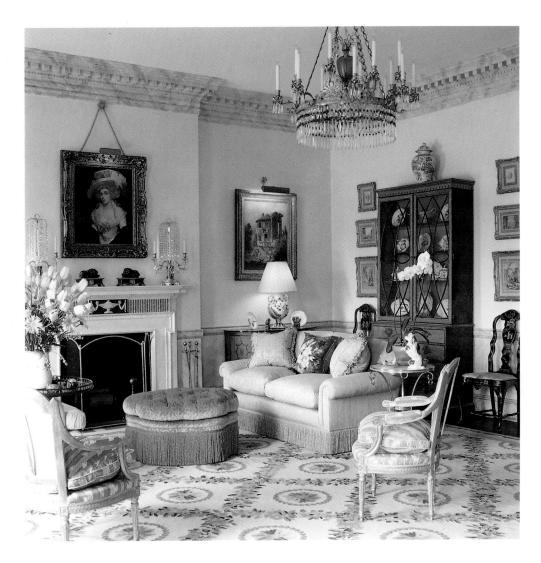

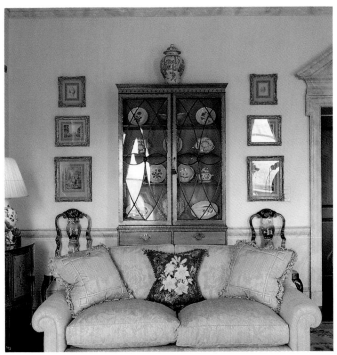

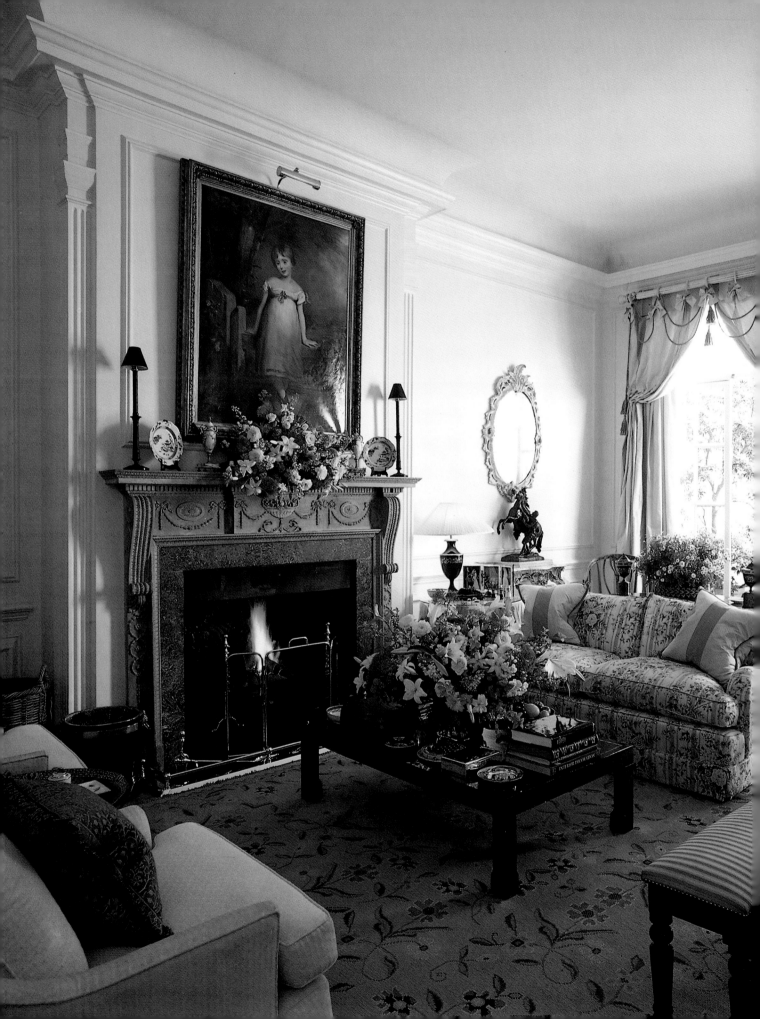

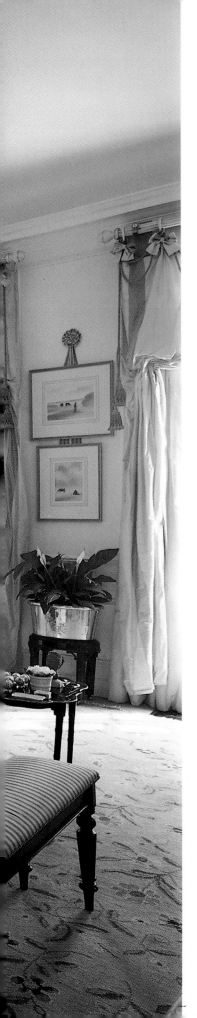

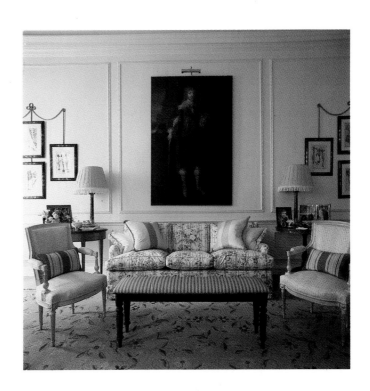

Detailed elegance

The harmony and distinction of this London drawing-room, decorated by Joanna Wood, is sponsored as much by the finishing touches and details as by the soundness of taste which underpins the scheme. Note the fine cording on the curtain heads, matched by the picture cords; and note the use of symmetry to generate a sense of restraint and order. Pictures are hung in twos and fours above chairs which, in turn, create perfectly balanced compositions with other pieces of furniture. The room's orderliness is offset by a lightness of touch and a halcyon prettiness which suits the airy aspect. The most important single element in the room is the eighteenth-century Portuguese needlework rug, for this was the cue for the blue-and-white colour scheme.

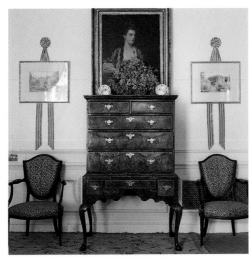

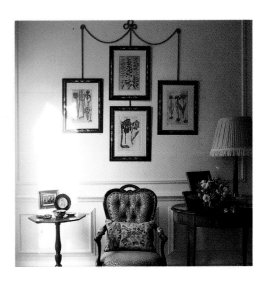

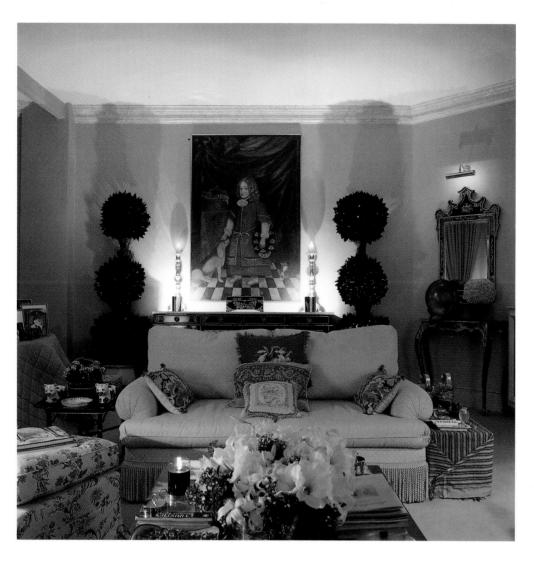

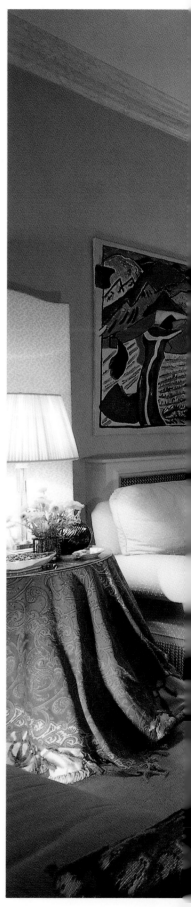

A neutral background

The thinking behind the choice of background colours in Hugh and Jillie Green's flat was that it should provide a neutral setting for a collection of artefacts in many hues, bought during travels abroad. Within the limited spectrum there are many subtle variations which give an interesting overall effect. The marbled cornice and woodwork tie in with the French marble chimneypiece; the wallpaper is unobtrusively patterned; and the sofas are covered in a light, two-tone weave. Symmetry makes a strong design statement, with two plant sculptures adding form and height to the wall opposite the fire, while dried moss 'trees' make an unusual garniture on the mantelshelf. Dramatic lighting gives the room a debonair theatricality. Lavinia Dargie, of Dargie Lewis Designs, advised on the fabrics and wall treatments.

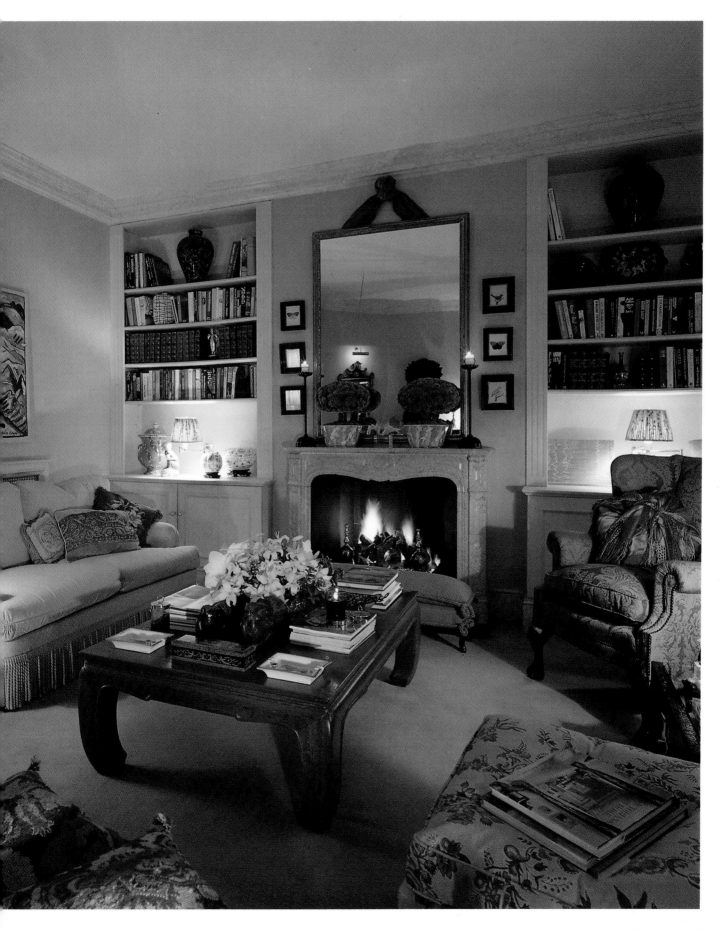

Decoration in detail

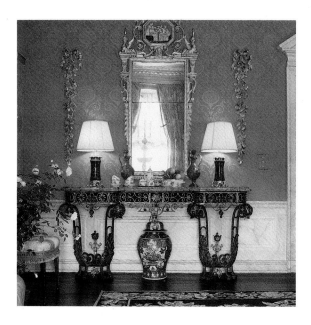

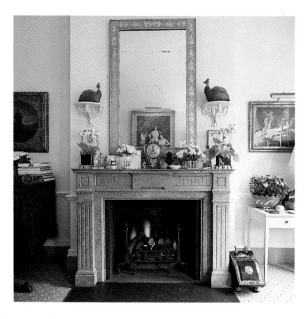

This arrangement in Carroll and Milton Petrie's apartment shows an exemplary balance between horizontal and vertical lines, and between simple and convoluted shapes. Gilded carvings enclose the composition, with lamps placed directly above the openwork supports of the gilt-iron side-table.

The chimneybreast in Penny and Guy Morrison's drawing-room is the setting for a quirky, symmetrical collection of decorative objects and a mirror. To either side of the mirror, birds are perched on carved brackets. All the plants have creamy-white flowers in harmony with the low-key colour-scheme.

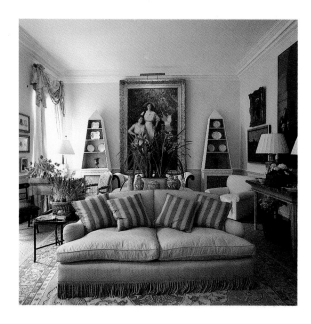

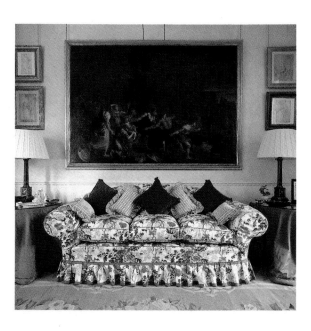

The long view of a room decorated by Penny Morrison demonstrates a keen sense of symmetry, starting with the sofa placed in the centre of the bordered rug. At the far end, a pair of painted antique obelisks displaying a collection of decorative plates rises alongside the life-size painting by Frederick Hall.

Symmetry need not imply stiff-and-starchy discomfort. Beneath a formal group of pictures in a London drawing-room, decorated with assistance from Jane Churchill, the ensemble of a chintz-covered sofa and a pair of red-clothed tables strikes a happy balance, looking inviting and relaxed.

Decoration in detail

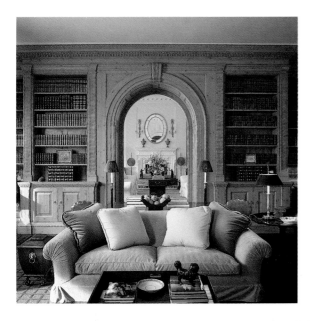

The book-lined wall between the library/sitting-area and the drawing-room in the Fifth Avenue home of Hethea Nye is pierced by an archway, creating a symmetrical vista of the chimneypiece. The panelling has carved enrichments based on eighteenth-century models. (The drawing-room is shown on page 11.)

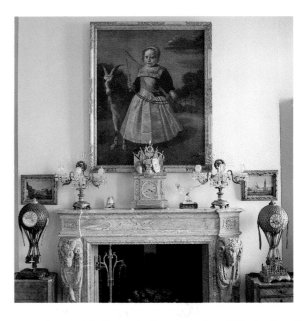

Two near-identical balloon clocks, one painted black, the other in gilt-ormolu, stand by an exceptionally handsome marble chimneypiece with neoclassical plinths. The room's unstrident wall colour is a sympathetic background for the golden hues of the highly ornamental Empire clock and paired candelabra.

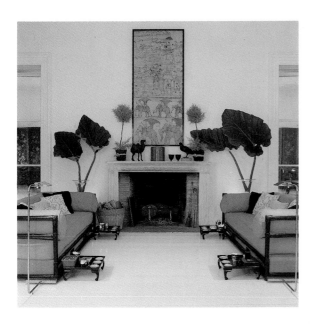

This fireside seating group is in a flat in Paris, decorated by Dreda Melé, but it has an oriental calm. Much of the furniture and objects was bought on travels abroad: the sofas are American; the painting above the chimneypiece is Burmese. The setting, also shown on pages 162–163, is entirely white.

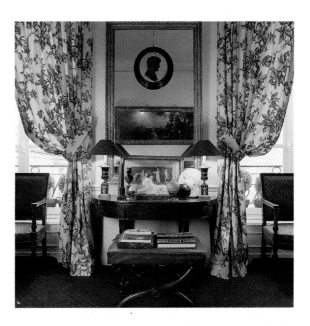

The windows in Etienne Dumont's flat are symmetrical and so, too, is the treatment of the space between them. A half-moon table supports a pair of urn-shaped lamps with Empire-style shades. The placing of the chairs in front of the windows, framed by the looped-back curtains, enhances the formality.

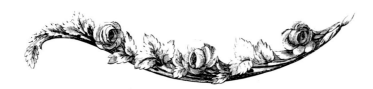

Double identity

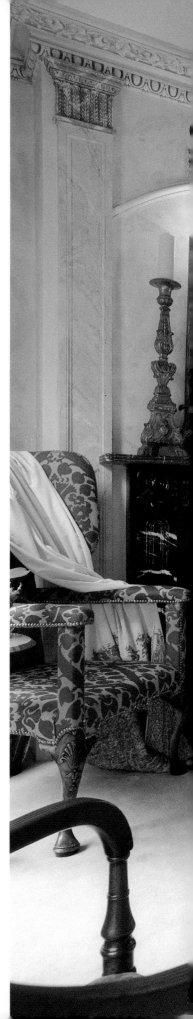

The typical, smaller Georgian and early-Victorian town house was built with two rooms per floor – one at the front and one, smaller, at the back. Sometimes the two rooms on the reception level were linked by double doors, but often they were quite separate, with separate entrances opening off a corridor or landing.

Nowadays, many people prefer to remove the intervening wall between the two adjoining rooms in order to form one large, L-shaped space. Numerous interiors in this book owe their existence to just such a decision, and the new-found space and proportions of these rooms undoubtedly offer an exciting challenge to the interior designer. Apart from the obvious advantages of more usable space, there are the less tangible but equally welcome benefits of longer and more interesting vistas. Why should we always think of vistas as exterior amenities?

In a few cases, the double rooms seen here have not been completely opened up. There remains a deliberate duality, but the decoration scheme considers the two spaces in relation to one another, sometimes using continuity as the decorative-spatial theme or, in other instances, showing a preference for a studied, stage-managed contrast. An accomplished example of well-articulated contrast is seen in the drawing-room and adjacent sitting-room on pages 38–41, decorated by Anne-Marie de Ganay. Here, the panelling and chintz wallcovering are boldly different but the interaction between the two rooms is especially attractive.

Of course, when two such rooms are linked by an arch, the architectural possibilities are vastly enhanced. In his flat shown on pages 52–53, John Wright has produced an idiosyncratic design using geometric forms in a highly innovative manner.

(Right) A first-floor drawing-room, decorated by Margaret Tiffin, has the typical London town house layout of two interconnecting spaces, the larger at the front of the building and the smaller at the rear, forming an L-shape. Although the two spaces have a cohesive scheme of decoration, using architectural adornment with panache, they have slightly different functions. The main part is a sociable sitting-area; the smaller part is a library-cum-music room.

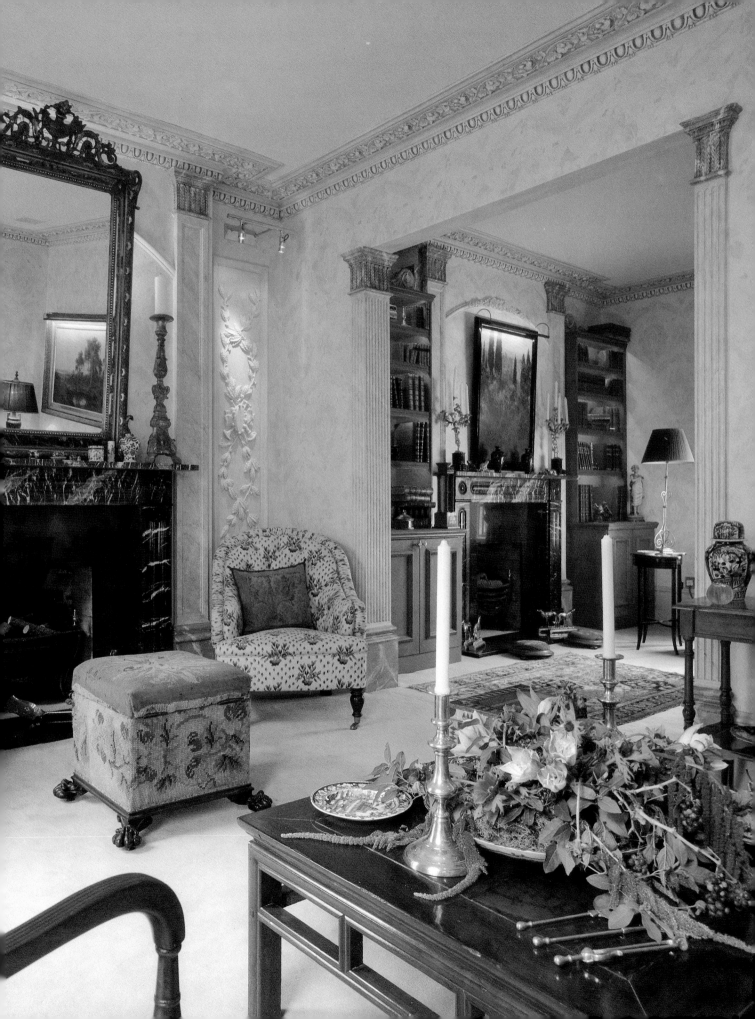

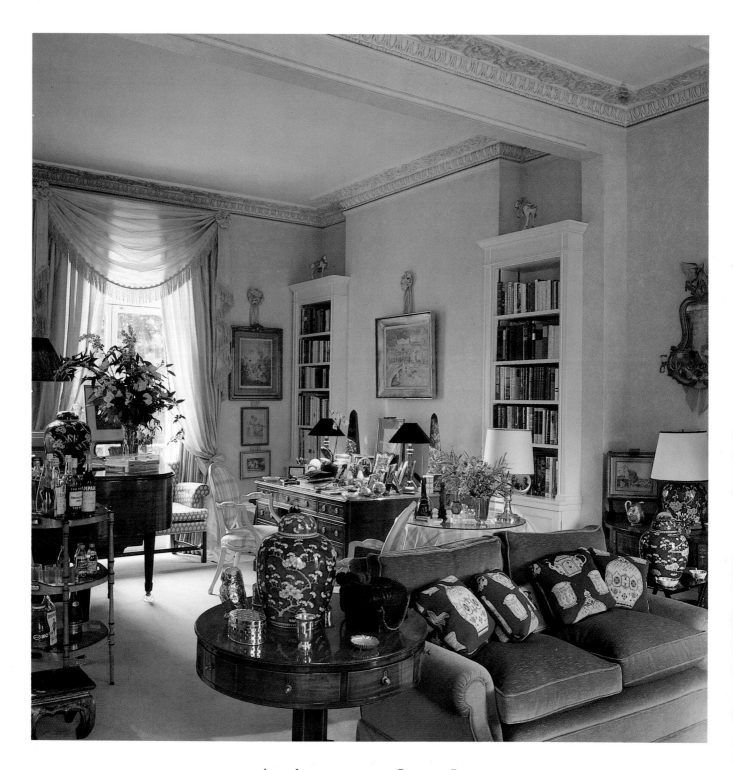

An integrated study

In a nineteenth-century London town house, a partition wall has been removed to form one integrated drawing-room. The chimneypiece in the rear part has also been taken out, thus providing wall-space for a desk flanked by bookcases – a well-contrived and practical study/writing area. The room's colour scheme was chosen specifically to complement the collection of blue-and-white objects, wittily parodied in the cushion fabric. Yellow silk top curtains and blue silk second curtains make a graceful window treatment. Karen Armstrong of Pavilion Designs assisted with the room's decoration.

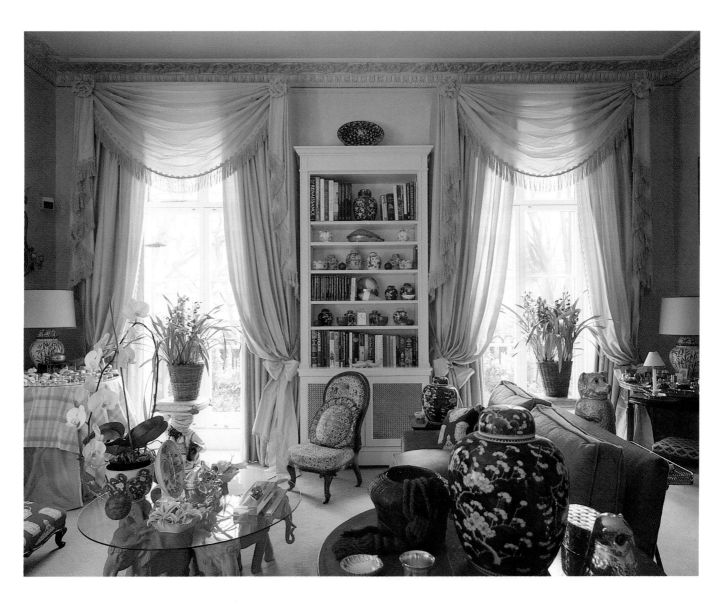

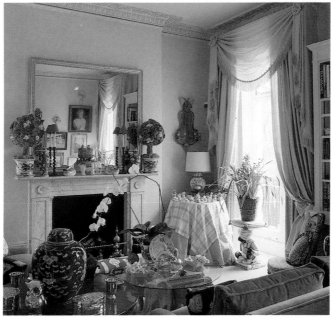

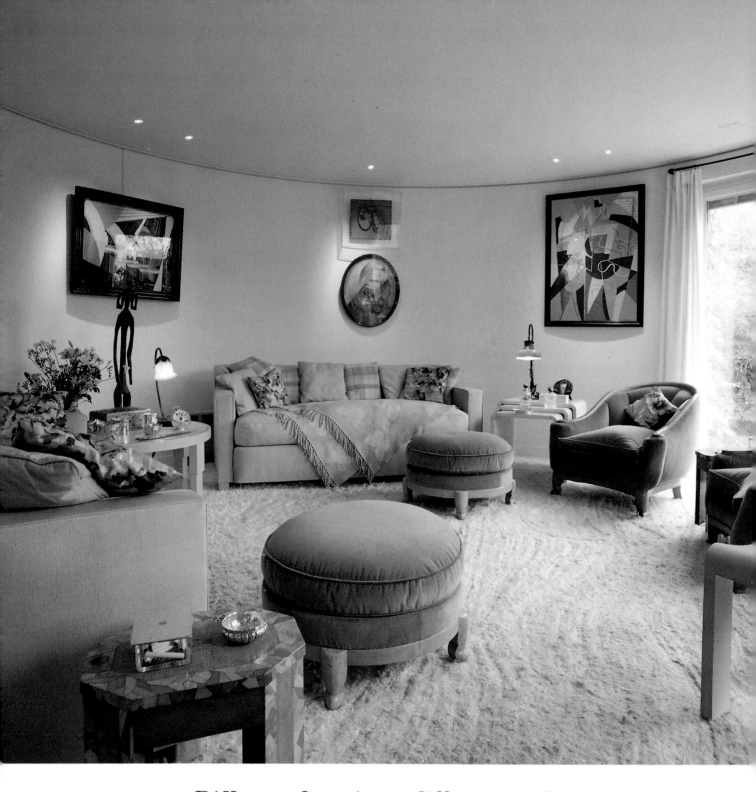

Different functions, different styles

Here are two closely interlocked spaces with emphatically different characters. The circular sitting-room, furnished with 1930s chairs and sofas, is pastel in tone and has an air of simplification. The walls are light and smooth. In contrast, the library area is much more intimate, with a mixture of seating, more pictures, patterned upholstery and rugs. Here, the painted walls are overlaid with thin panels of sycamore, giving the impression of rusticated stone. With age and exposure to light, the wood is developing an especially lovely honey colour. The architect for the flat was Serge Caillaux.

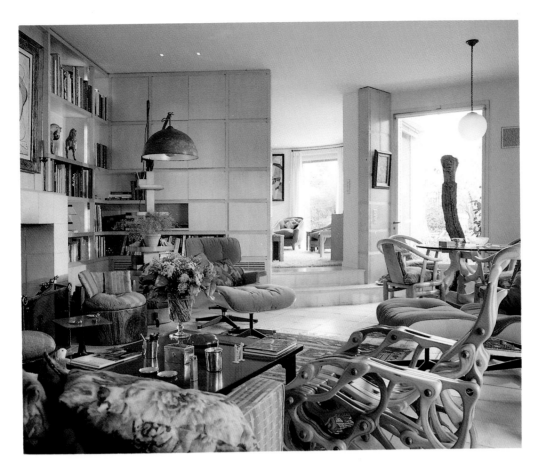

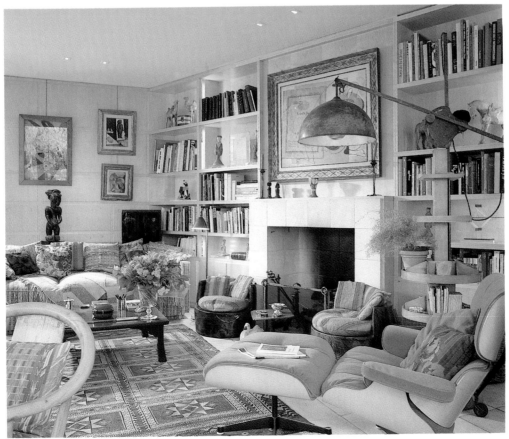

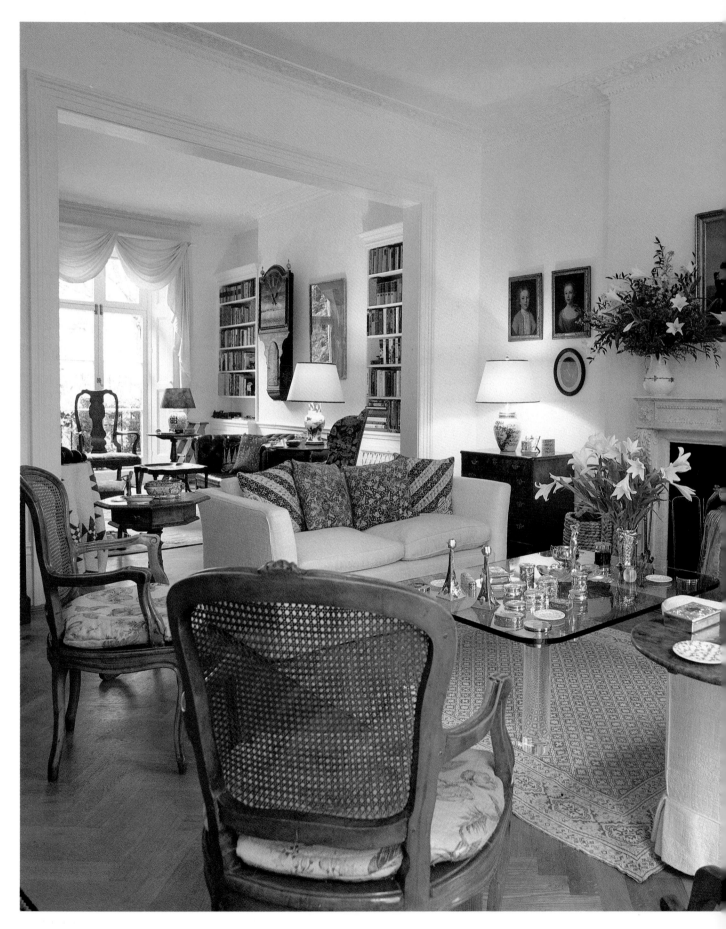

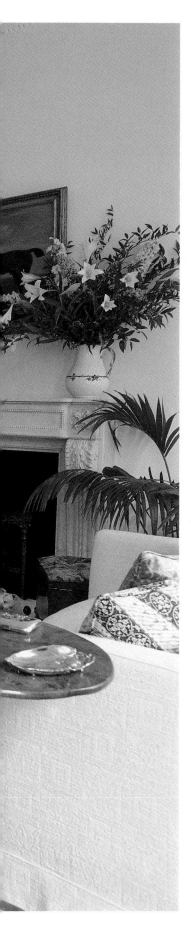

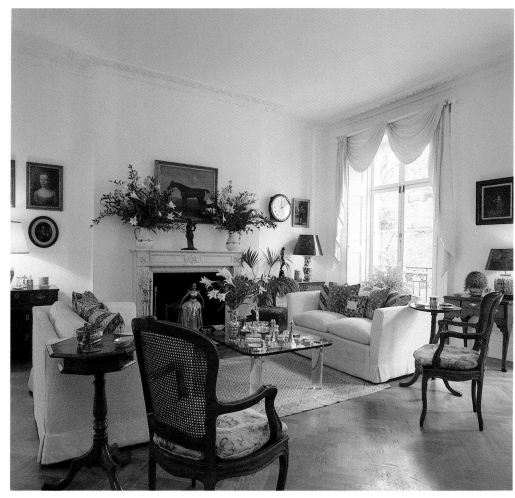

Simplicity and equilibrium

This L-shaped drawing-room in a London town house achieves a satisfying equilibrium with restrained colours and an appearance of simplicity. The walls are painted warm-white; there are no curtains; and the parquet floor is left largely uncovered. Although the owners are interested in antique furniture, and are collectors of paintings, especially of naïve pictures of children and early-nineteenth-century portraits, the room is agreeably unencumbered. The mantelpiece displays a single figure and a pair of vases, but the arrangement has great impact, thanks to the dramatic scale and exoticism of the flowers. The narrower end of the room is more intimate, with a deep-buttoned Chesterfield and bookshelves in the recesses to either side. The furniture here is arranged less formally, and the textiles are richer, but the overall impression of the room remains light and uplifting.

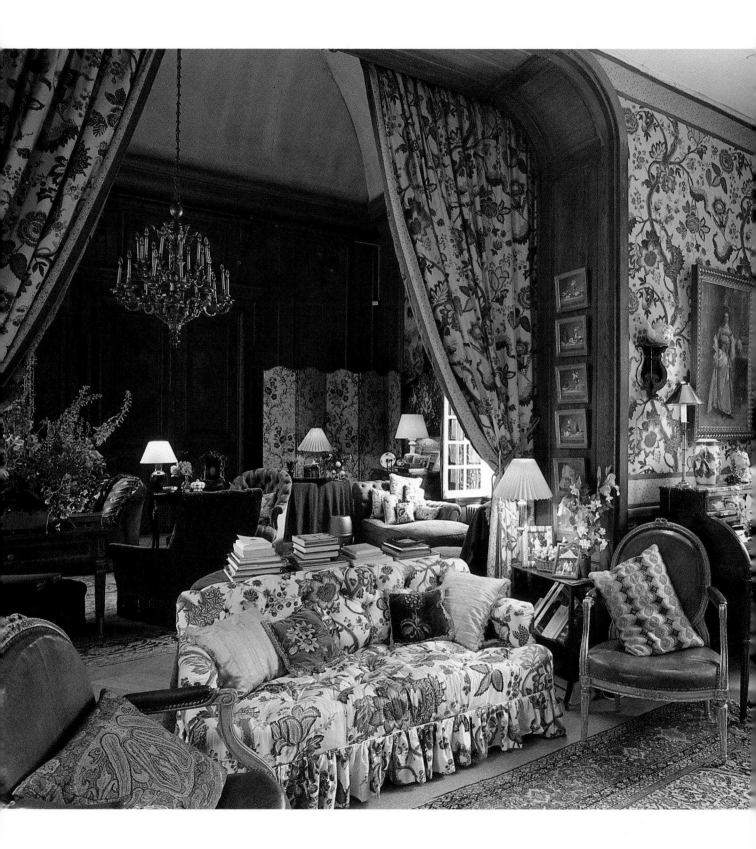

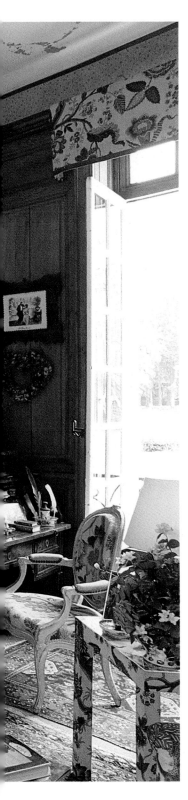

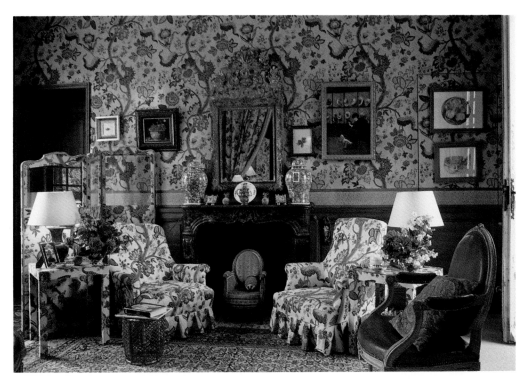

Within a French château

In a wing of a magnificent château, just outside Paris, Anne-Marie de Ganay has decorated her double sitting-room in suitably grand, yet intimate, style. It is grand, mainly because the scale of the panelled part of the room demanded large, impressive furniture, such as the boulle *armoire*, chaise-longue and tall, embroidered screen. But it is also cosy, due to the plentiful and welcoming appearance of the seating and the pretty, floral chintz at the opposite end of the room. This latter area is arranged as a snug place for reading by the fire or for writing at the desk. It is a deliberately nostalgic, >

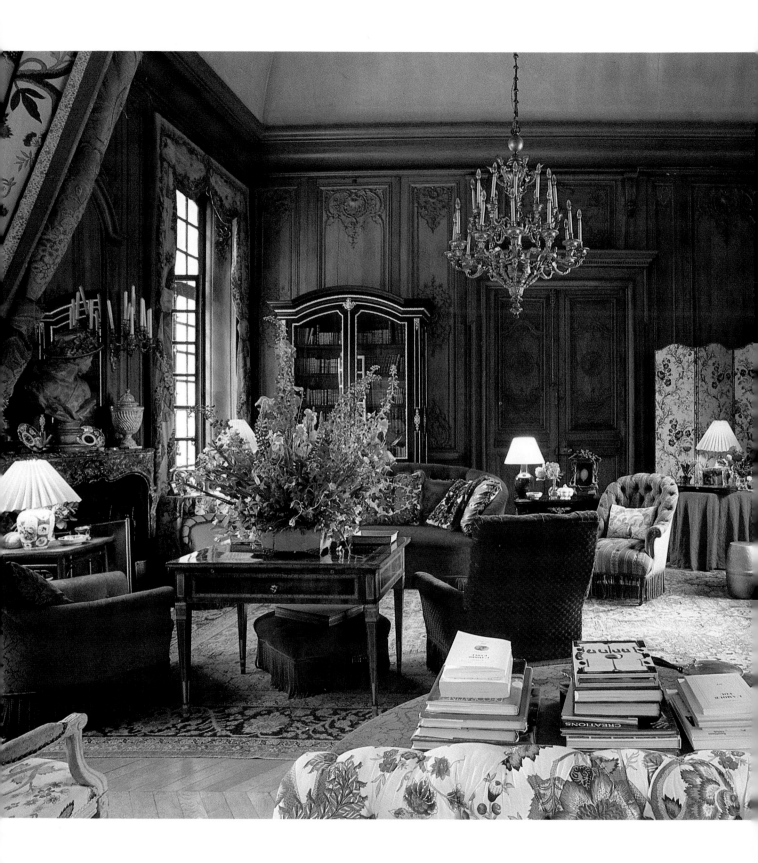

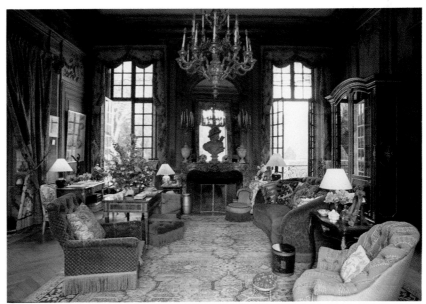

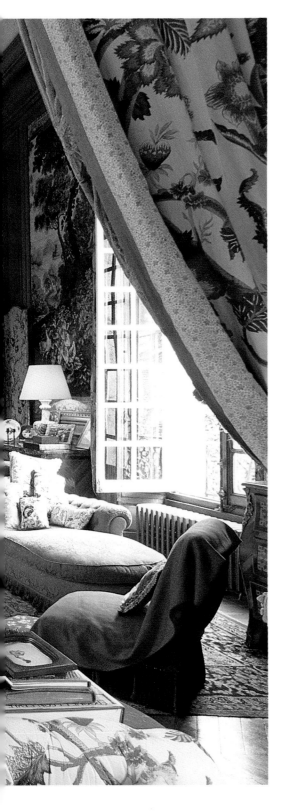

< companionable space, with many mementoes of childhood. The frieze is made from a child's dress fabric, while a child's chair is placed in front of the chimneypiece. The two parts of the room are linked by a wide archway draped with the same chintz as that used on the walls of the small sitting-area. Red, a favourite colour of Anne-Marie de Ganay, is particularly noticeable in the main room, where it is used for much of the upholstery and appears in the pattern of the antique carpet. Flowers are also favourite features in Anne-Marie de Ganay's interior decoration, and here they make a natural, enlivening contribution to the polished *mise en scène*.

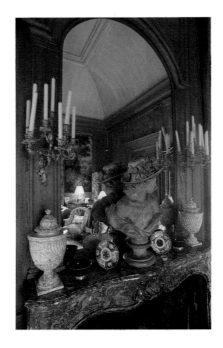

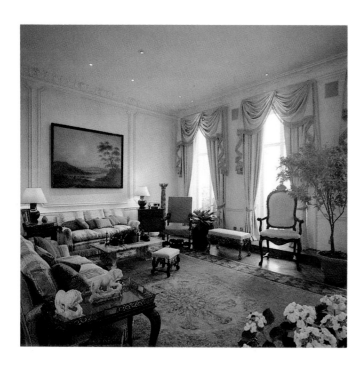

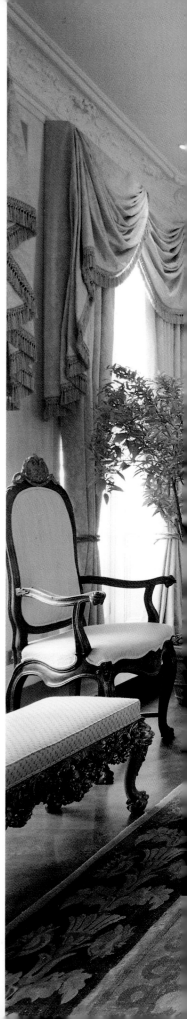

Serene and even

In redecorating one of the very few remaining single-family houses in London's Eaton Square, Marie-Luis Charmat effected a virtuoso transformation which includes a serene, L-shaped drawing-room with linking arch. Many of the elements were bought specially for the room, but the even tenor of the colours and the unjarring nature of the patterns result in a supremely well-balanced scheme which, in spite of its newness, looks as if it has always existed. The walls were given an 'antique' paint finish by Hannerle Dehn, and the fabric on the sofas was used in reverse to achieve an older, softer appearance. Two fine seventeenth-century walnut armchairs, with high backs and exuberant carving, add an unexpected quirkiness to the room.

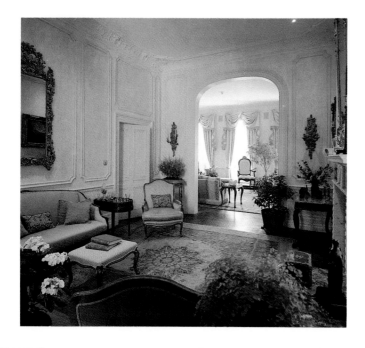

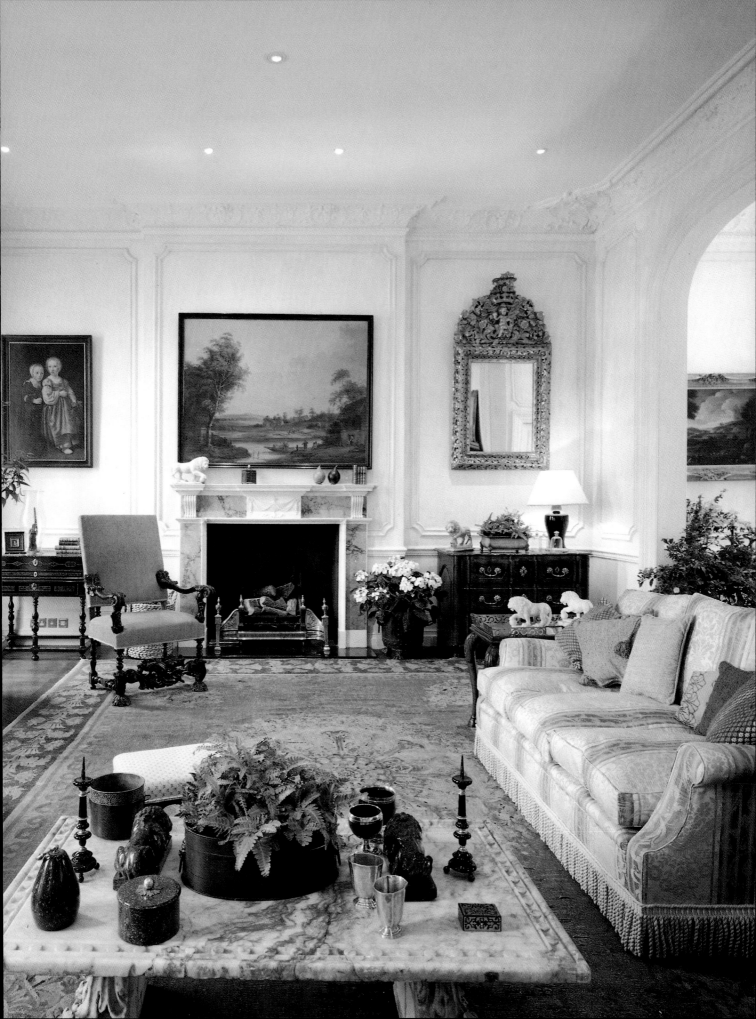

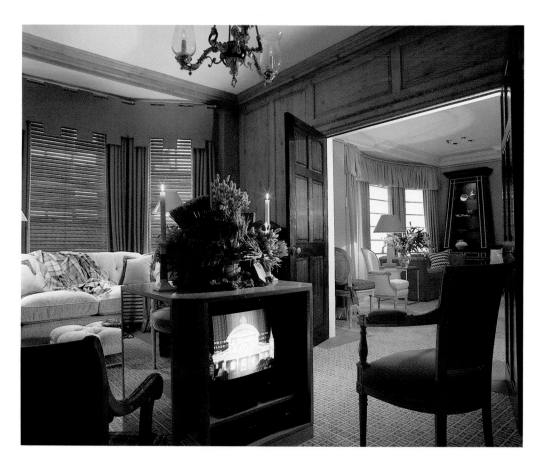

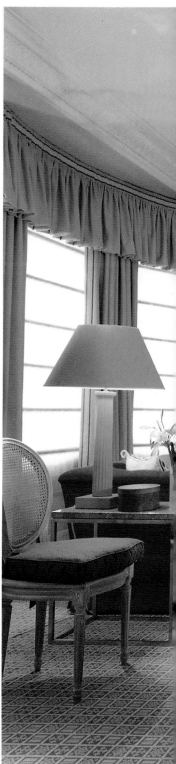

Contemporary but classic

Designed by Stephen Ryan of David Hicks International, this sitting-room and library have 'classic Hicks' hallmarks. Updated interpretations of classic forms are punctuated by strong blocks of colour and arranged with precision. The two spaces are linked by the same carpet and complementary colours, though the tones in the library are more muted.

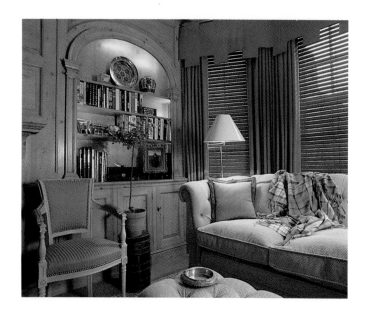

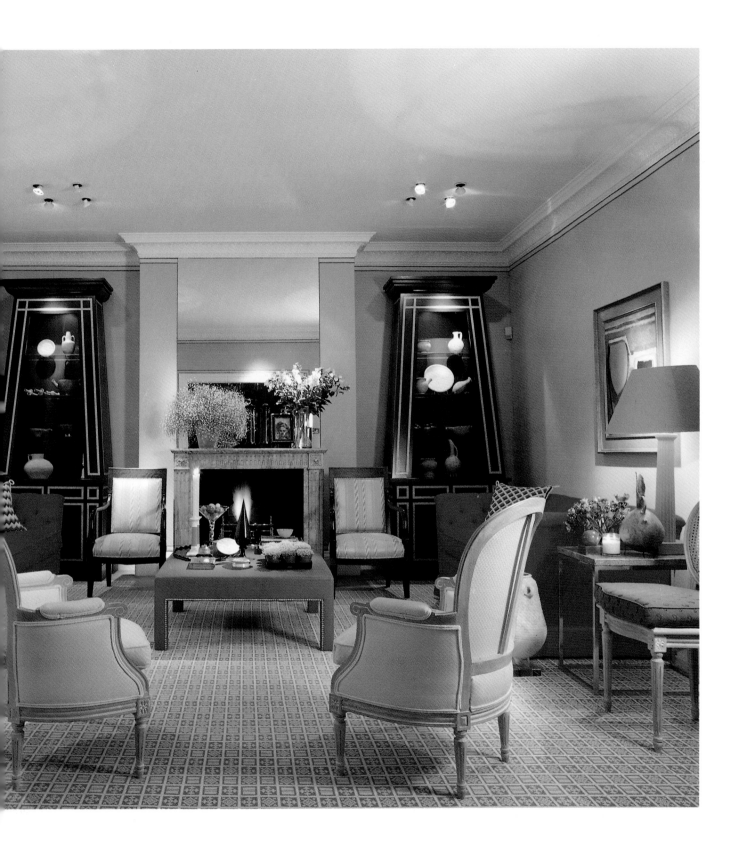

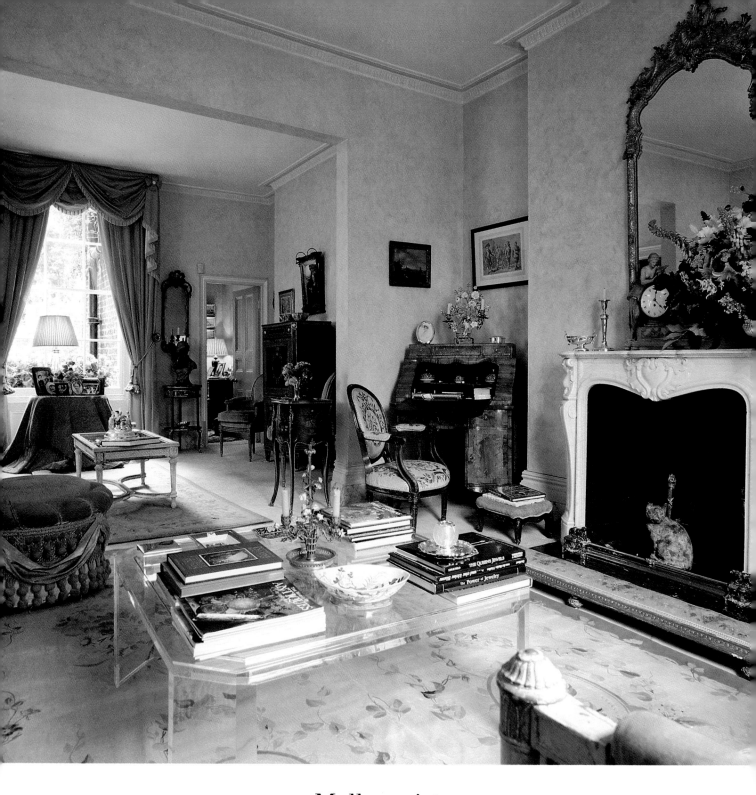

Mellow vistas

This sitting-room, though recently decorated, is satisfyingly mellow in appearance. The subtly mottled walls, painted by Graham Carr, are a flattering backdrop for the paintings and a complement to the curtains which were made twenty years ago and have faded to an exquisite lime-green. The line of vision between the two parts of the room has been kept as free as possible: furniture is low, and the coffee-table in front of the marble chimneypiece is transparent acrylic, creating minimum visual interruption. The room was decorated with advice from Gunilla and Madeleine Douglas.

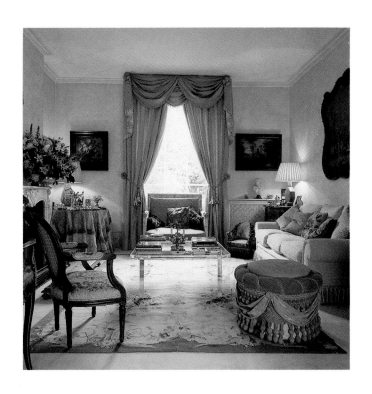

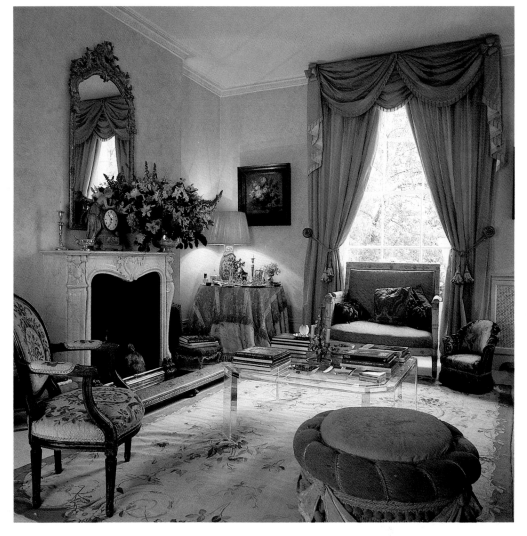

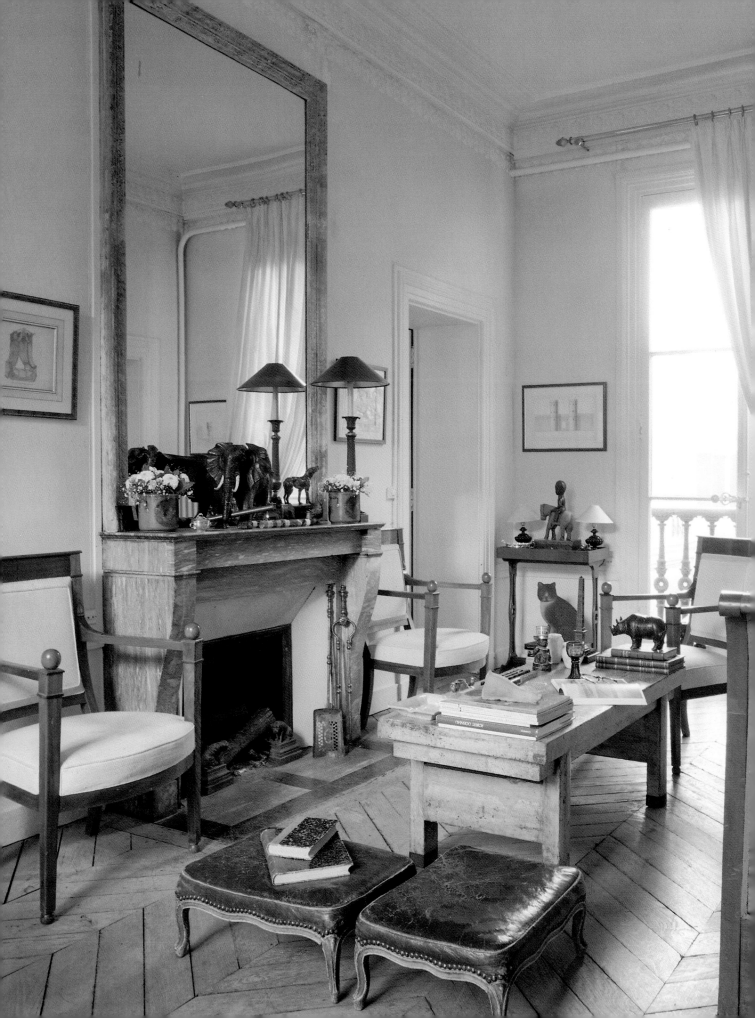

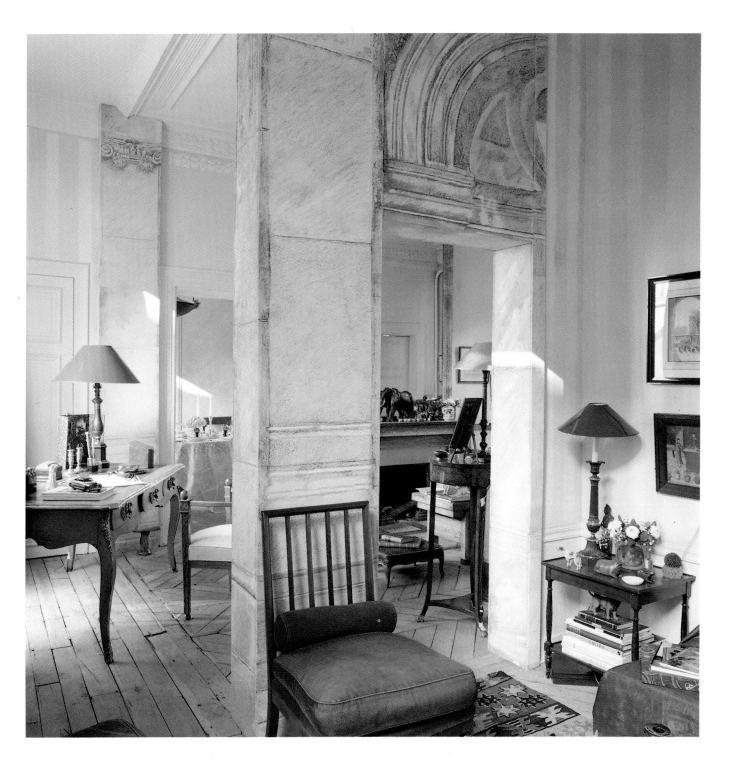

An ancient fragment

The two interconnecting sitting-areas in Nicole Mugler's *appartement* in Paris were originally separate rooms. Although the main room (left) was a well-proportioned space with a balconied window at each end, it gave no access to the flat's large and attractive terrace. The small, adjoining box-room was a wasted space but had the advantage of doors leading directly outside. The obvious way to improve the flat's layout >

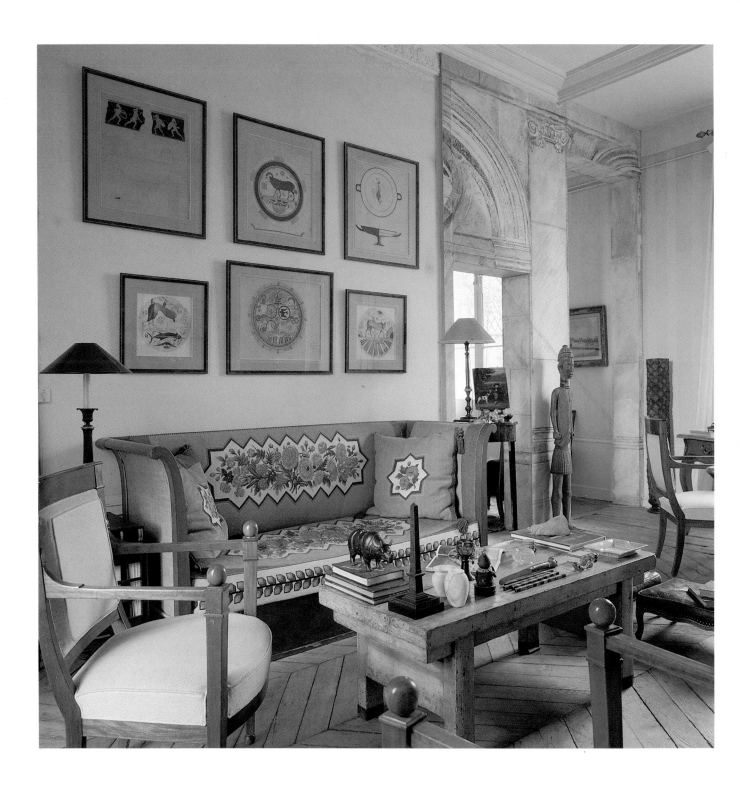

< was to demolish the dividing wall between the two rooms, but for structural reasons this involved major reinforcements with unsightly beams and posts. Making a virtue of necessity, a brilliant piece of disguise was thought up. A plywood casing was made, then stained and painted by Jean Oddes to look like a fragment of an ancient stone arch, absorbed by a later building. The stonework is echoed by a *trompe l'oeil* pilaster on the opposite wall, alongside the door to the dining-room.

The decoration and furnishing of the flat is low-key in colour

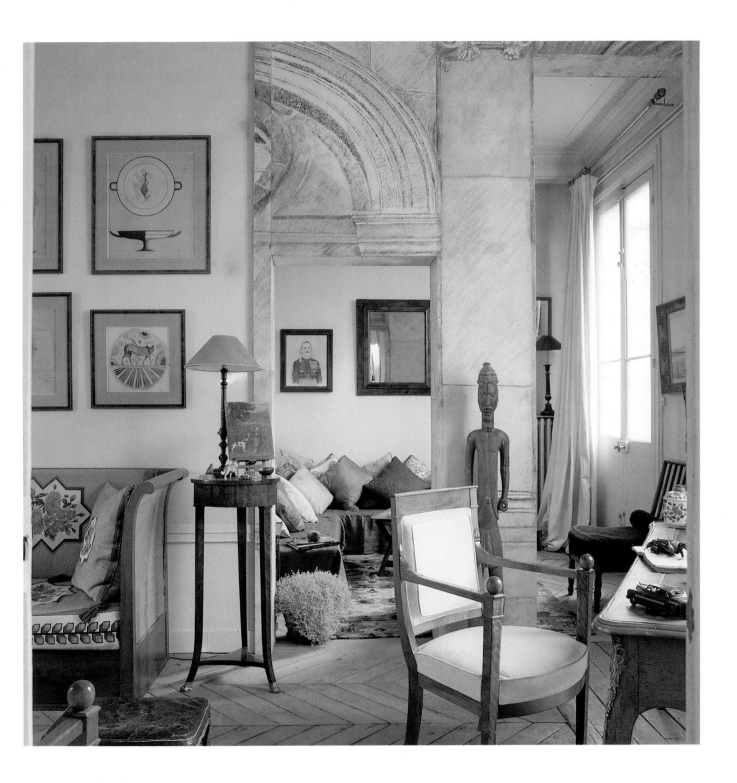

and appears very understated, yet it incorporates some
extremely interesting pieces. One of the most unusual is the
early nineteenth-century Russian sofa with its original cover.
There is a preponderance of pale woods and natural textures.
The walls are lined with plain cotton which has been painted
with subtle stripes in a yellow/peach colour; the chimneypiece,
which previously had gilded embellishments, is now marbled;
the wooden floor is left bare except for a kilim in the smaller
sitting-area.

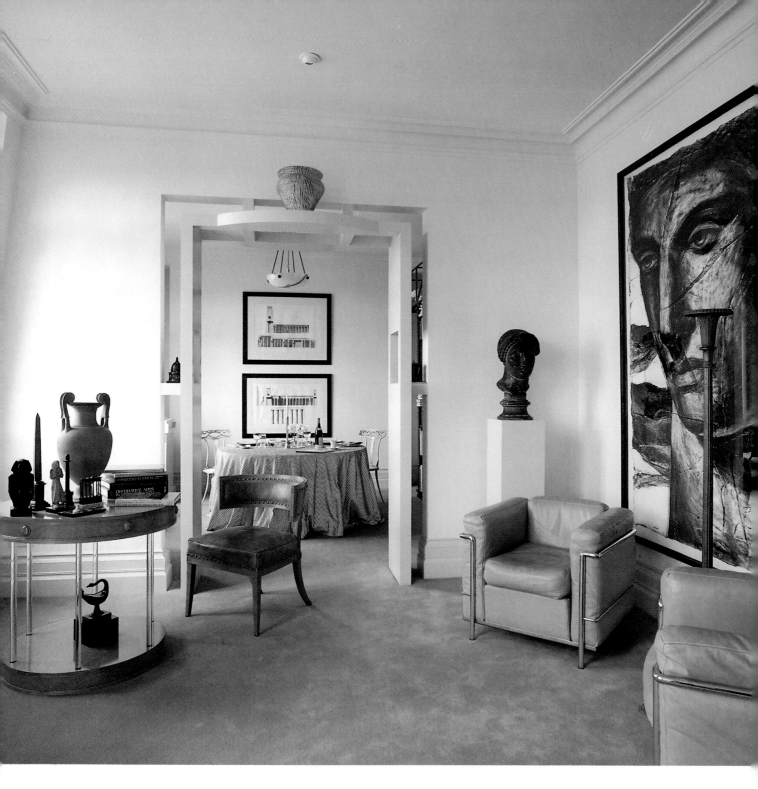

Eclectic influences

Essentially a post-modernist, John Wright prefers to be inspired by period styles rather than reproduce them to the letter. In the double living-room of his flat on the top floor of a London mansion block, there is minimalist decoration yet, paradoxically, multifarious influences. There are Danish chairs, vases and a *torchère* dating from the 1800s; classical archaeological artefacts sit on a 1930s bird's-eye maple table;

chrome-and-leather 1920s armchairs by Le Corbusier stand in front of an immense, contemporary charcoal drawing by Alison Lambert. And, in the dining-area, a bookcase made of ebonized wood and bronze, designed by John Wright, pays a sort of homage to the late-Georgian architect, Sir John Soane. The dividing arch has a strikingly modern architectural treatment, in keeping with the room's cool, uncluttered decoration.

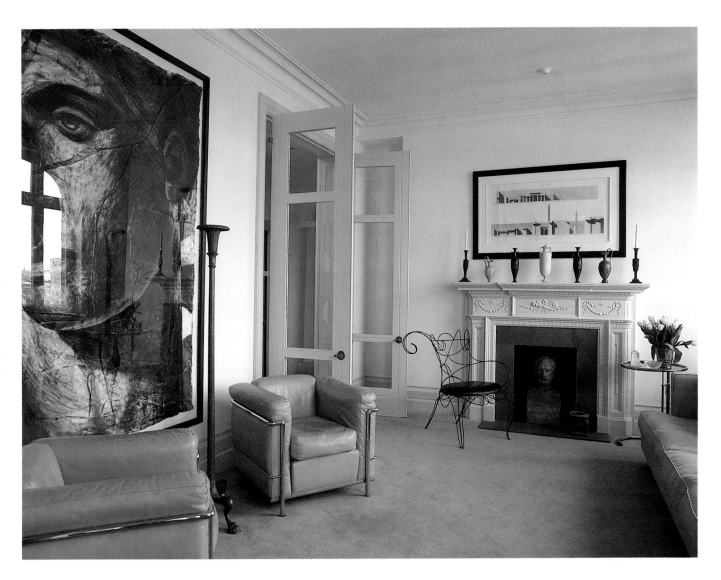

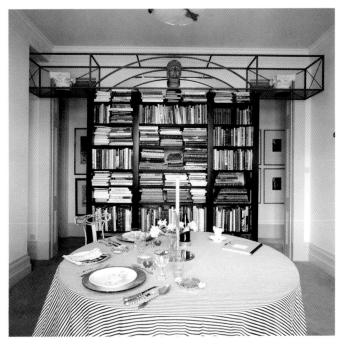

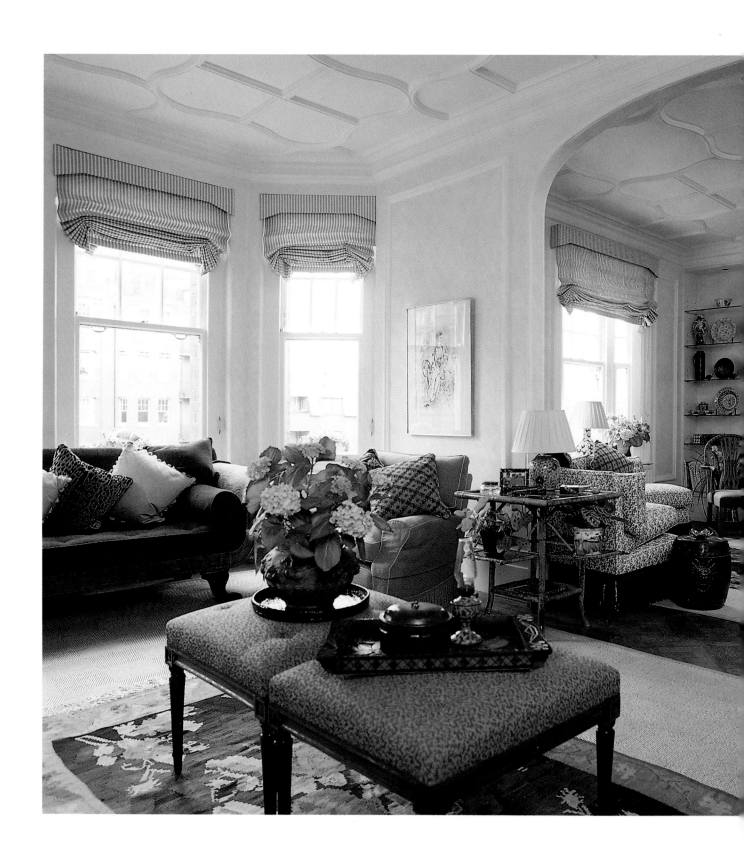

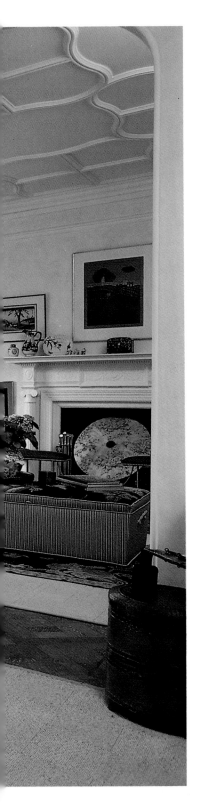

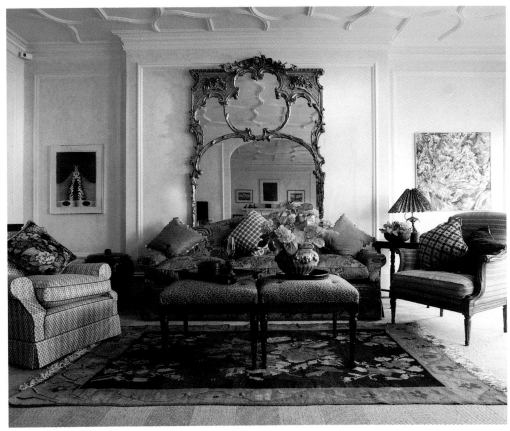

Pleasingly proportioned

The shallow archway between the two sitting-areas in a flat in Holland Park is particularly pleasingly proportioned. It is high and wide enough to imply a single room, yet there is sufficient wall expanse to either side to create interesting shapes and a feeling of enclosure in both sections. The room is in an Edwardian block and has fine period mouldings, especially on the ceiling, which provide a decorative affiliation between the two areas. The paint finish, by Barbara Broun, uses subtle shades of 'old ivory', an accommodating, tranquil background for a variety of patterned textiles, ranging from checked silk taffeta to simulated leopard-skin. Ivory is also well-attuned to the numerous paintings and the collection of blue-and-white porcelain displayed on glass shelves to either side of the chimneypiece. A huge and splendidly ornate mirror is placed on the wall opposite the chimneypiece to reflect light from the large windows and to aggrandize the space. The interior decorator was Simon Playle.

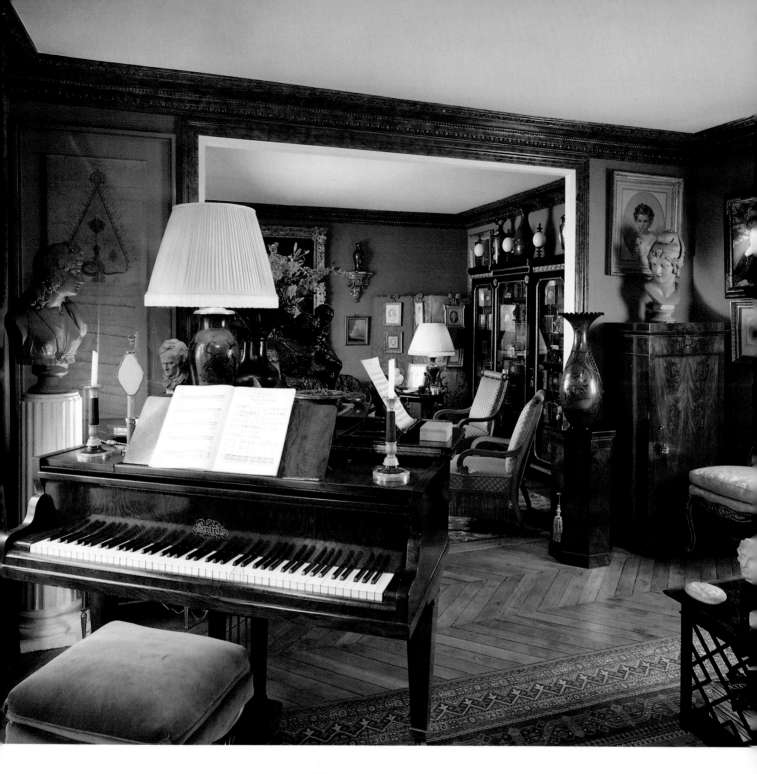

Two into one

This double sitting-room in a flat in Paris was once two small, separate rooms linked by a narrow doorway. Alain Goiot enlarged the opening to form a more usable – and more elegant – space, which still retains a sense of cosiness but offers greater scope for entertaining. In some ways, the style of decoration is rather sombre, based on heavy colours and patterns, but this was intentional as the client wished for a room with a lived-in, long-established persona. He also wanted a room for use primarily in the evenings, and thus it has to respond well to artificial light. The warmer tones of natural wood figure prominently in the furniture and painted architectural mouldings.

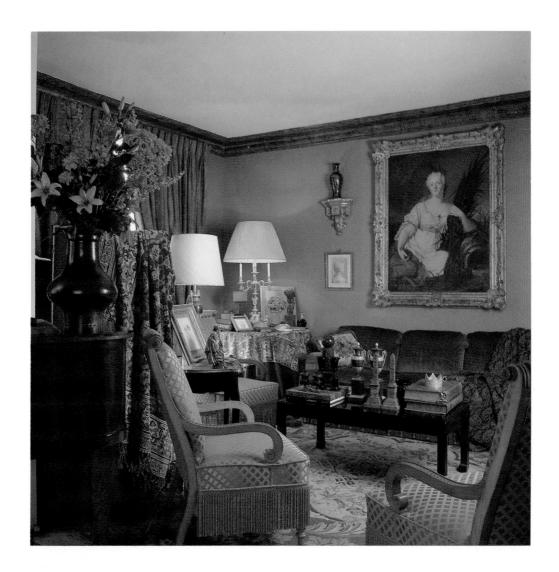

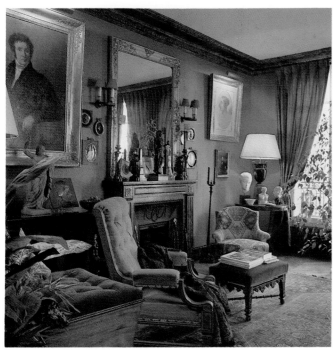

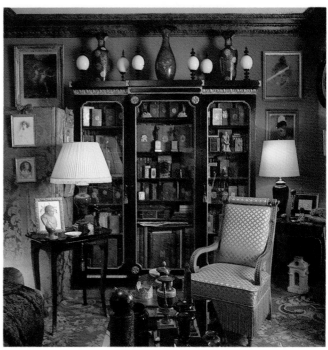

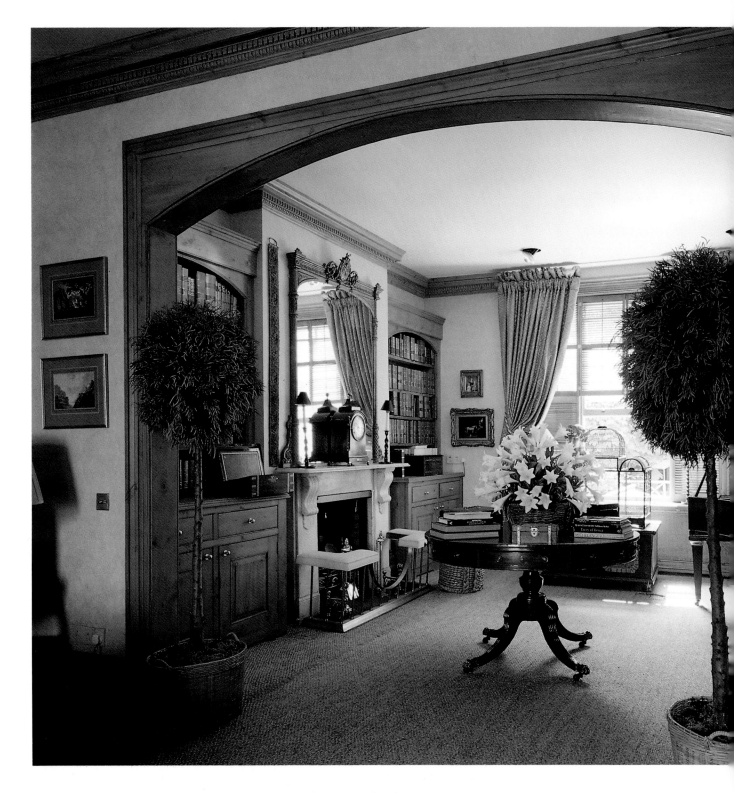

Something in between

'Not quite English and not quite American; not quite London and not quite country' – that was the brief to Sarah Tillie, the decorator for this drawing-room, originally two separate rooms, in an 1866 house in London. The walls have been drag-painted in an old-gold glaze, and the cornice has been grained to match the wooden doors and cupboards. Sisal matting provides a rural-looking underpinning for antique Persian rugs.

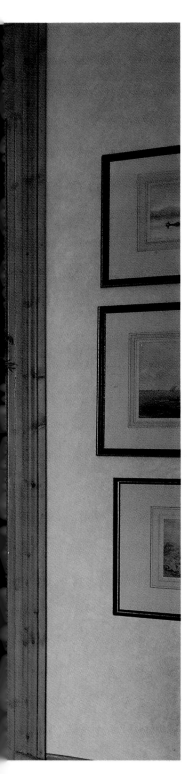

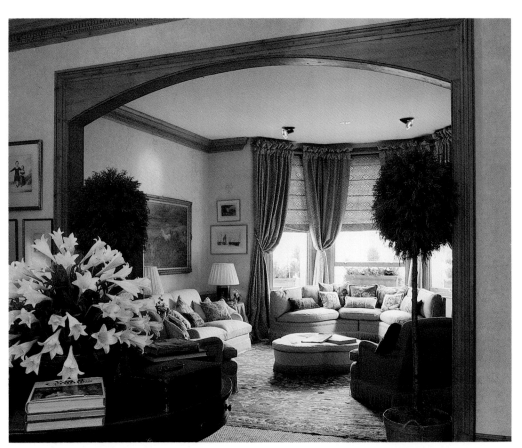

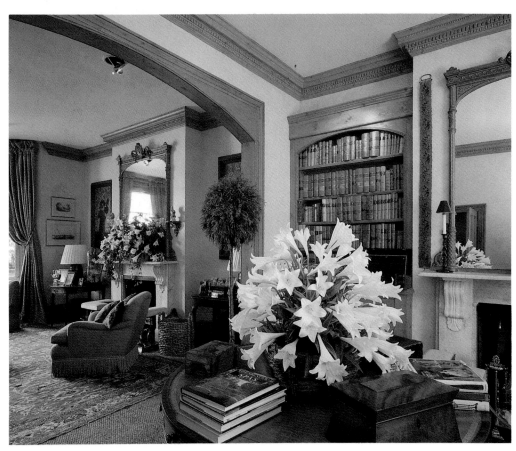

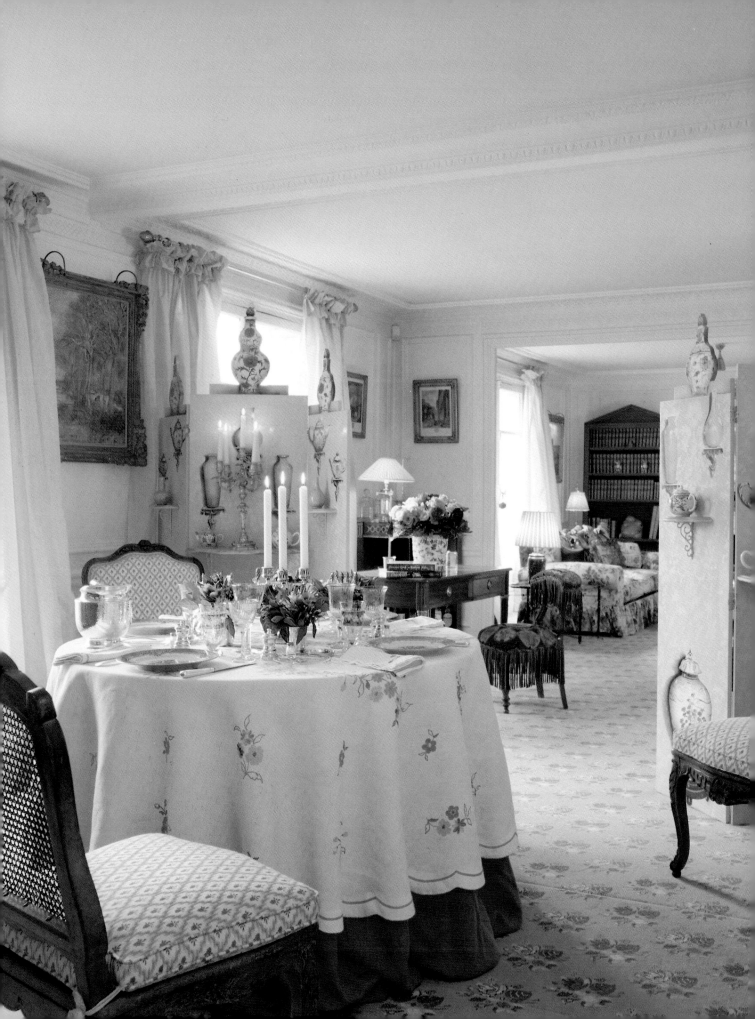

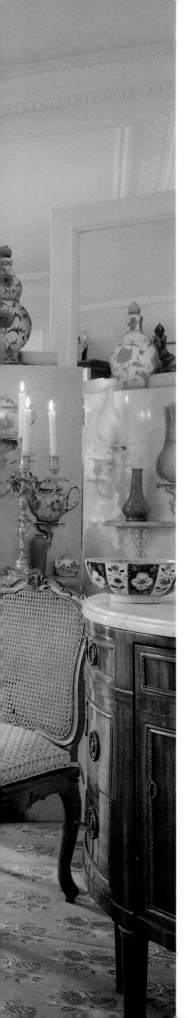

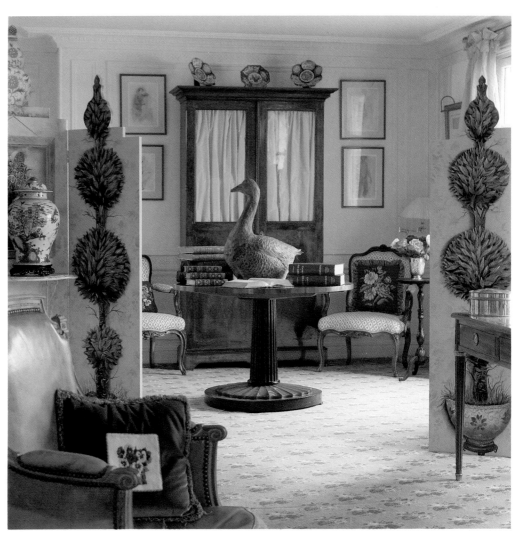

The colours of sunshine

This interior, decorated by Sabine Marchal, could be described as a triple, rather than double, room. One half of the floor space is a sitting-area, with deep-upholstered sofas to either side of the chimneypiece. The other half is an informal dining-area, loosely sub-divided by screens to form a third area used for writing. The screens are arresting works of art, as pretty and humorous as they are practical. Cut-out shapes are perceived as pots and urns on one side but, when seen from the other side, they are magically transformed into topiary plants. To add further confusion, real china jars are displayed on shelves fixed to the screens.

The three parts of the room are united by the palest cream >

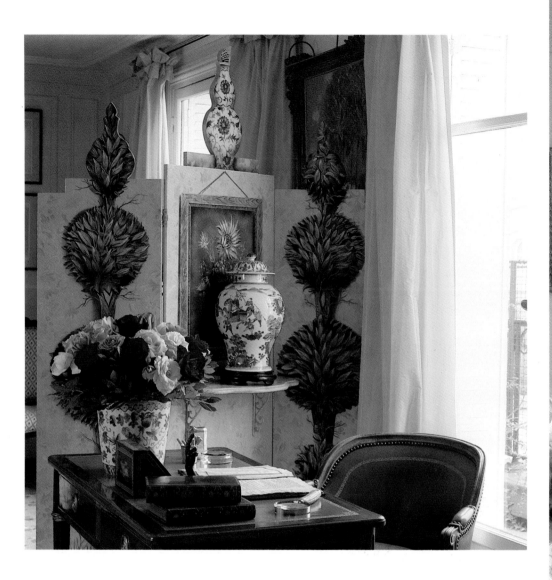

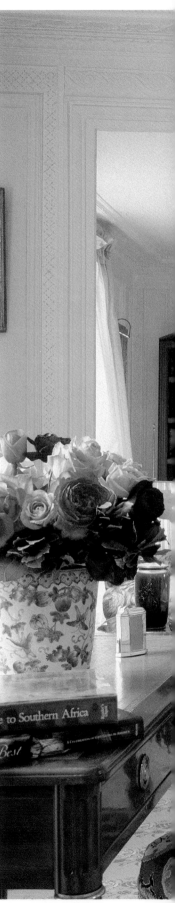

< wall-colour and delicately stencilled trellis-work frieze. The same carpet, based on an eighteenth-century Russian original, is laid throughout. The dominant colour in the room is yellow, though splashes of pinky red appear in the fabrics and book-shelves. The fireplace end of the room is set out with precision, with paired bookcases, paired sofas and paired urns on the chimneypiece. The dining end of the room is more idiosyncratic, with some unusual pieces of furniture, including an 1830s Viennese pedestal table which, overlaid with an embroidered cloth, doubles as a dining-table. A Louis XVI desk is placed by one of the room's four windows, all of which have vivid yellow taffeta curtains.

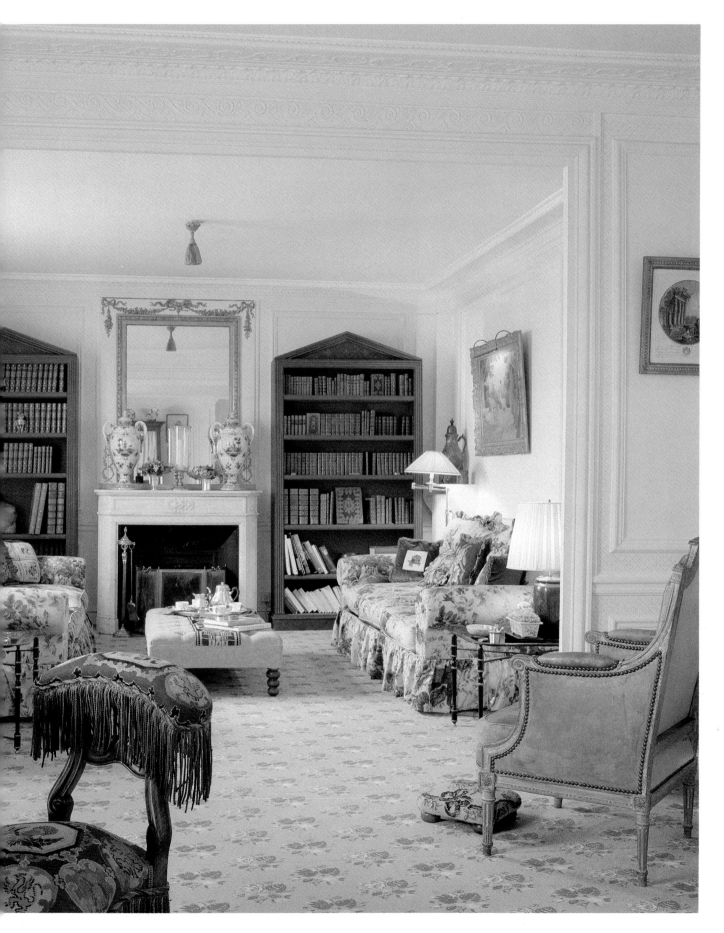

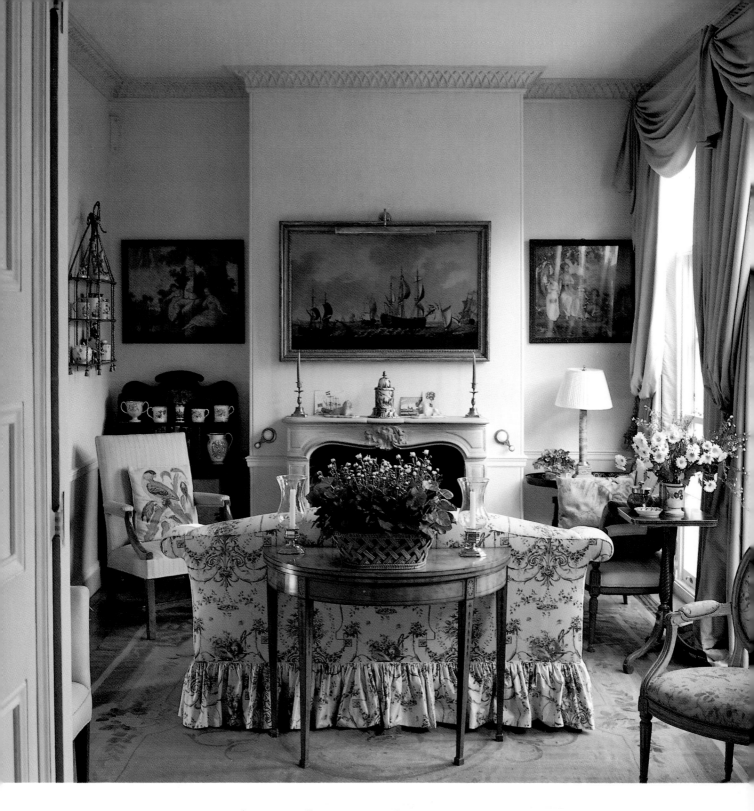

An understated equanimity

This London drawing-room and adjoining
dining-room evoke, in miniature, the style of a
stately home. The floor area is small but there
is a timeless correctness and equanimity in
the assemblage of furniture, objects and
colours, which transcends fashion. The

drawing-room is a recent addition to a 1750s
house and was designed by James Mather
with appropriate gothick detail in the cornice
and windows. Cornelia Faulkner oversaw the
paint effects, which have just the right degree
of understatement.

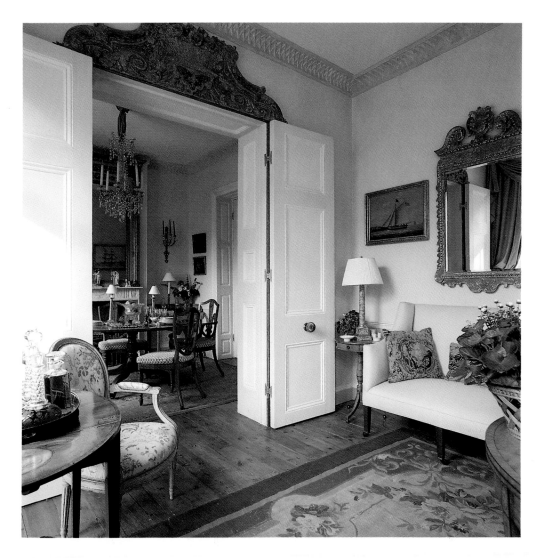

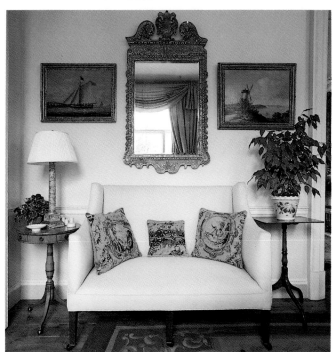

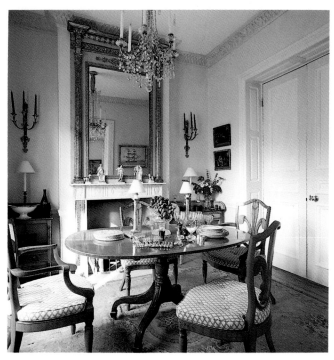

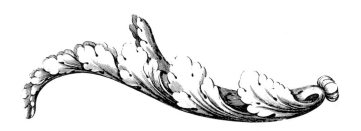

A place for books

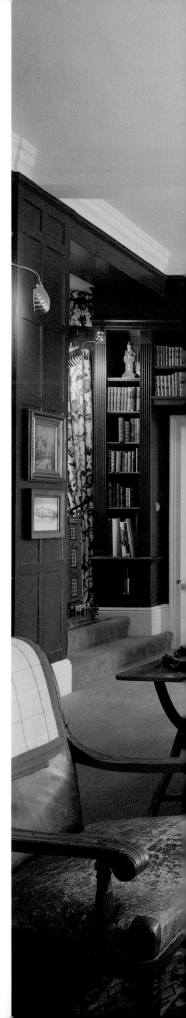

In the more constrained days of the eighteenth century, books were thought improper in the drawing-room, presumably because the setting was intended purely for socializing, and if people wished to read they retired to a study or library. Happily, contemporary drawing-room mores are less starchy. Reading a book while others are in the room may still be frowned upon, but nobody seems to find the physical presence of books offensive. On the contrary, most of us believe that books give a drawing-room a more lived-in, more welcoming ambience. Books are visually stimulating and sometimes, one suspects, are valued as much for their appearance as for their literary promise. The so-called coffee-table book sums up everything. This lavish production incites browsing, conveys an instant degree of knowledge and, more importantly perhaps, plays a significant role in interior decoration. Large and impressive, it is unashamedly designed to be part of a total *mise en scène*, to be given a prominent place on a table rather than relegated to obscurity on a shelf.

Many drawing-rooms are now furnished as part sitting-room, part library. The distinction between the two functions has become blurred, but the aesthetic results are often immensely successful. From a practical point of view, the main thing is to get the right housing for the books, whether a free-standing antique bureau-bookcase or specially designed, built-in shelves. If you opt for the latter, it is essential that their form and finish are as sophisticated as the most covetable piece in the room – anything less can look depressingly mean and out of keeping in an otherwise carefully-judged drawing-room. Then there is the need for good, directional lighting and, finally, for easy – but not too soporifically inductive – seating.

(Right) Shelves painted in a deep, bookish green have an attractive and practical lighting arrangement using brass lamps fixed to the vertical supports. The tone of the paintwork relates well to the bindings and is continued over the wall panelling. Green reappears in the upholstery and fringed curtains. The room is in a house in Dorset, decorated with advice from Nina Campbell.

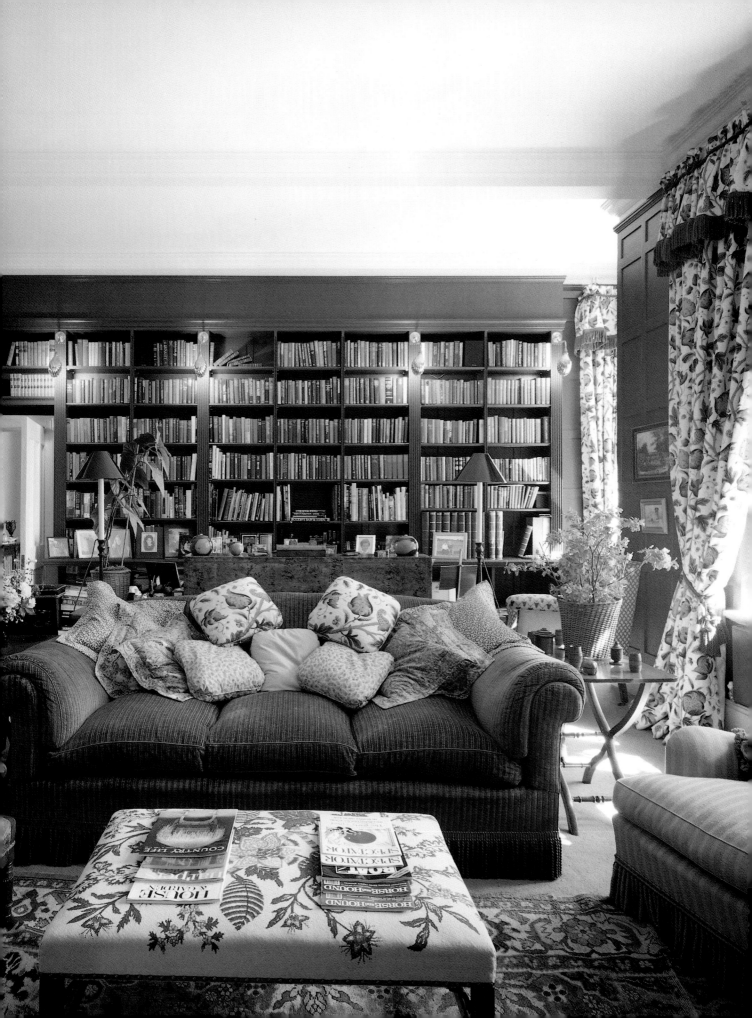

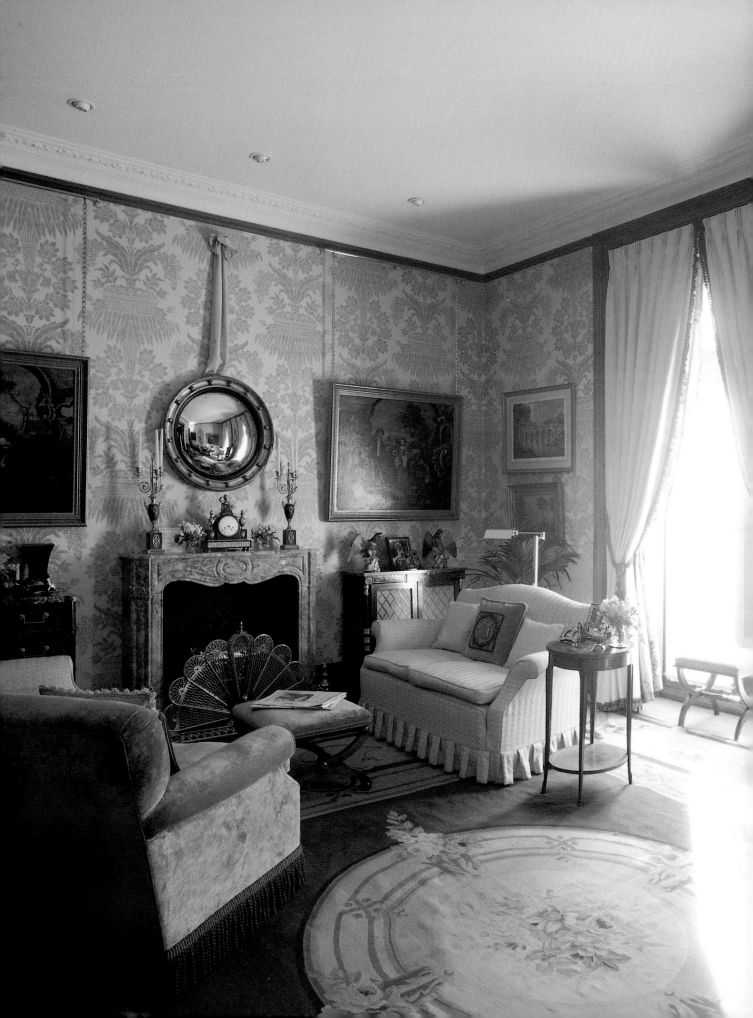

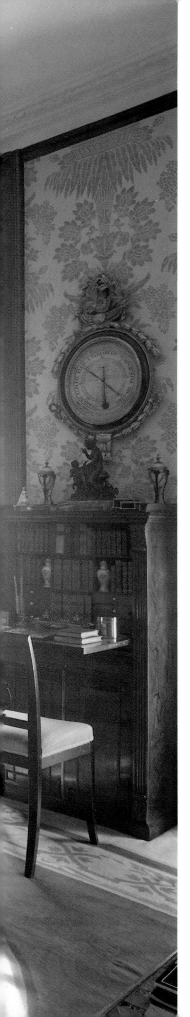

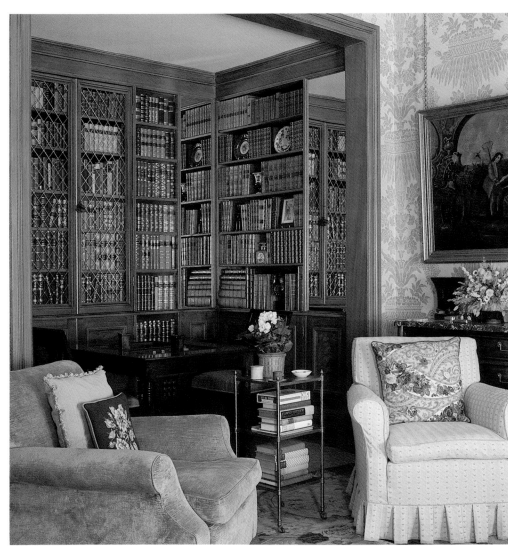

Putting the books aside

Space is at a premium in this *pied-à-terre*, yet the impression is uncramped and luxurious. The flat is in one of London's earliest purpose-built blocks, which dates from the 1880s and, externally, is a mixture of Victorian and French styles. The traditional architecture and French association influenced the decoration and furnishing of the room. The chimneypiece is French; so, too, are the Aubusson rug and the wallpaper. Even the curtain treatment is a traditional French arrangement of dress curtains and inner curtains. All the books have been kept together in an alcove, thus freeing the walls in the main room for pictures, a convex mirror and a handsome barometer. The mini-library has shelves and cupboards of wood, a mellow complement to the leather-bound books – some of which are merely spines mounted on a panel to conceal the television.

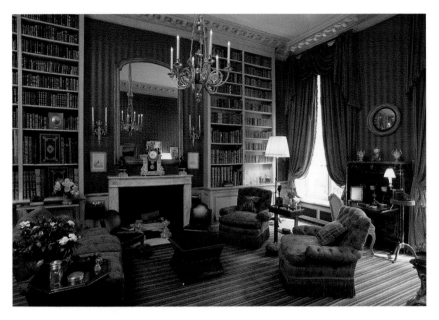

An integrated series of stripes

Sandy de Yturbe describes the book-lined sitting-room of her apartment in Paris as a family room, used for relaxing, watching television, listening to music and reading. But it is a family room of a very sophisticated order, with good furniture, red-fabric-lined walls and complementary red-striped curtains. The carpet is striped, and so, too, is the upholstery of the deep-buttoned chairs, though the latter stripe is a freer variant, with a woven floral motif. The specially-designed bookcases, painted by René Louis Picherit in varying tones of greens, browns, pistachio and grey, integrate with the room's architectural embellishments. The top of the bookcase has been painted to match the frieze of the cornice, and the plinth has been marbled to blend with the skirting-board. The furniture includes a fine Louis XV Chinese lacquered bureau and four signed, carved-wood chairs by Cresson. The richness of the room is enhanced by golden highlights which appear in numerous guises, ranging from the elaborate gold-leaf detail of the book bindings to the ormolu arabesques of the chandelier and wall sconces.

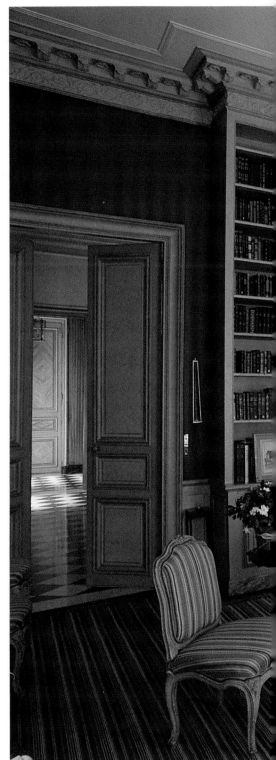

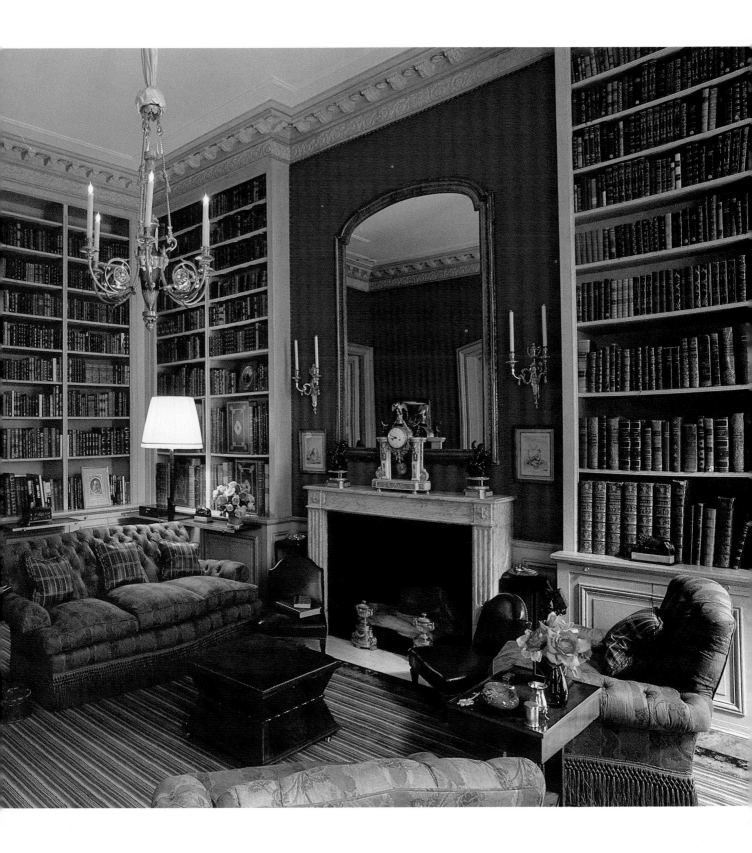

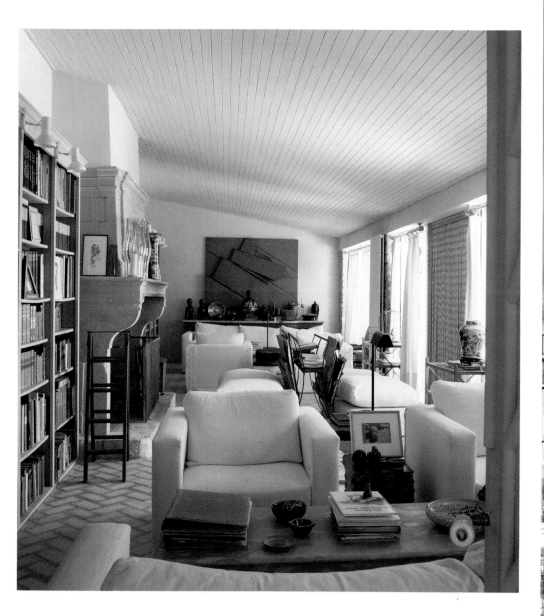

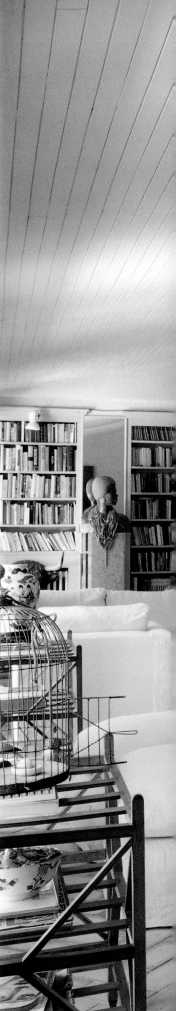

A distinctive clarity

The exaggerated length of this drawing-room in a one-time café in Provence, converted by Dick Dumas, made it a difficult space to decorate, but dividing it into three distinct seating-areas has worked well, both visually and practically. Bookcases line two walls, one of which has an imposing seventeenth-century stone chimneypiece. The wall above the mantelshelf has been skilfully painted to extend the stonework to range with the top of the bookshelves, giving continuity of line and clearer definition beneath the sloping ceiling. Spotlights, fixed at regular intervals along the bookcases, are simple and functional. The clarity of the room's decoration is reinforced by the bold shapes and unusual character of the ornaments.

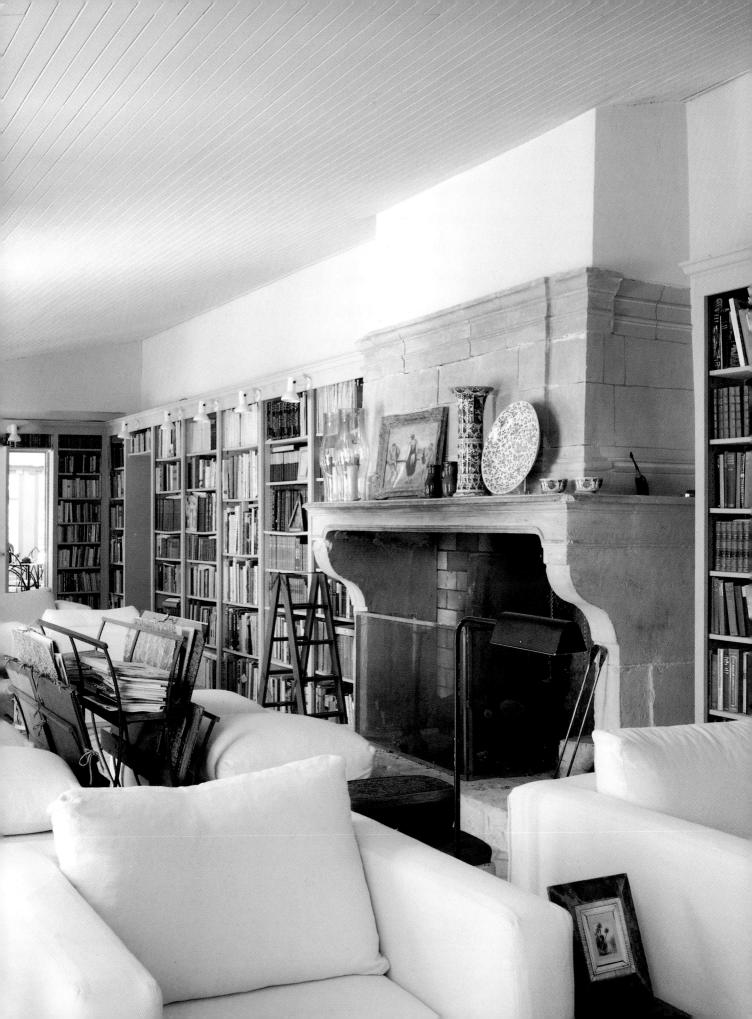

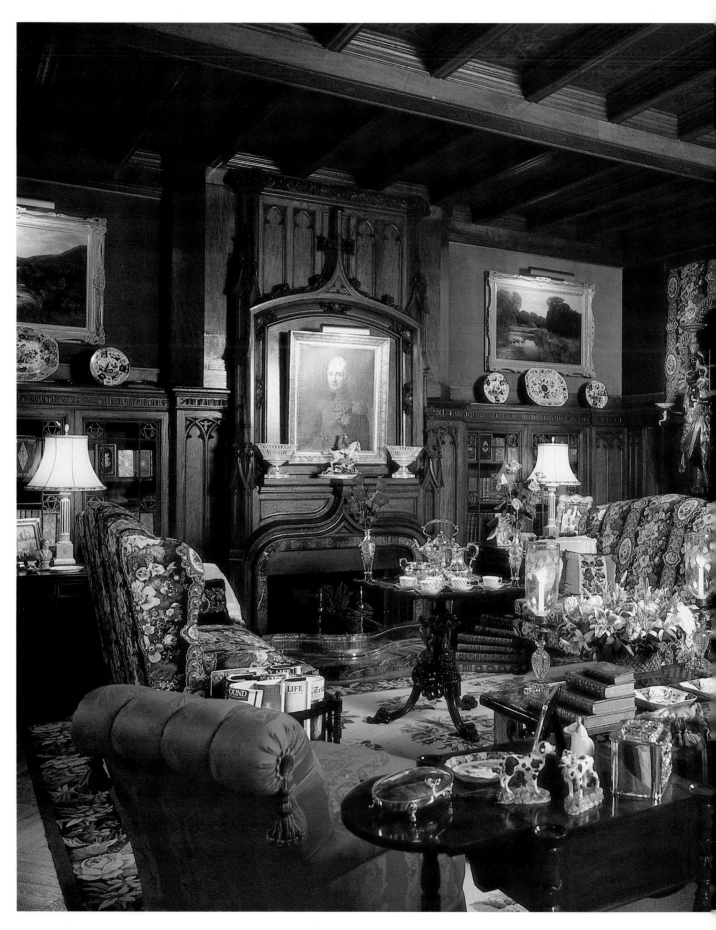

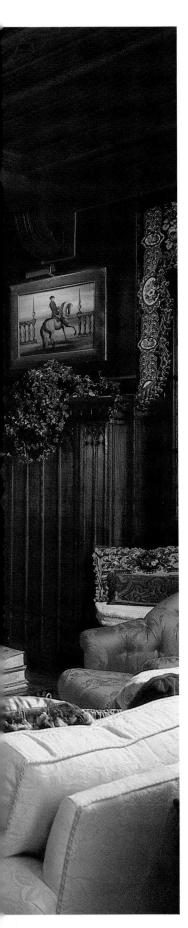

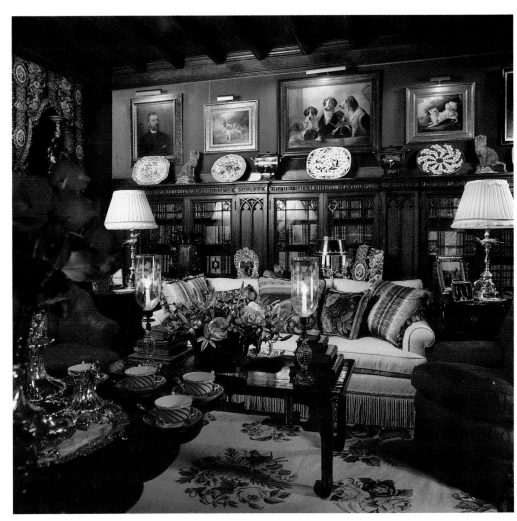

An air of tradition

There is something very satisfying about a room which
combines rich, deep colours with carved wood. The
combination has an affinity which seems especially agreeable
in a library setting such as this, designed by Richard L. Ridge
for a fund-raising show-house for the Kips Bay Boys' and Girls'
Club in New York. The room is in a house built in the first
decade of this century, and the present scheme conveys a
suitably established, traditional aura. Books are housed in
glass-fronted cabinets which are low enough to allow paintings
to be hung above and to provide an ideal, eye-level stage for a
series of plates. Snug seating, covered in three different
fabrics, is grouped on a colourful, rose-patterned rug in front
of the gothick chimneypiece.

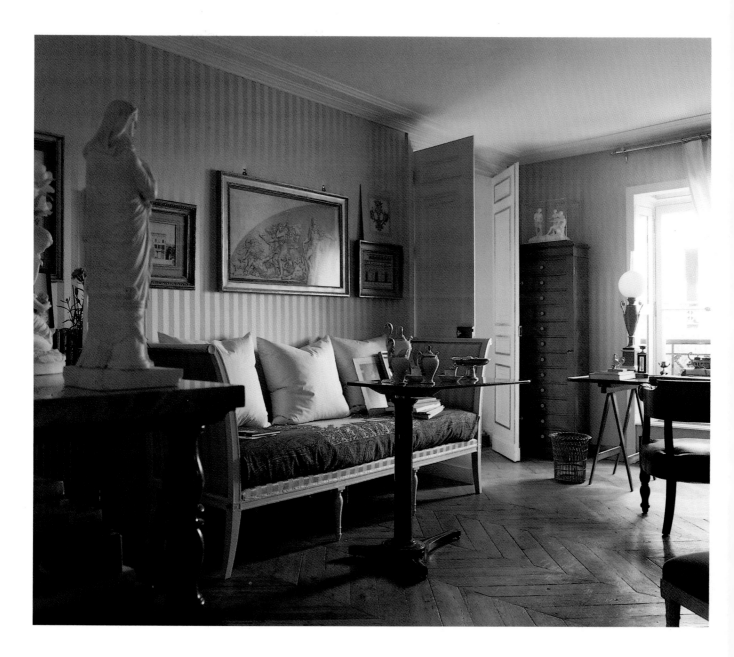

Purist decoration

This rather reserved room in Paris is not only a working library, containing art reference books, but also a showcase for a remarkable collection of rare tomes, including first editions, with their bindings displayed Empire-style behind glazed doors. The room's ceiling is fairly low, so collector-decorator Pierre-Hervé Walbaum faced the walls with a striped fabric to give the illusion of greater height. A narrow band of the same powdery blue is used to edge the pure white silk taffeta curtains. White recurs in the collection of Sèvres figures and in the painted late-eighteenth-century sofa and neoclassical chair. Pierre-Hervé Walbaum is a purist who never hangs pictures in different media in the same room. Here, he has limited his selection to drawings, mainly of architectural subjects, including some by Meynier relating to the Arc de Triomphe and the Palais Bourbon.

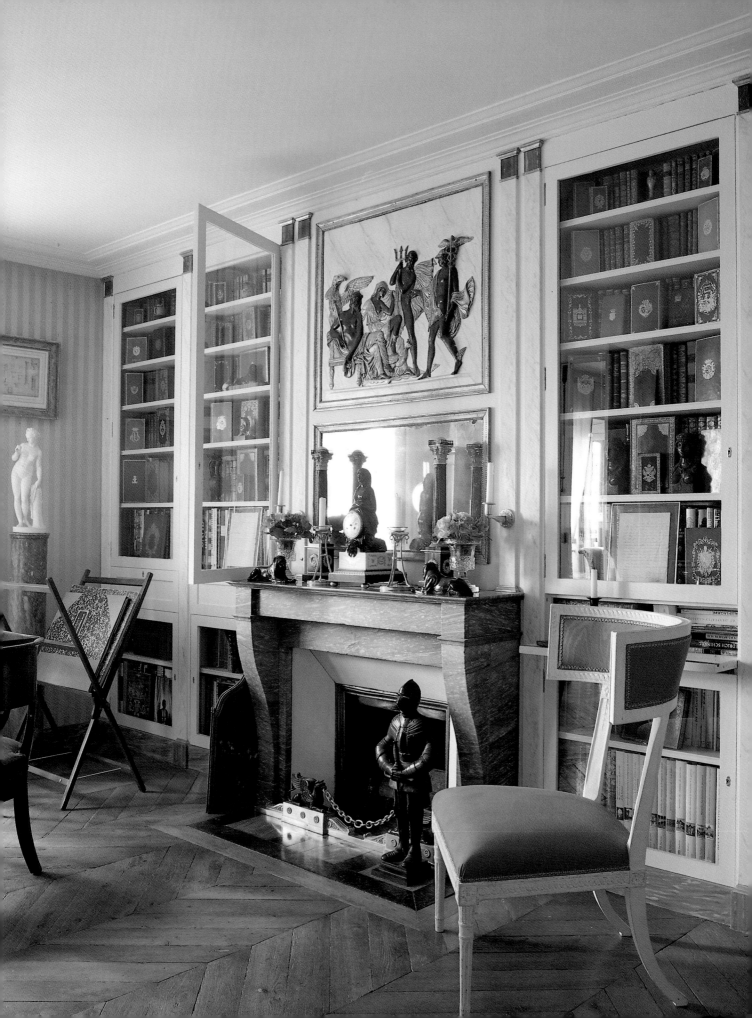

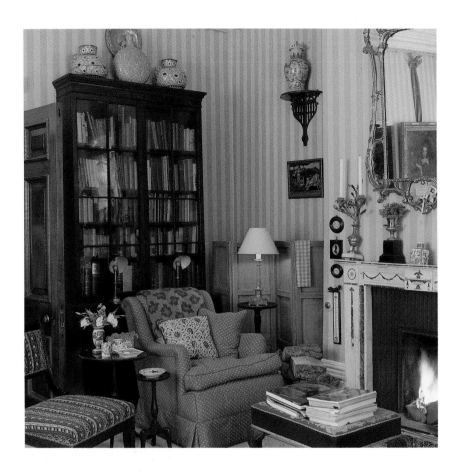

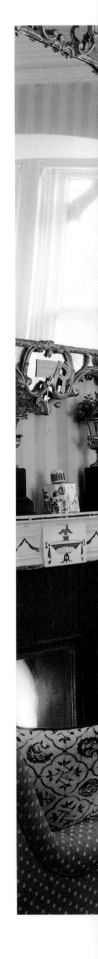

Inviting and undemanding

With its deceptively carefree arrangement of furniture and objects, this room in an erstwhile rectory in Berkshire epitomizes the English country-house style of decoration. Comfortable and warm, it is cluttered in the nicest possible way, and the ambience is totally undemanding. Although the room doesn't pretend to be a library, it invites sitting and reading, with soft seating and two glazed bookcases to meet the needs of such languorous pastimes. The striped wallcovering and checked upholstery on the sofa are important counterbalances for the more flamboyant chintzes and for the curvaceous pots and mirror. The room was decorated by Roger Banks-Pye of Colefax and Fowler.

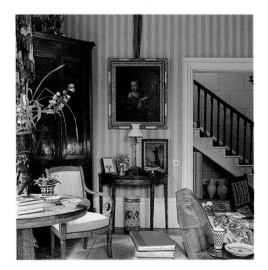

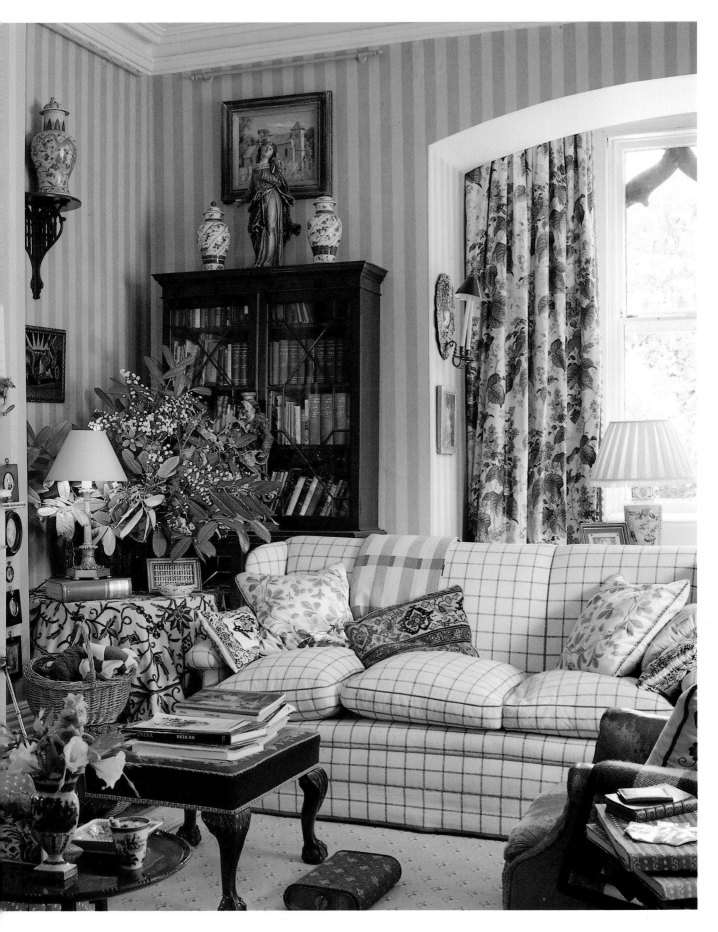

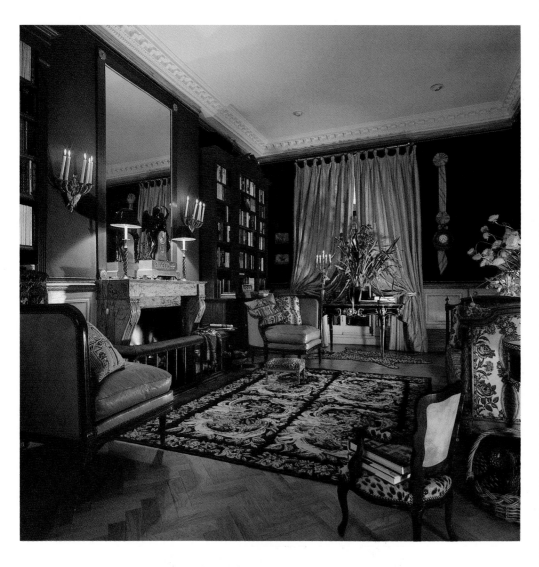

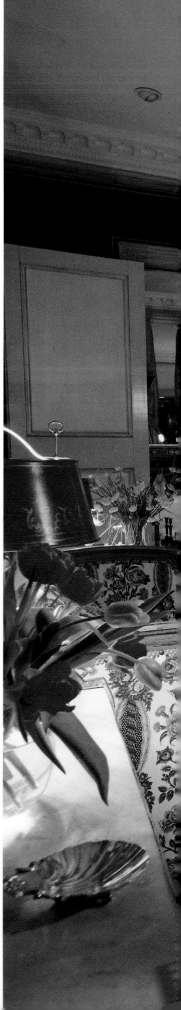

Perfect for winter reading

When a room is decorated with such élan and grandeur as here, well-designed lighting is essential to complement and, in a sense, stage-manage the drama. Spotlights recessed in the ceiling give good overall light and can be directed towards particular pieces of furniture and objects. The grey marble chimneypiece and ceiling-high mirror are given added prominence by magnificent five-candle wall sconces and a pair of candlestick lamps with Empire-style shades. With light bounced off the mirror, the effect is truly sparkling, a lustrous foil for the dark green baize above the painted dado. With two large, handsome bookcases, an open fire and comfortable chairs, this room is the perfect setting for evening reading. André de Cacqueray assisted with the decoration.

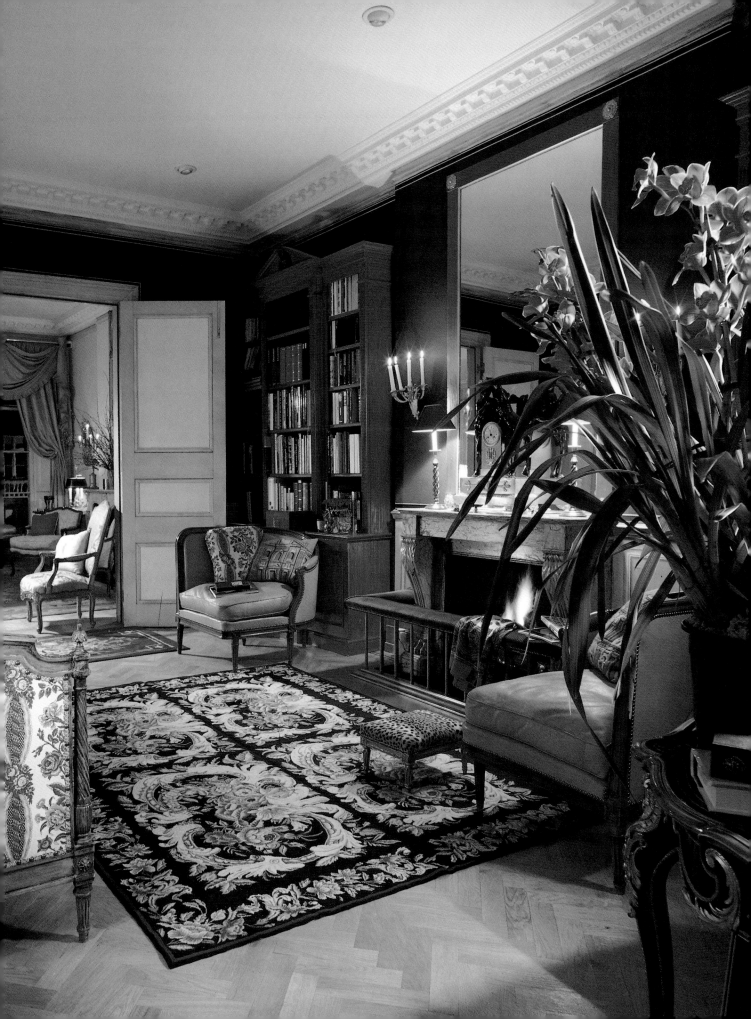

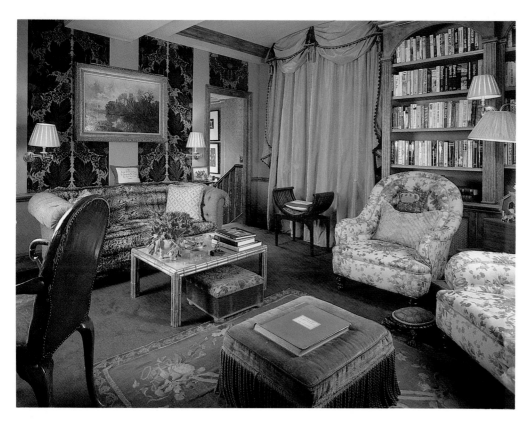

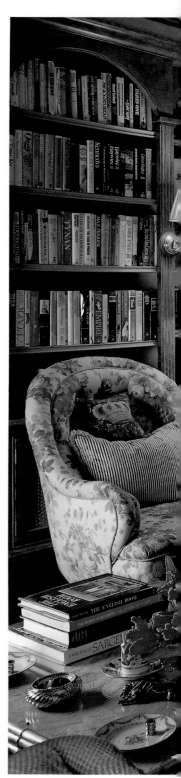

A literary ambience

Apart from well-organized shelving for books, there are three
essential elements in every traditional library/sitting-room –
and this room, decorated by Sally Metcalf of George Spencer
Designs, incorporates them all. The first is comfort, for no one
enjoys reading when sitting in an unyielding chair. The second
is good lighting. The third is less tangible: an atmosphere
conducive to quiet, even solitary, hours of bookish pursuits.
Here, the books are housed in arched bookcases painted in
faux bois to match the cornice. Wall lamps with pleated silk
shades illuminate the books and provide light for readers
ensconced in the buttoned chairs and sofa. Additional light
comes from the brass pole lamp with gathered silk shades. The
upholstery fabrics, though new, have a faded, antique
appearance, well tuned to the room's nostalgic ambience. The
muted colours of the rug are equally pleasing and appropriate.

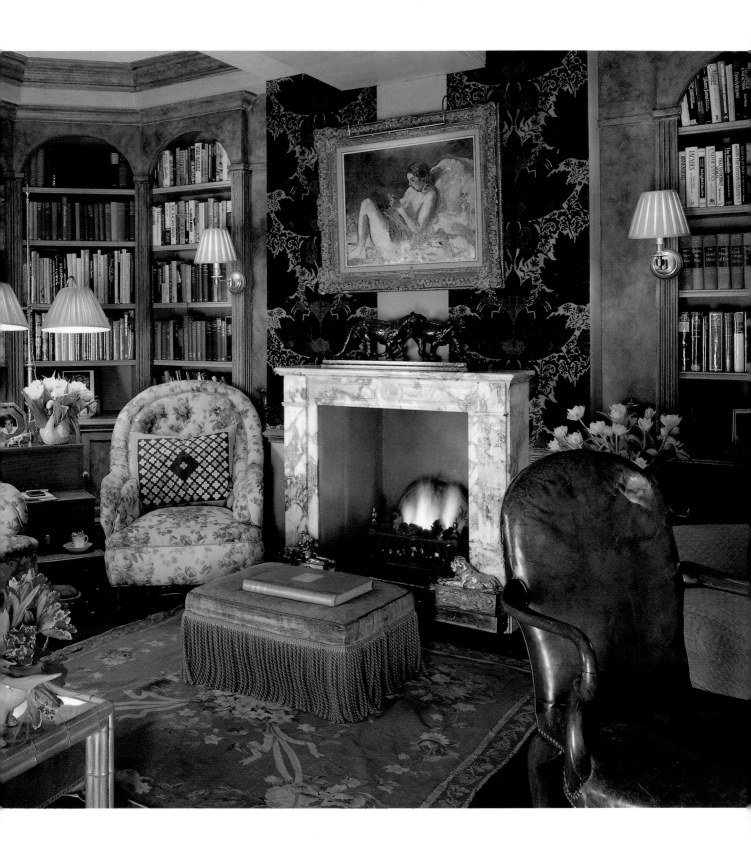

Decoration in detail

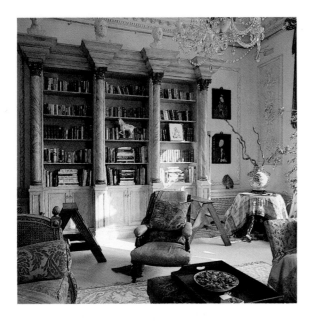

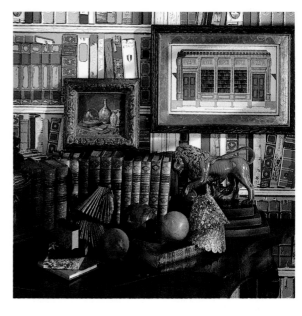

The substantial size of this drawing-room in London, decorated by Margaret Tiffin, requires furniture of equally prodigious proportions. The design for a bookcase, with a massive cornice supporting busts, was the starting-point for the room's decoration. It is painted in Florentine green with sienna columns.

Books are the decorative story here, but only a few are real. The rest are pure fiction. The background for this arrangement by Anne Hardy is wallpaper, printed with all kinds of readable-looking tomes, and the books on the table include a Victorian book-box and some volumes made of marble.

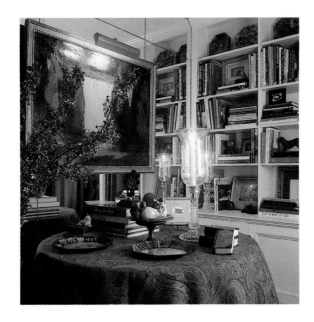

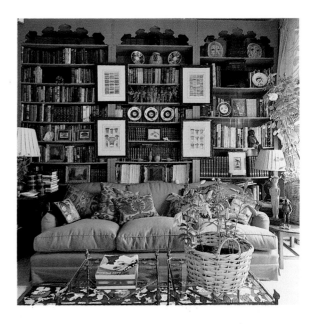

In one corner of a room by Paula Perlini, there are two different, but complementary, wall treatments. The wall clad with mirror not only adds depth to the modestly sized setting but reflects the adjacent bookcase, giving the illusion of continuity while providing an unconflicting background for a painting.

The arches of this tripartite bookcase are unusual and slightly oriental. Equally unusual is the manner in which prints are hung against the vertical supports, breaking up the rigid lines of the shelves. Plates, pots, pictures and other small ornamental pieces mingle with the books, making a lively composition.

Decoration in detail

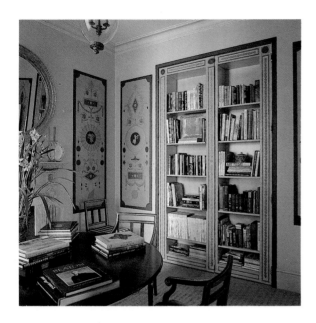

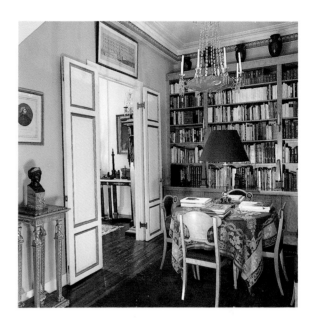

These double doors, designed by Katharine Fortescue for a small flat in London, are a brilliant solution to the problem of having too many books and too little wall space for shelving. The doors are built with shelves on one side, with an architrave painted to echo the wall panels by Barbara Brown.

A fine collection of blond-wood furniture, including a set of Biedermeier chairs, prompted the paint-finish of the bookcase designed by Håkan Groth for Rupert Cavendish's home in London. The bookcase fills the width of the room but stops short of the ceiling, allowing space for a row of classical vases.

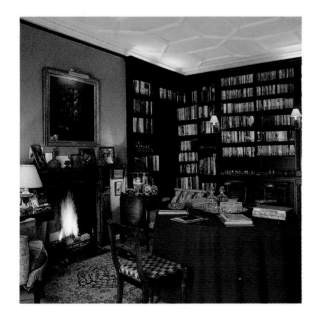

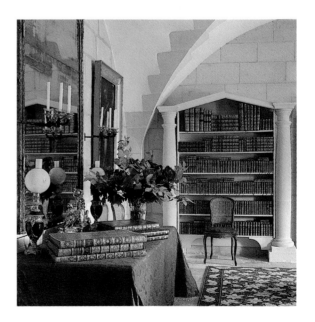

Though an uncommon choice for built-in bookshelves, black is a good foil for colourful bindings. Furthermore, black makes the gaps above the books less obtrusive, as they disappear in total shadow and fuse with the bookcase framework. The room was designed by Liz Smithers of Sloane Decorators.

A modern version of a neoclassical bookcase, designed by Elga de Caraman for her home in the Loire Valley, has an architectural severity which stands up well to the stone walls and vaulted ceiling. The quietude of the setting, combined with the uniformity of the brown leather bindings, has a collegiate timelessness.

Gilded highlights

Among the most immediate and glamorous ways to enrich any surface – whether painted wall or printed textile – is to add golden highlights. In spite of its opulent, rarefied image, gold is a most accommodating ally in interior decoration, combining sympathetically with other finishes and colours. With white, it has a purity which is supremely sophisticated. With dark colours, gold gives a rare richness. In schemes embodying bright colours, it imbues a jewel-like brilliance.

There are two schools of thought about the amount of gold a room can sustain. One advocates a restrained approach, with gold used merely for accents; the other favours a dazzling and lavish directness, with gold dominating the entire setting. Either way, and in whatever measure, gold suits today's traditionalist, revivalist mood. Gilded furniture and picture frames, ormolu clocks and brass-inlaid furniture are wholly in keeping with a richer, more confident style of interior decoration.

One of the most sumptuous wall treatments illustrated in this chapter (on pages 94–95) is, paradoxically, the subtlest, with gold glinting in occasional, random flashes from beneath a textured paint finish. More conventional is the use of gilding on architectural mouldings, which makes a resplendent and appropriate background for antique furniture, especially for French furniture of the eighteenth and early nineteenth centuries. The revival in the use of gold in interior decoration is undoubtedly linked to the current fashion for the English Regency and French Empire styles, when brass and ormolu were such important materials for embellishing furniture and decorative objects. The drawing-rooms on pages 88–89 and 92–93 are just two of many in this book which display these neoclassical influences.

(Right) This is a Gilded Chamber in every sense. The walls, painted an appropriate period green, are lavishly embellished with gold leaf, as is the compartmented ceiling with allegorical themes by Pierre-Edmond Hédouin. The Louis XVI giltwood chairs and exceptional marquetry furniture with ormolu mounts take the golden theme to even greater lengths, extravagantly reflected in huge mirrors. The room, in Jean Lupu's house in Paris, was decorated with advice from Jacques García.

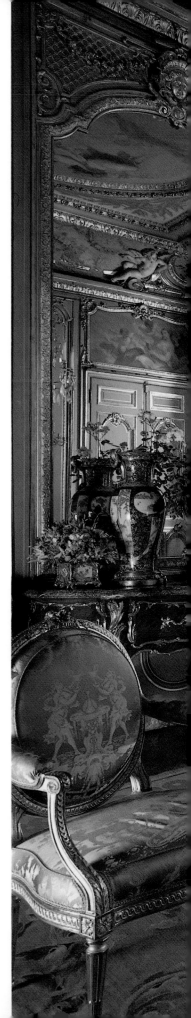

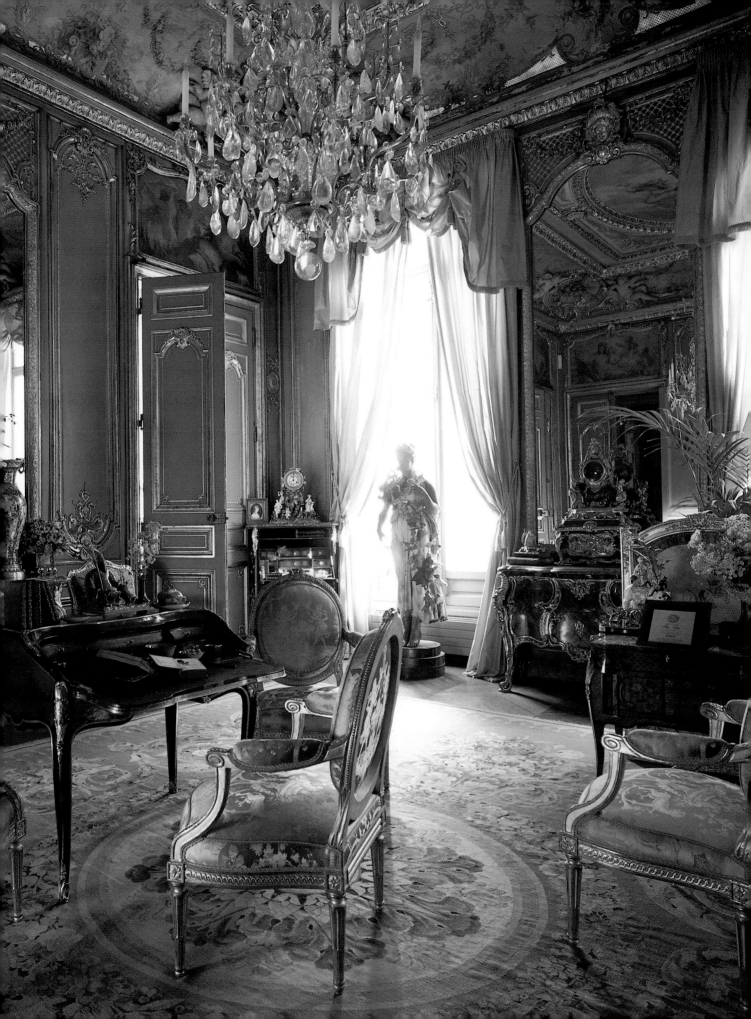

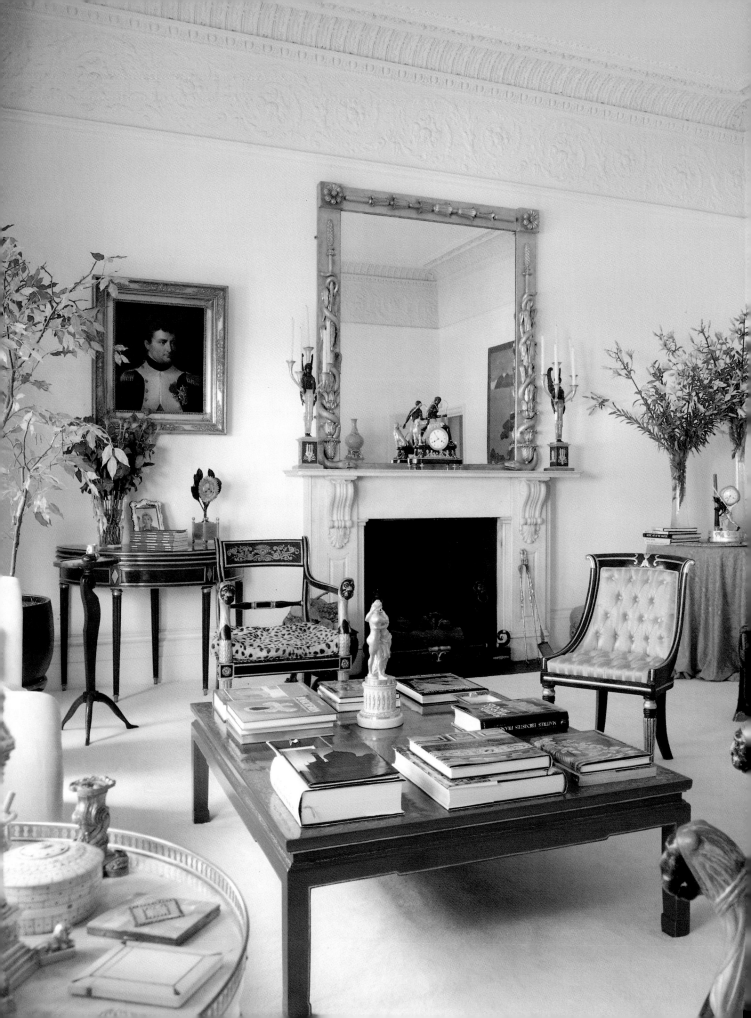

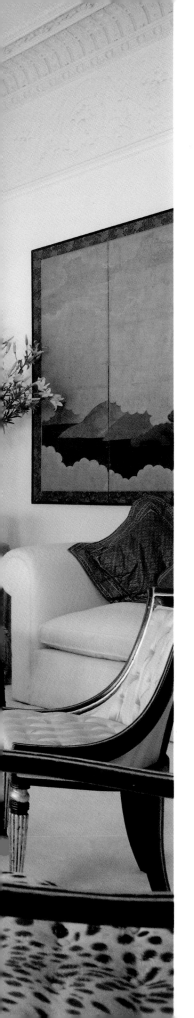

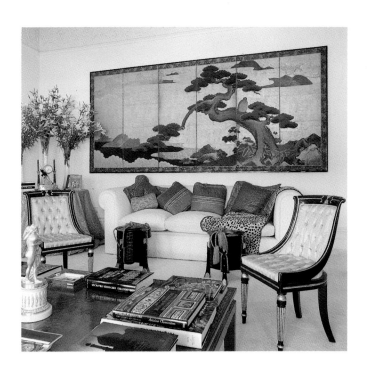

White gold

All the architectural planes in this room, decorated with advice from André de Cacqueray, are white, giving the impression of an artist's canvas on which the furniture, fabrics and objects have been 'painted', then highlighted with gold. White is usually the most chaste of backgrounds, yet, when combined with gold, it takes on an entirely different character. It becomes luxurious and indulgent. Here, luxury is instilled by the seventeenth-century Japanese screen, depicting the four seasons, and by the black-and-gilt chairs, which include a magnificent pair with lions' heads and claw feet by Thomas Hope. Gold reappears, *inter alia*, in the red-lacquered coffee-table made from an eighteenth-century panel, and in the Swedish neoclassical mirror.

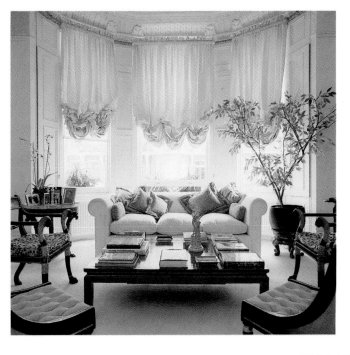

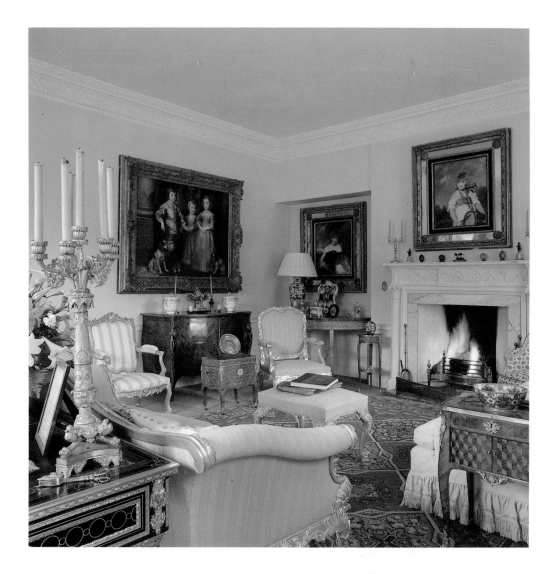

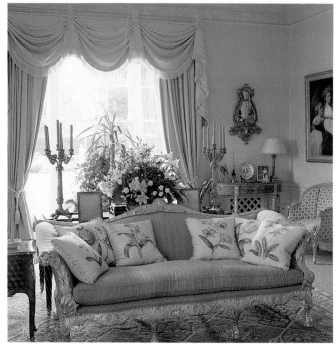

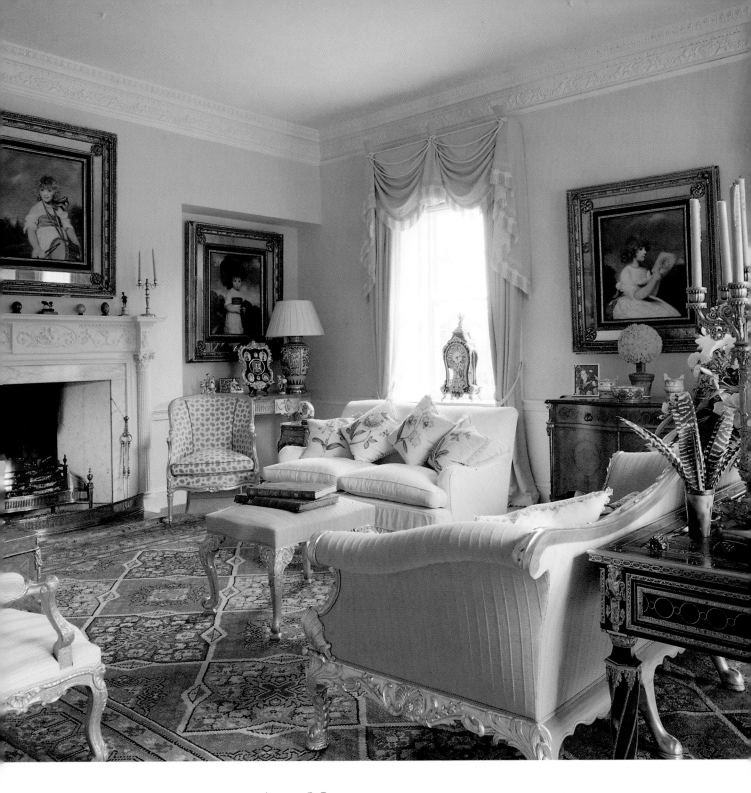

A golden presence

The shape and proportions of this drawing-room in a late-eighteenth-century house in the West Country called for furniture, especially seating, with 'presence'. The large gilt sofa, partnered by two giltwood armchairs and a stool, is compatible with the space and sets the tone for a whole range of golden accents. The latter are seen in the furniture mounts, in the candelabra and, most notably, in the frames to the portraits. The frames on the chimney wall and above the commode by the window are especially unusual, having inset strips of mirror. Melissa Wyndham was consulted for the room's decoration.

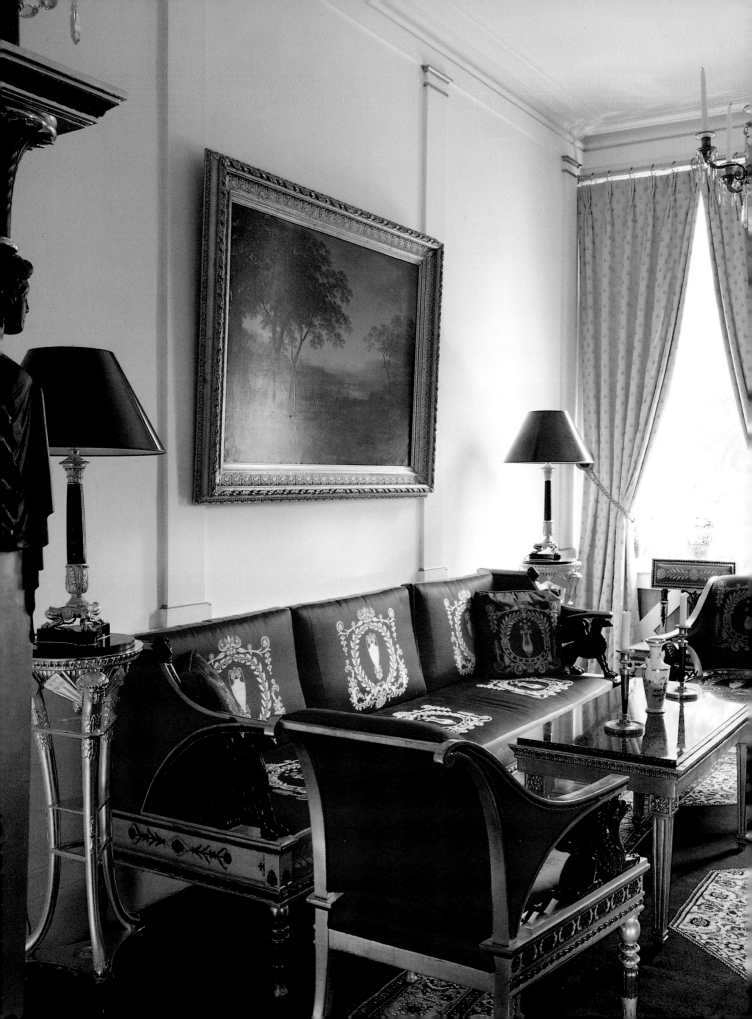

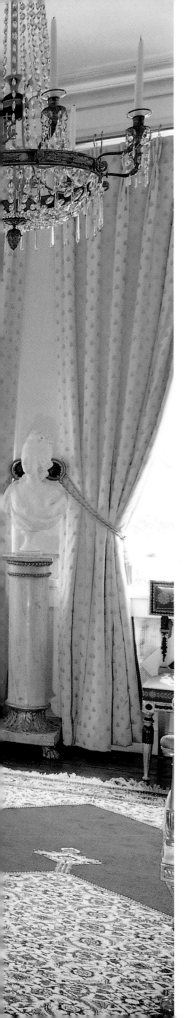

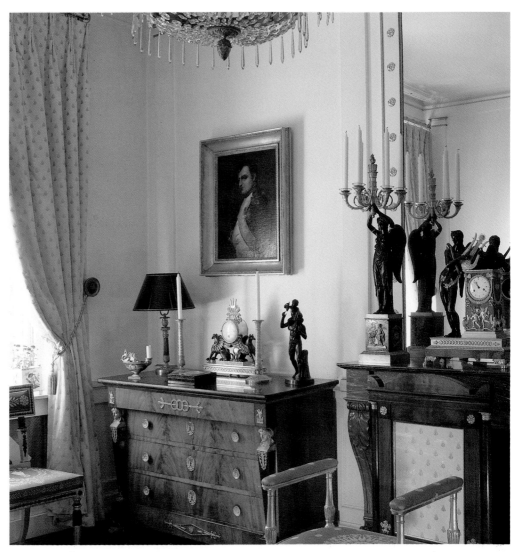

Powerful imagery

Gold is a vital ingredient in this augustly decorated sitting-room in London, where the only sign of reticence is in the use of white for the walls – but even this is picked out with gold. Rupert Cavendish is an ardent admirer of, and dealer in, Empire furniture, so it is hardly surprising that his flat reflects the confidence and historical imagery of that expansive style. Here we see allusions to classical Rome in the wreaths and palmettes of the upholstery fabrics, as well as to ancient Egypt in the griffins supporting the arms of the chairs. Appropriately, a portrait of Napoleon presides over a French Empire commode, and French Empire candelabra flank an ormolu and porphyry clock with a figure of Apollo. Napoleon is also acknowledged in the curtain fabric which is patterned with bees – one of the Emperor's favourite symbols.

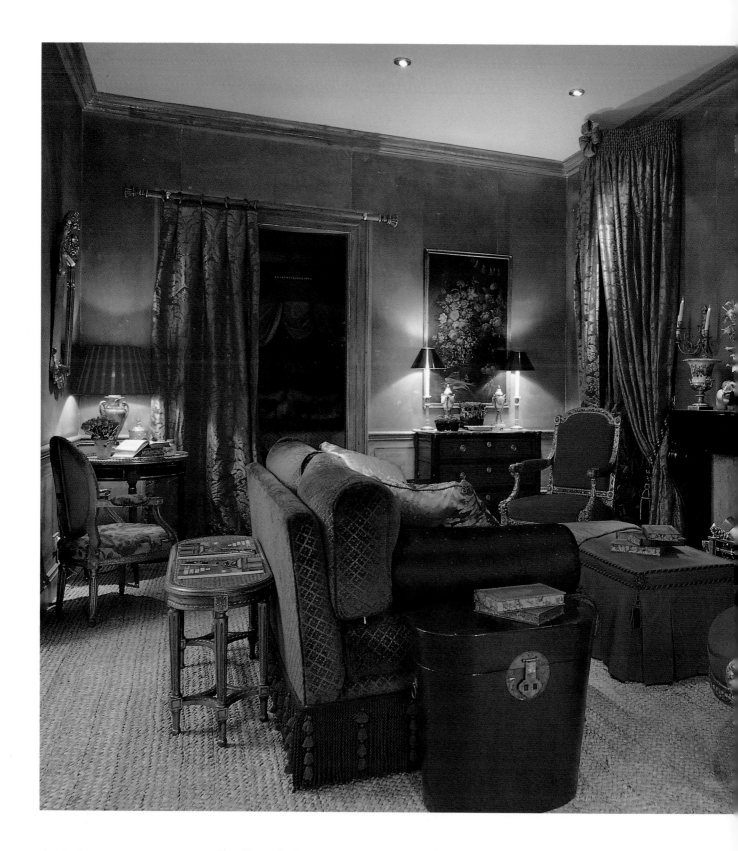

All for the Midas touch

The all-enveloping sense of *luxe* in a sitting-room by Monika Apponyi of MM Design springs from the sumptuous fabrics and colours. The interplay of reds, ranging from cardinal to deep plum, is thrilling yet cosseting. The walls shimmer with flashes of gold randomly appearing through the subtly textured paint finish carried out by Geoffrey Lamb. The finish is a magical foil for gilt furniture and silken textiles.

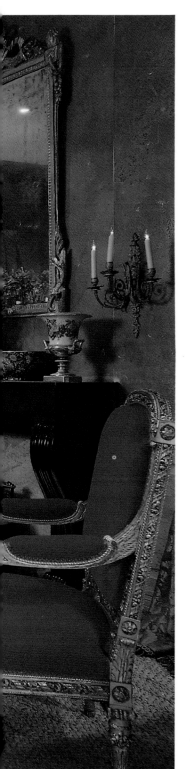

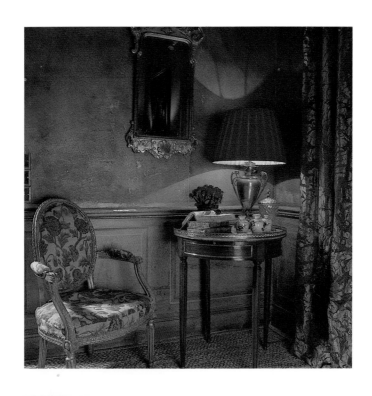

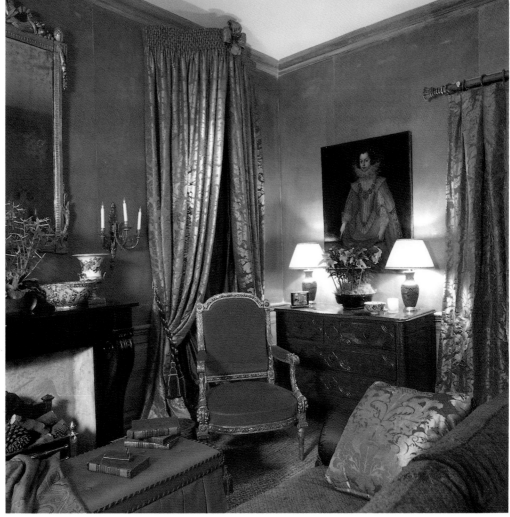

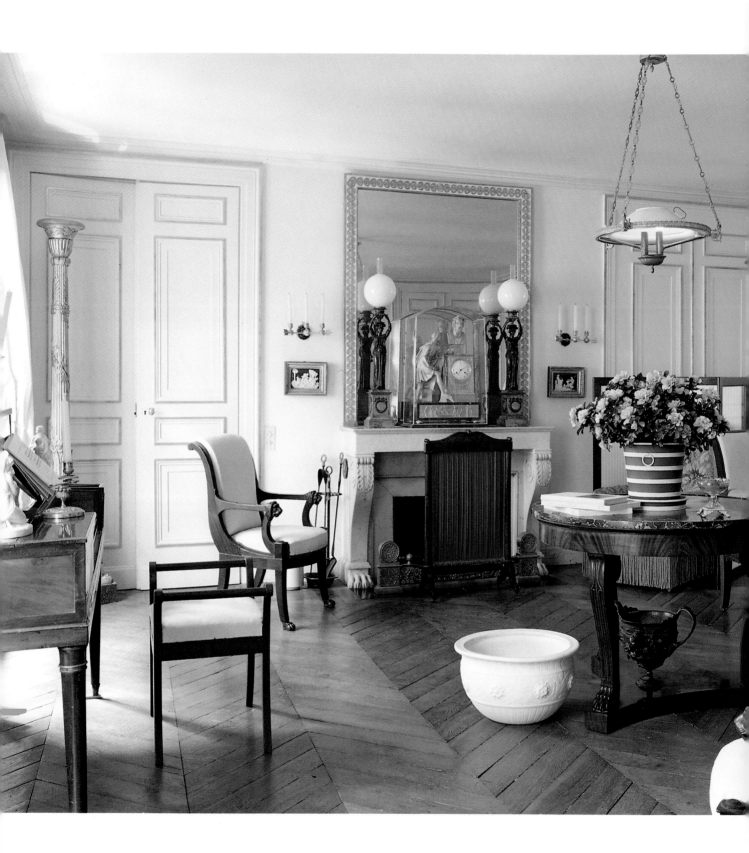

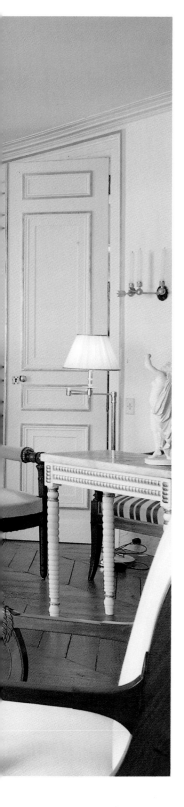

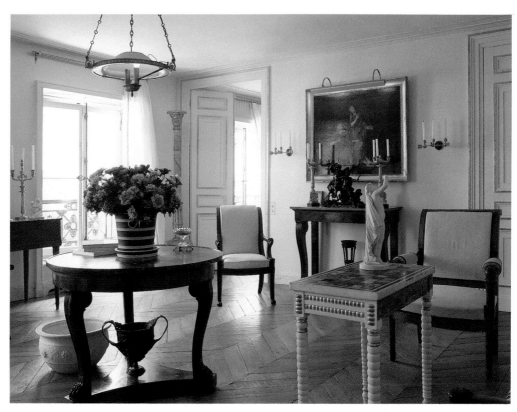

For a disciplined collector

Collector and decorator, Pierre-Hervé Walbaum, demonstrates an uncluttered aestheticism in the salon of his nineteenth-century *appartement* in Paris. The severe, disciplined scheme, based on historical precedent, is lifted by the gold-leafed mouldings, by the tall, gilded *torchères*, and by the ormolu clock and wall sconces. The room is notably lacking in pattern and textiles: there are no curtains, no carpet.

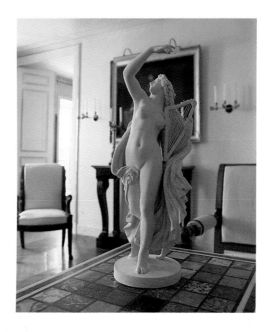

Decoration in detail

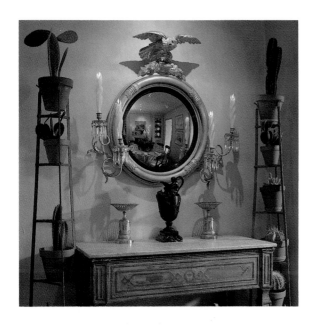

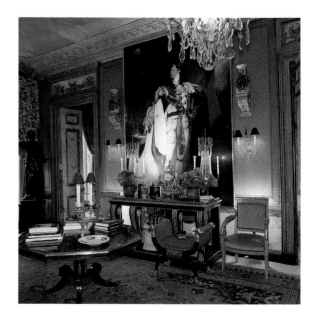

Although there is harmony in the colours of this composition, the materials are as opposite as can be imagined – but that antithesis is what makes the display so attractive. Cacti in terracotta pots, *au naturel*, are set on iron stands beside a gilded table triumphantly surmounted by a golden, eagled mirror.

All the furniture in this room by Brian Juhos has golden highlights: an octagonal table with brass inlay, an ebonized console with gilded carving, a neoclassical stool with gilt detail, and two painted armchairs with gold decoration. Even the brackets supporting the vases are gilded.

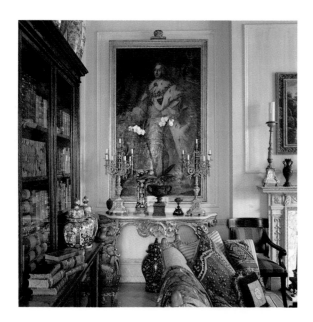

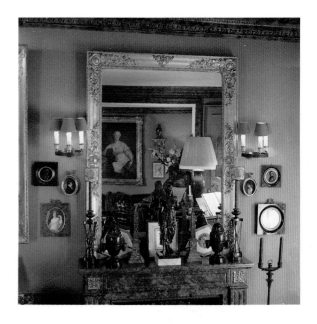

Seen against warm beige, as in this setting by Margaret Tiffin, gold has a subtler, less contrasting impact. The giltwood table and pair of candelabra are exuberant but are not overpowering. Likewise, the gilded frame of the portrait melds into the 'aged' paint finish. (See, too, pages 102–103.)

The sparkle of glass and gilt cannot fail to have an enlivening effect in a traditional context. Here, the handsome mirror looks especially lustrous against the rich tones of the wallcovering. Bronze ornaments encapsulate the browns, golds and siennas of the surrounding colour-scheme. (See, too, pages 56–57.)

Decoration in detail

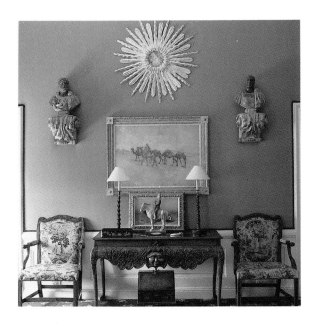

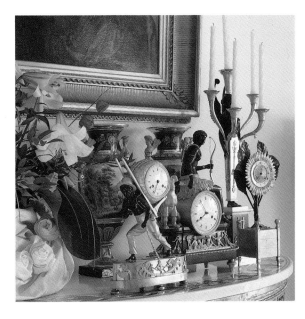

A brilliant sunburst rises above a substantial arrangement of furniture and objects in a room in Carroll and Milton's New York apartment, decorated by Pauline Boardman. The gold is picked up by the picture frame and busts on carved brackets, forming a marked contrast with the brown-wood table and chairs.

On an inlaid marble table, a collection of French Empire clocks in bronze and ormolu has anecdotal interest combined with superb craftsmanship and sheen. The sunflower clock is particularly rare, but the clocks mounted with figures reflect the fascinations of the period. (The room is also shown on pages 88–89.)

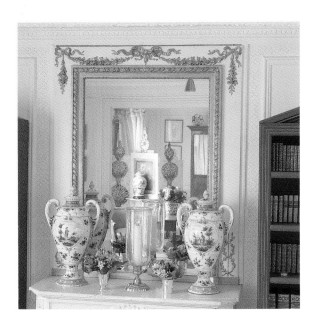

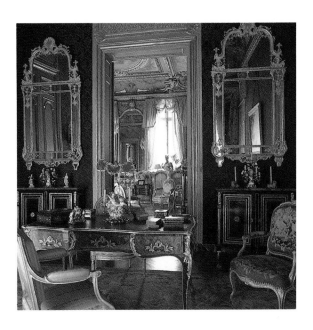

Here, the use of gold is restricted to the mirror-frame and carved swags. Its application is delicate and pretty rather than lavish and forceful, a charming enhancement to the 1820s urns, delectably decorated in pink and green. The group, put together by Sabine Marchal, has a deft lightness. (See, too, pages 60–63.)

The restoration and painting of the *boiserie* in a spectacular salon in Jean Lupu's house in Paris was advised on by Jacques García. The restoration uses ink-green for the walls, together with highlights of gold-leaf. The gold embellishments set the tone for the highly gilded character of the room's furnishing.

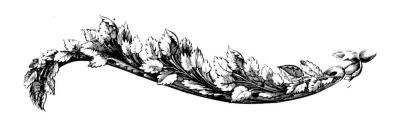

The art of display

Most of us have a natural instinct to arrange our possessions in some sort of order, if only for the very practical purpose of knowing where to find them when we need them. But when those possessions have an aesthetic appeal, we like to display them in a manner which, in itself, has artistic merit.

An awareness of the art of well-thought-out picture-hanging and object-arranging has doubtless gained momentum – and inspired many an enthusiastic practitioner – thanks to the wider availability of magazines and books devoted to interior decoration. Although connoisseurs and collectors of fine art have always been mindful of the aesthetics of displaying their possessions, most people, until comparatively recently, felt that their decorative whims were too modest to be highlighted and made the focus of attention. But now that so many magazines parade galleries of beautiful photographs showing lively arrangements of even quite commonplace objects – driftwood, old bottles, inkwells – everyone has been able to see that these items can take on a new interest. The crux of the matter is, of course, the individuality of the display. Victorian kitchen plates stacked reticently on a shelf may seem of little significance, but when hung in a group against a suitably coloured wall, or ranged boldly on a dresser, they become infinitely more noteworthy.

The framing and hanging of pictures are such crucial factors in any artistically orientated home that they deserve an entire book in their own right. The careless hanging of paintings and prints, however good their quality, can destroy their impact, whereas a well-considered arrangement is a joyous enhancement.

(Right) This room, designed by David Easton for Carroll and Milton Petrie, is a superb example of a scheme in which the pictures and interior decoration have a reciprocal richness and theme. With its Chinoiserie-fret border, the Chinese-yellow dado alludes to the Chinese subjects of the paintings, while the gilding of the frames is echoed by the giltwood moulding which outlines the walls. The symmetrical arrangement of pictures is centred on an eighteenth-century elephant clock on a carved bracket. The display is made even more effective by the sumptuous background of damask-design silk velvet.

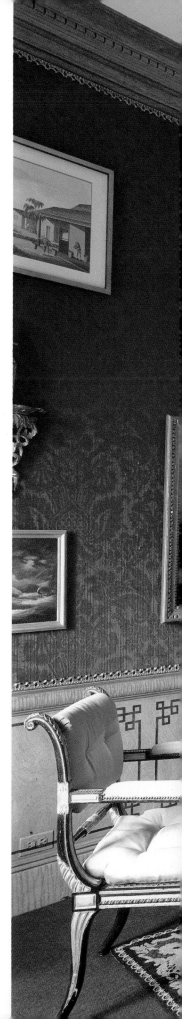

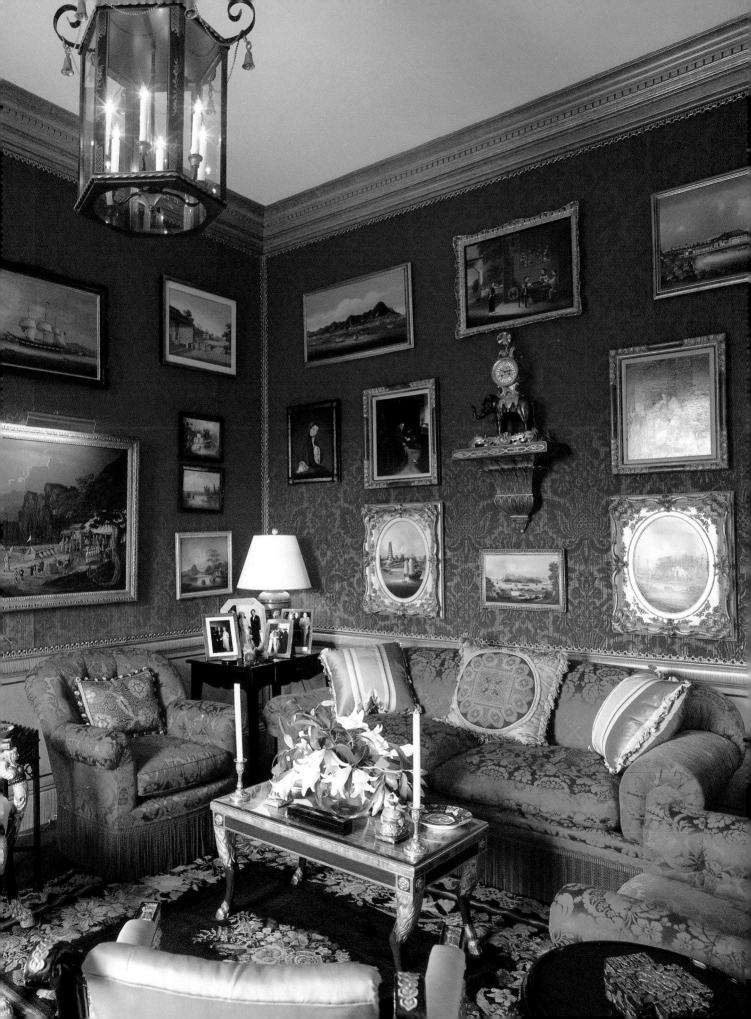

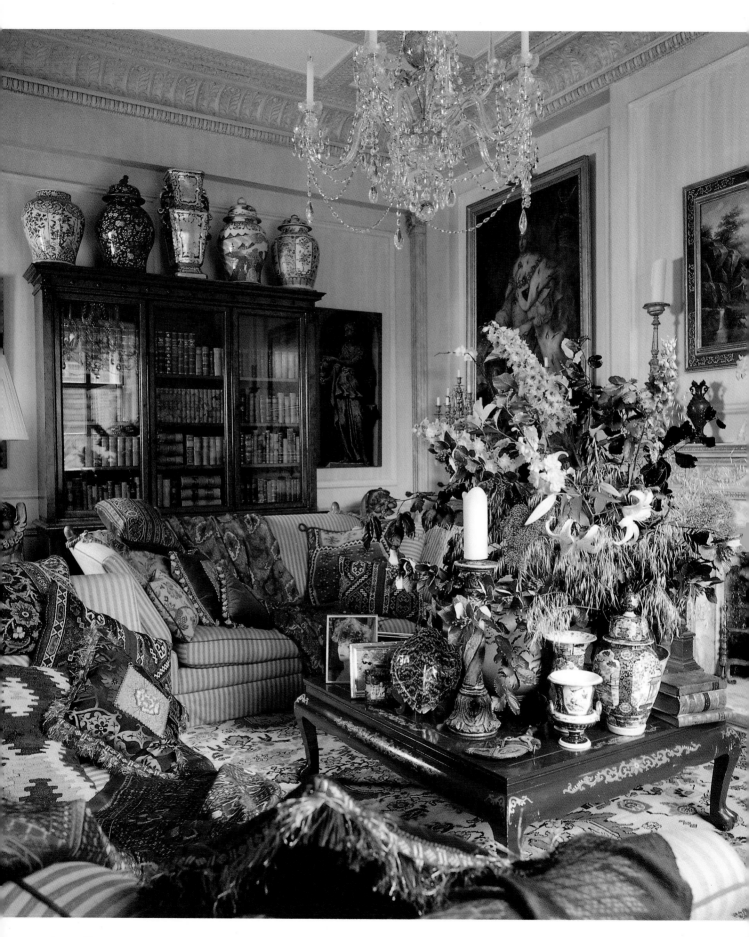

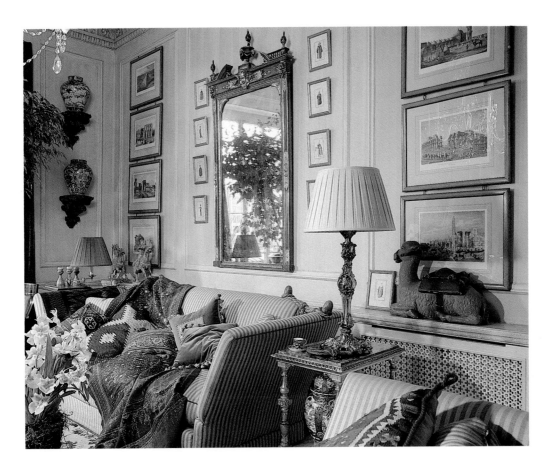

Controlled profusion

Designed by Margaret Tiffin, this is a complex room but the profusion is held in check by the controlled colour scheme and by the arrangement of the objects and pictures which is managed with skill and authority. On the chimneypiece and atop the magnificent 1810 bookcase, the objects are placed symmetrically. The set of small Turkish watercolours and Egyptian prints by David Roberts are also positioned symmetrically, centred on a French mirror, but, in contrast, the things on the lacquered coffee-table, the kilim cushions and the huge display of flowers look serendipitously unplanned.

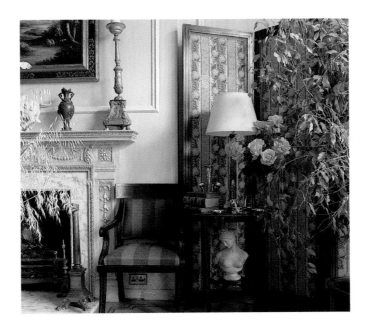

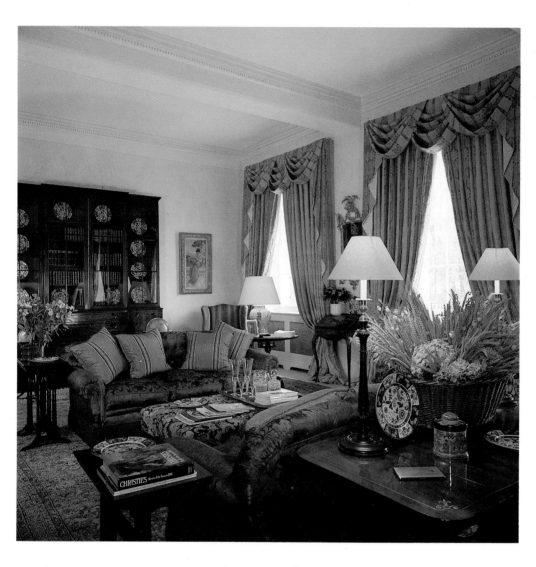

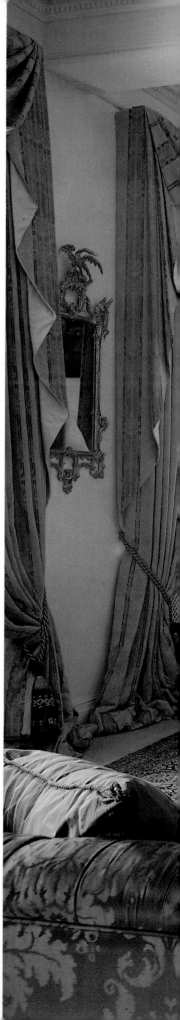

Unframed and unconventional

Conventionally, traditional paintings are displayed in frames, but in this instance the absence of frames for the full-length eighteenth-century portrait and quartet of still-lifes makes the paintings seem even more striking. They take on the quality of painted panels, rather than easel pictures, and their intense colours are emphasized by the direct juxtaposition with the low-key, honey-beige walls. The stippled paint finish was chosen to complement the subtle print of the curtain fabric. The room, which was designed by the Langton and White partnership, has an interesting, unpredictable combination of bright and subdued colours.

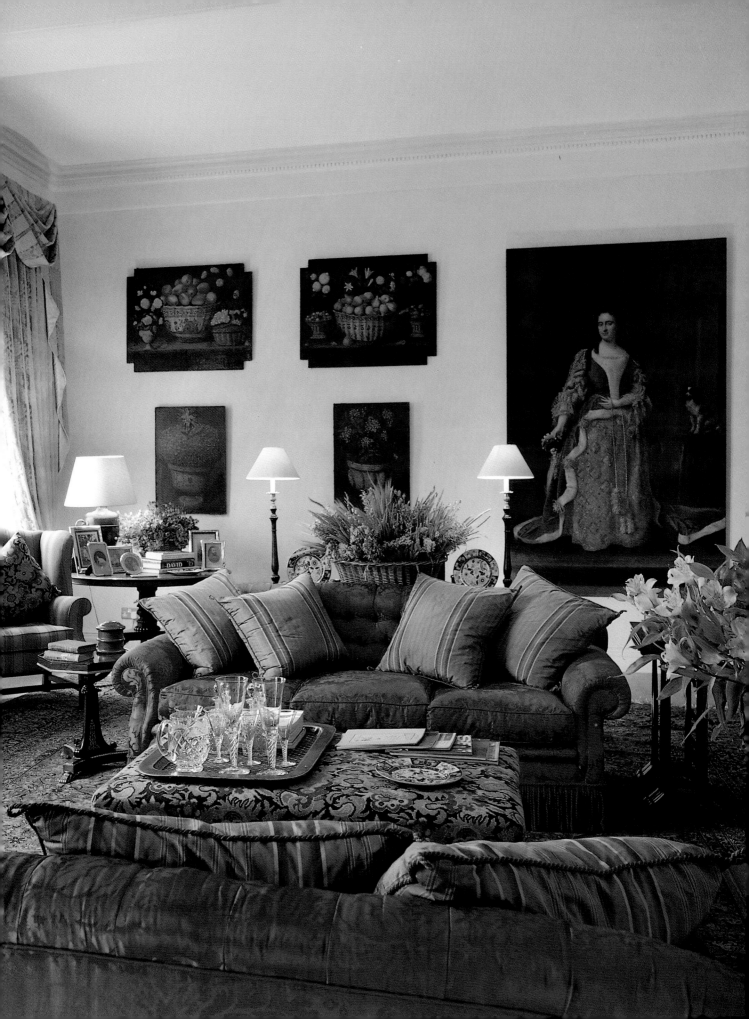

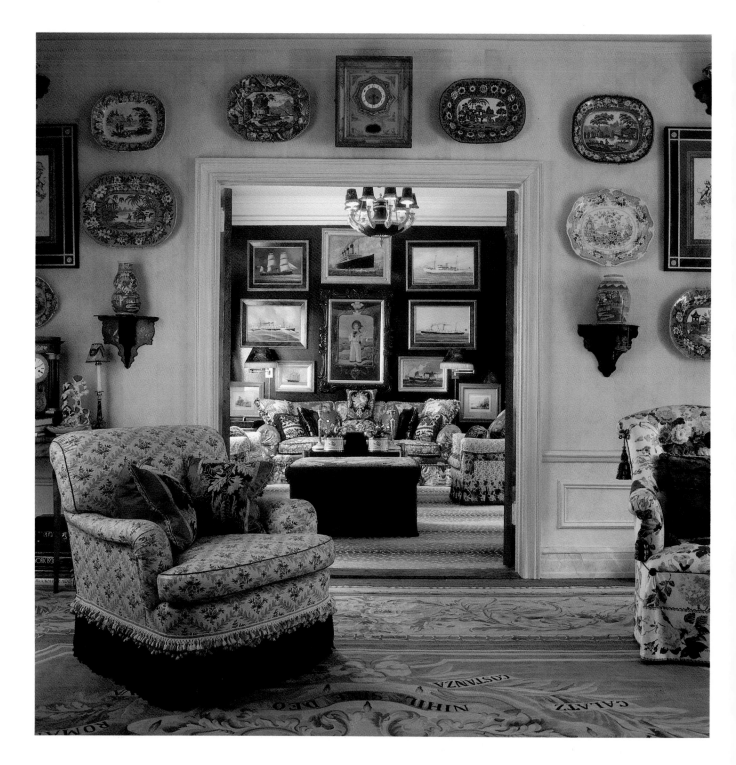

Visual indulgences

This sitting-room and adjoining library are
visual feasts. First, there are the unusual
colours: a heavenly, translucent blue paint
effect decorates the walls in the first room,
while a metallic green foil wallpaper lines the

walls in the second. Then there are the
patterns. A beautiful early-nineteenth-century
Aubusson rug abuts 'tiger-skin' carpeting; and
myriad chintzes upholster the seating, cover
the cushions and drape the windows. Add to >

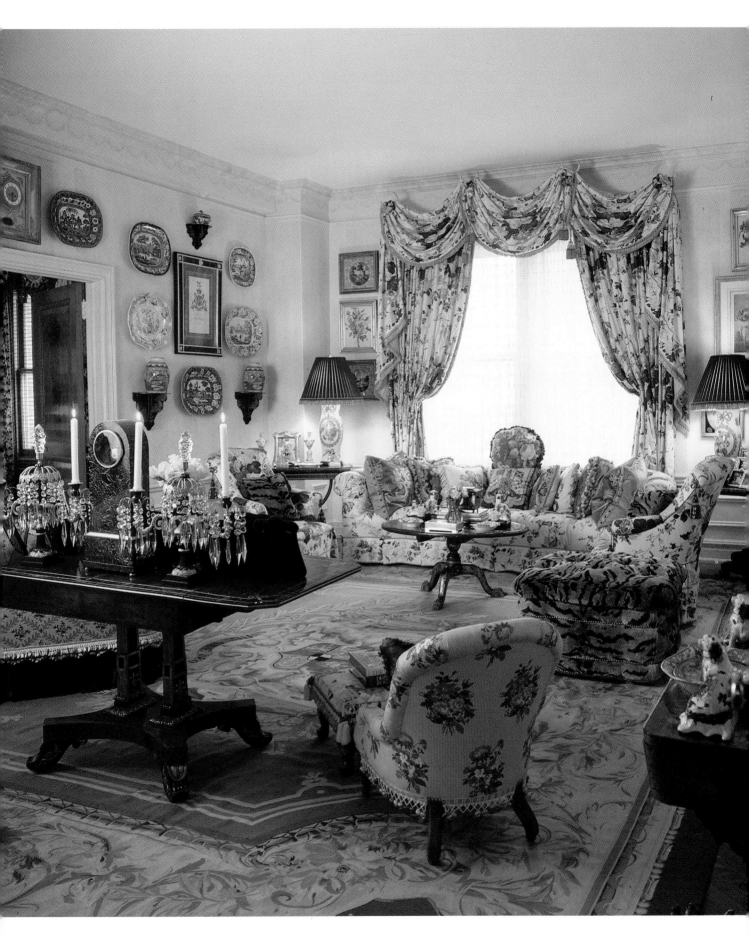

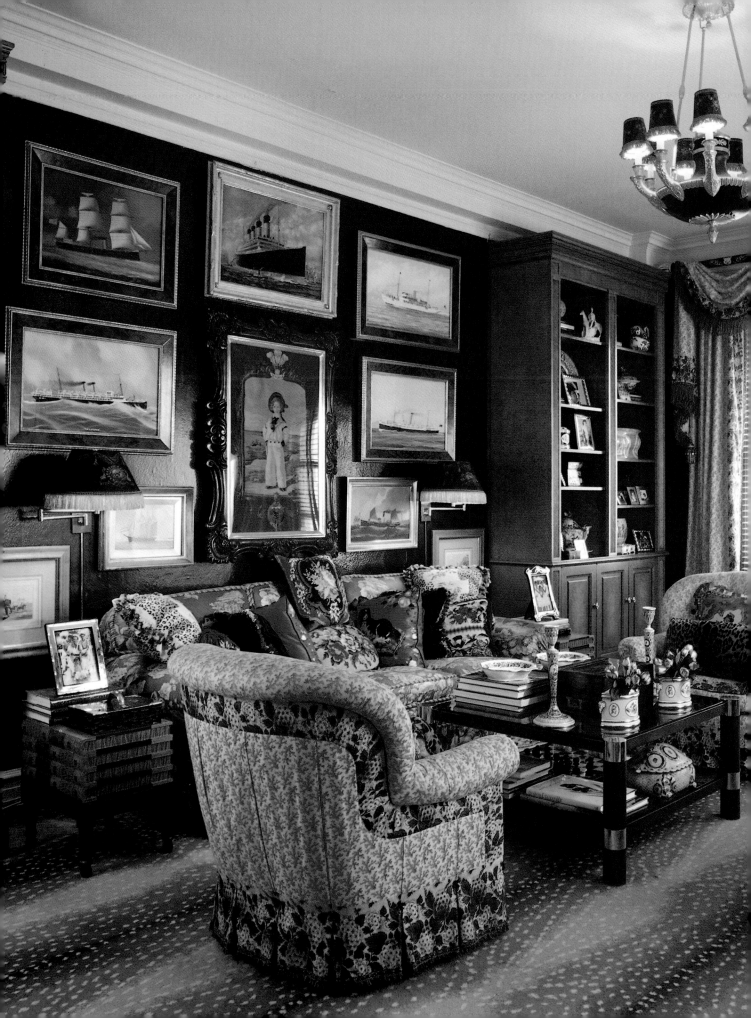

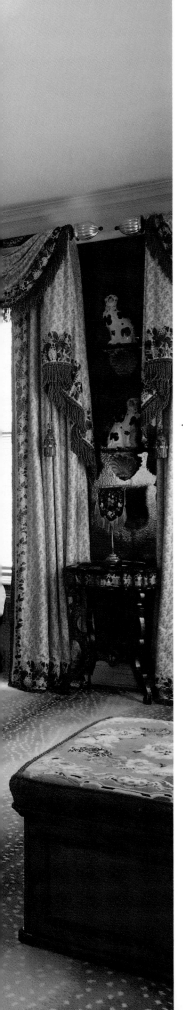

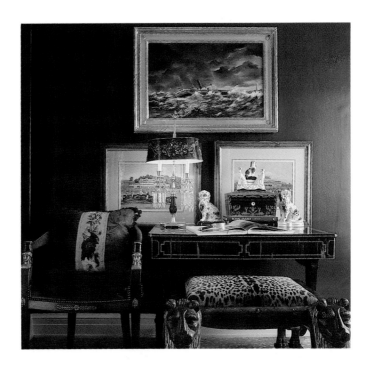

< all this a collection of blue-and-white china plates, lots of pictures and silver photograph frames, and you have an exceptionally stimulating environment. This is the home of New York designer, Ann Le Coney, and reflects her passion for collecting and her unhesitating way of putting all her favourite things together. The prospect from the sitting-room to the library is an essay in symmetry, with plates surrounding the opening between the two areas and, beyond, a sofa and armchairs set on the axis of the archway.

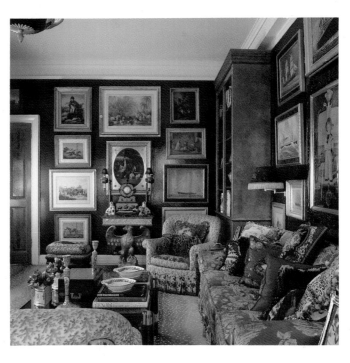

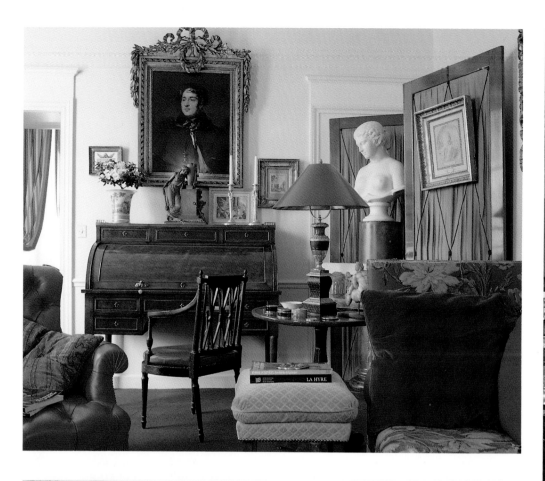

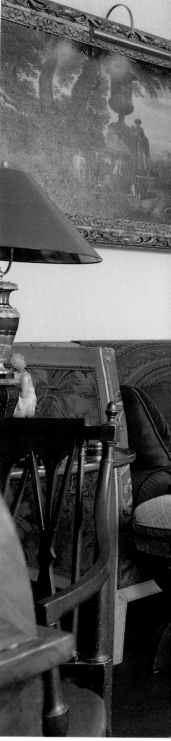

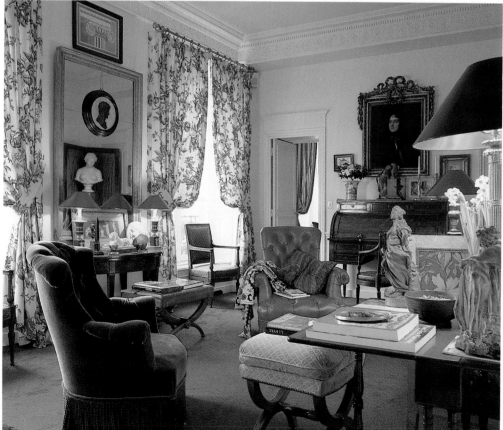

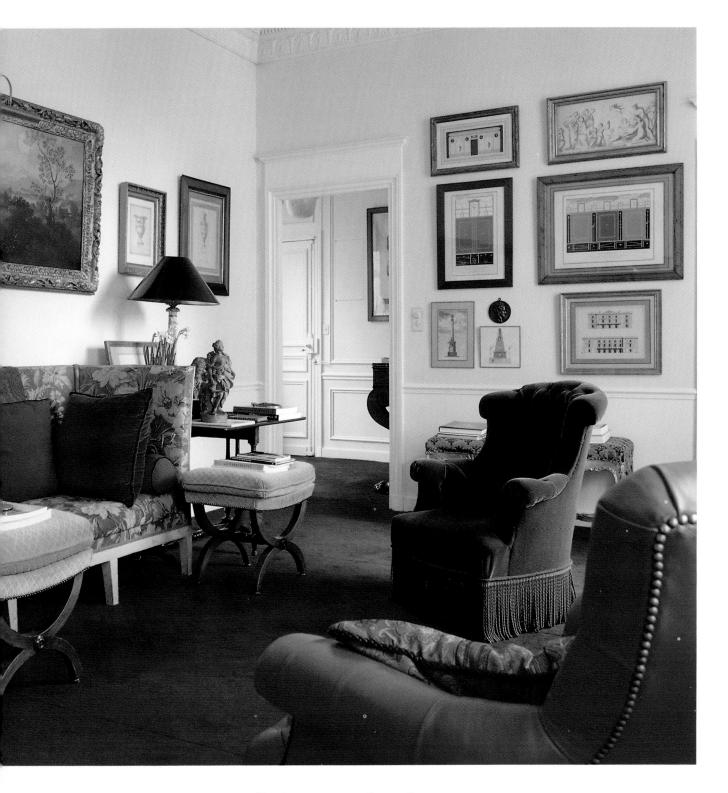

Colour and culture

The theme of the pictures and *objets* in
Etienne Dumont's vividly coloured Paris
apartment, decorated with advice from Pierre-
Hervé Walbaum, is the Grand Tour. The
grouping of the pictures is carefully related to
the wall spaces and furniture. Typically, the
horizontal format of the seventeenth-century
Italian oil painting forms a linear unity with
the sofa. And note the use of a screen as a
backdrop for sculpture and pictures.

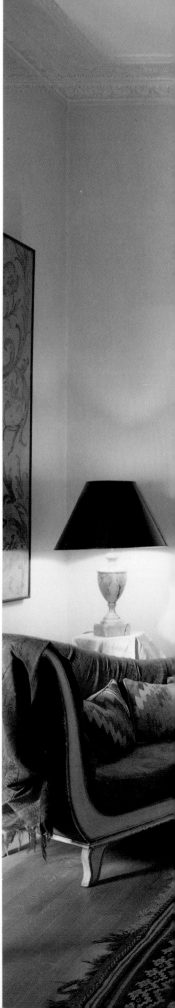

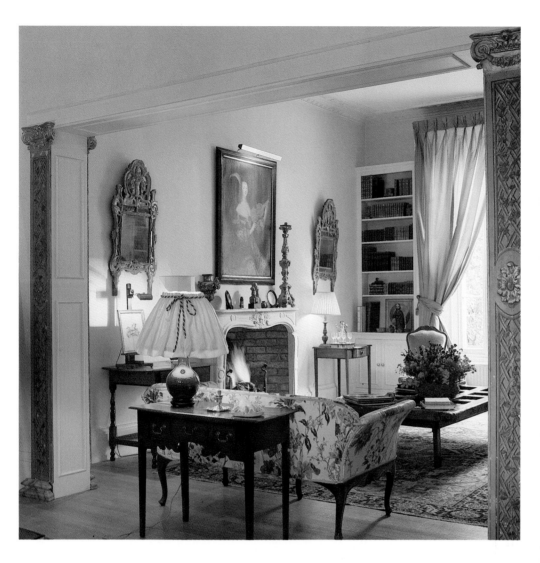

Sophisticated and unfussy

What is especially interesting about the way in which the trio of portraits is hung by Stanley Weisman in this double sitting-room is that the central painting is lower than the flanking paintings. A more predictable arrangement would have set them all at the same level or, possibly, put the side ones lower than the middle one. Yet this nonconformist method of hanging has a strange, rather compelling, quality which works well in a room which has a sophisticated unfussiness. The entire space seems like a carefully composed still-life, the artistic allusion heightened by another striking display idea: an easel supporting a carved wooden panel with musical emblems. This and the painting of a girl playing an instrument, seen at the other end of the room, are particularly apt as the setting is often used for musical and theatrical soirées. The coffee-tables are made from old Guatemalan doors.

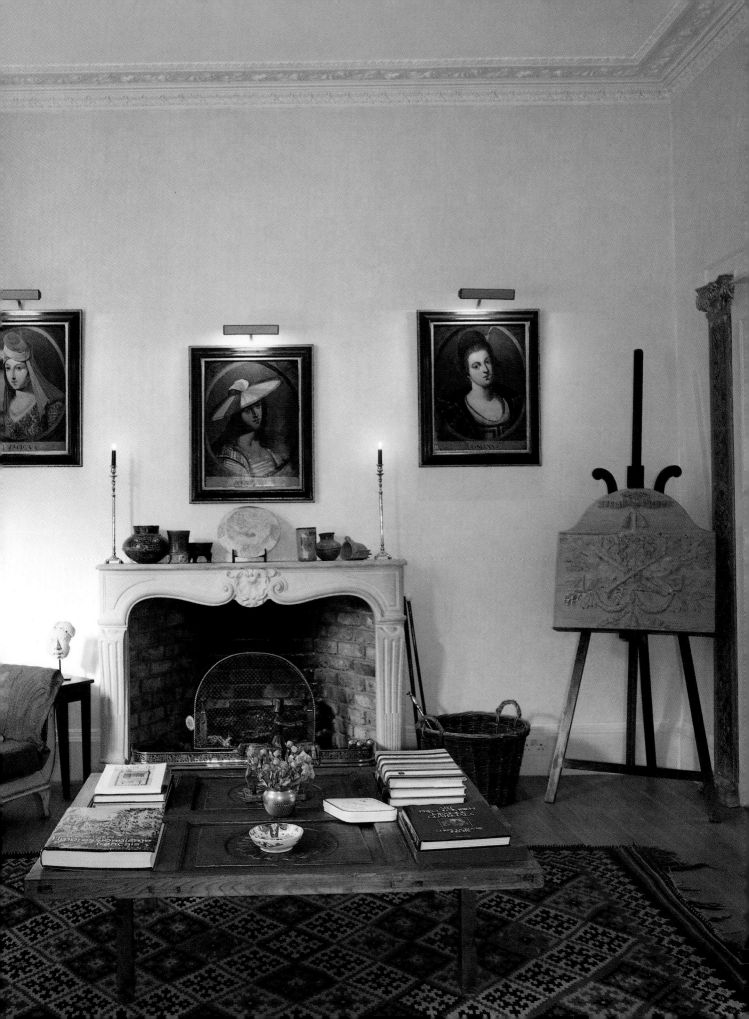

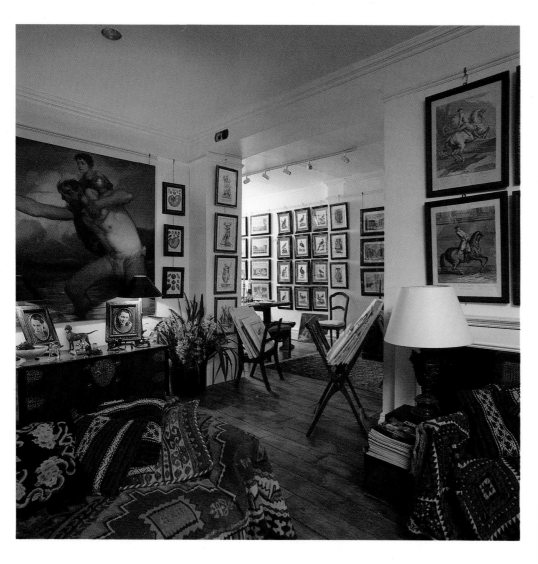

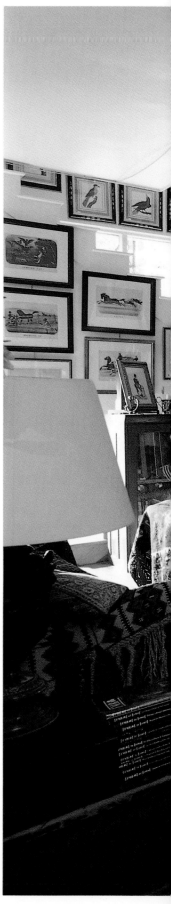

A nice dichotomy

This mews house presents a dichotomy of the most agreeable and stylish kind. The seating-area is distinctly casual, with sofas loosely covered in colourful kilims and strewn with cushions, but the hanging of the pictures, which are such an important element in the overall scheme, is unusually taut. Small pictures, all beautifully framed, are hung in close formation, especially in the dining-area which opens directly off the sitting space. Although the prints have individual interest, they have even greater impact when clustered together, almost giving the impression of a single, large picture. The portrait of St Christopher is the only image without a frame, emphasizing the contrast in the scale and medium of the oil painting and the engravings. Not surprisingly, perhaps, this picture-filled interior is the home of a dealer and framer, Julia Boston.

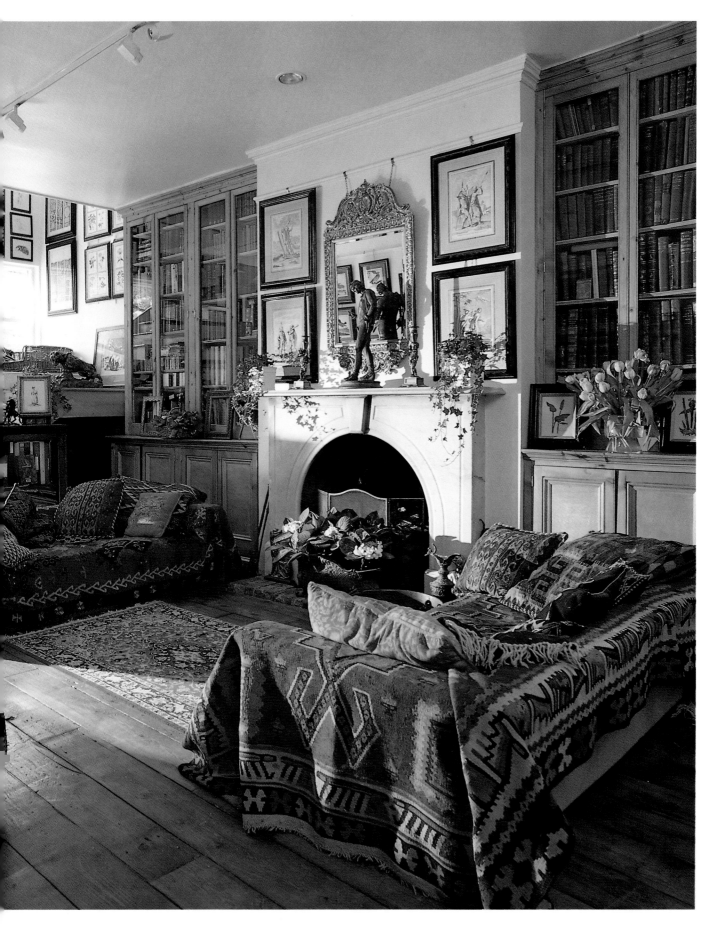

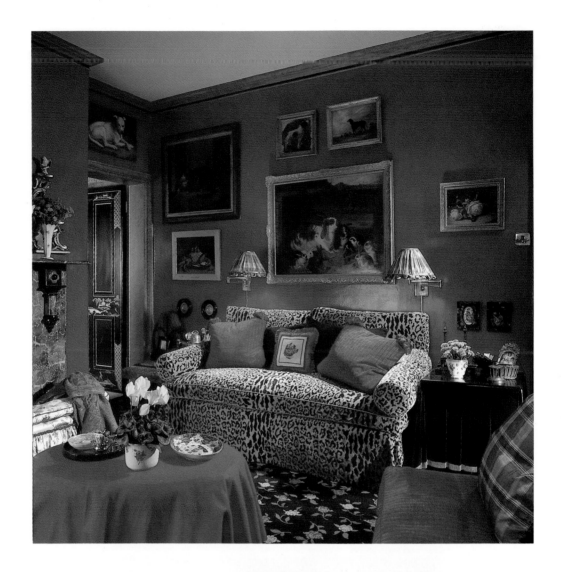

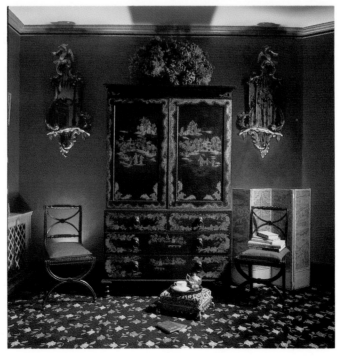

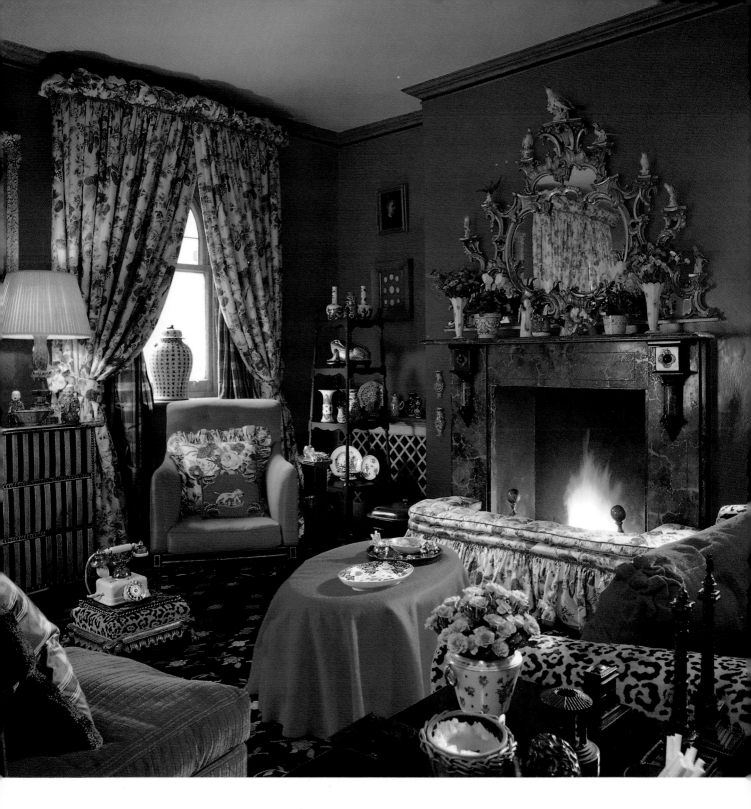

An animated assembly

Few sitting-rooms are more daring in their use of colour and pattern than this *tour de force* by Diana Griffin-Strauss. Especially well-suited to winter, the scheme is deliberately inward-looking, focusing on the Victorian marbled slate chimneypiece and nineteenth-century giltwood mirror with its delightful garniture of birds. The deep-red background brilliantly offsets the porcelain, pictures and lacquered furniture.

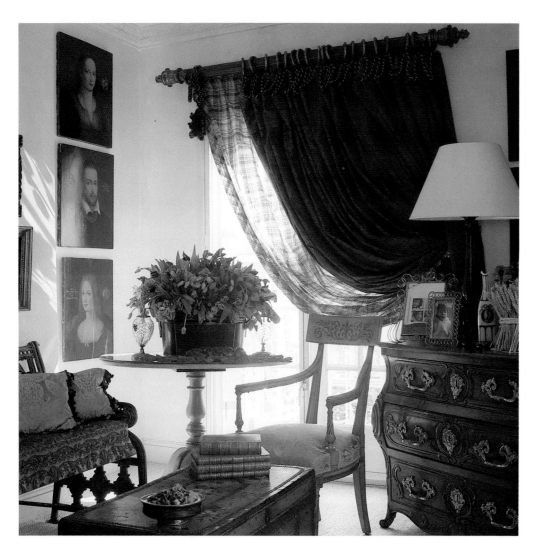

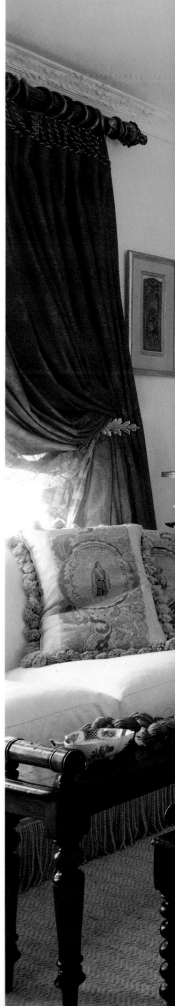

A certain *joie de vivre*

The homes of collectors can all too easily become over-bearing, with too many possessions and too little light, but this room in a late-eighteenth-century terraced house in Chelsea is just the opposite. It has a cheerful, outgoing disposition, radiating *joie de vivre*. The room belongs to Stephanie Hoppen, a picture dealer with a particular interest in interior decoration and with a keen, original eye for arranging and displaying her collections. The three main themes in this room are pictures, coloured glass and candlesticks. The pictures are many and varied but all are hung in related patterns. The group above the chimneypiece is centred on an unusual early-eighteenth-century Peruvian painting of the Archangel Gabriel and is bounded by a pair of highly decorative sconces. Horizontal mirrors with foliated gilt frames make interesting shapes >

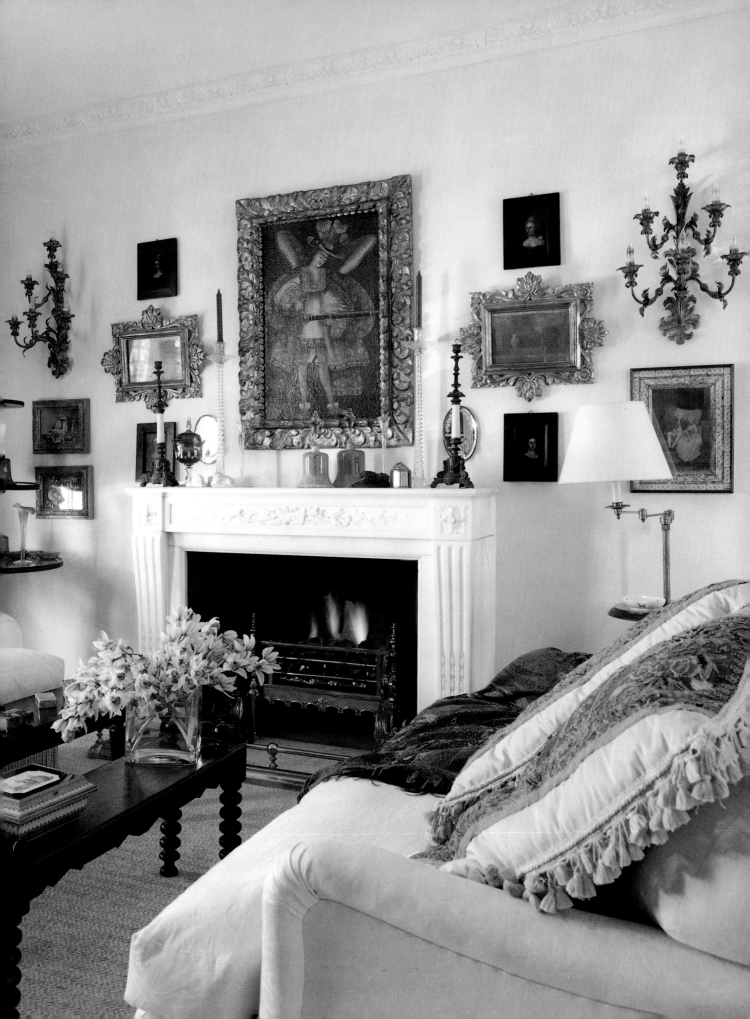

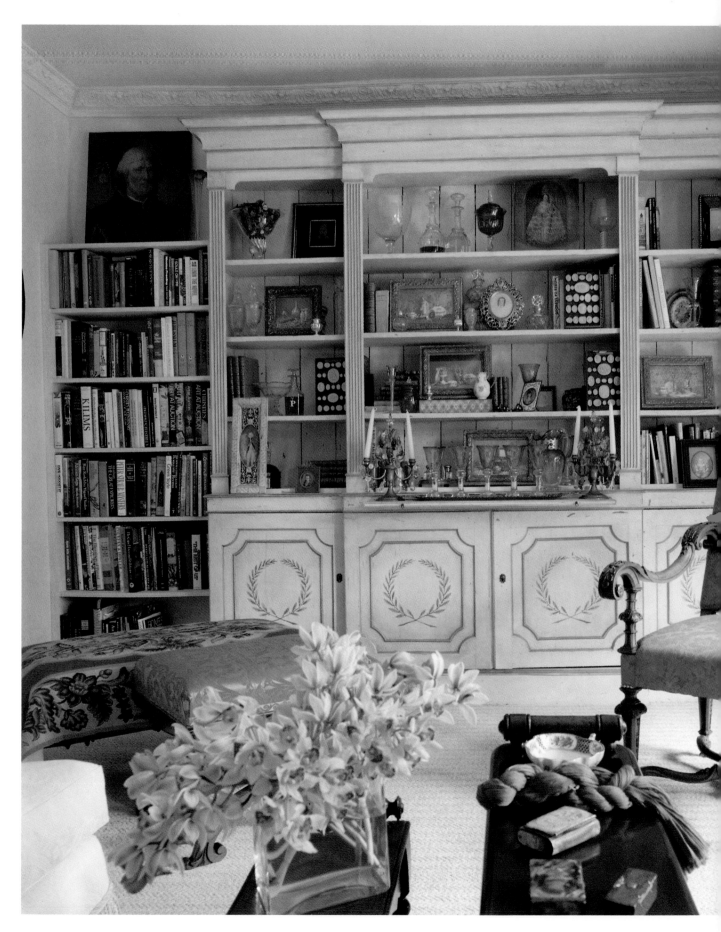

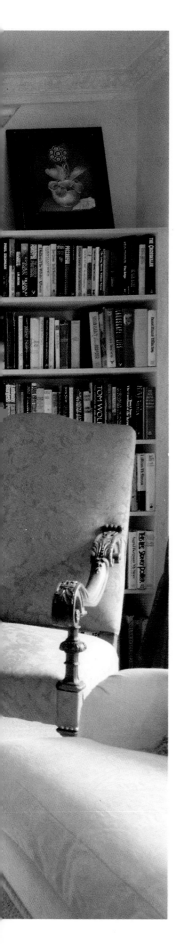

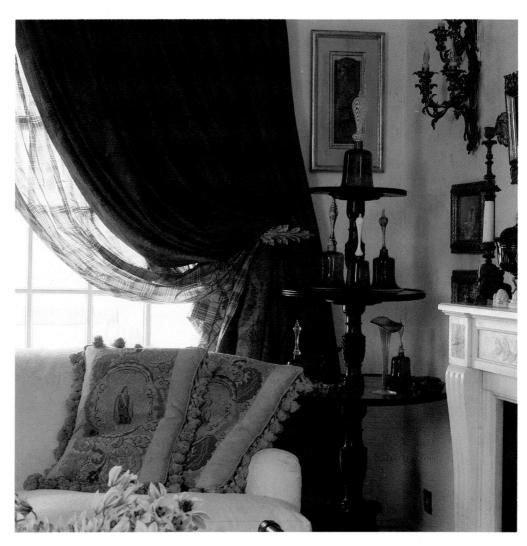

< within the group's overall composition. In contrast, the series of French family portraits is hung without frames.

The collection of pink glass, which includes numerous bells, is seen especially well on the three-tiered dumb-waiter, which allows light to shine through the glass from all sides. Favourite candlesticks are displayed on the chimneypiece, where their tall, elegant forms punctuate the spaces between the pictures. But the room's most engaging displays are seen in the bookcase painted by Lauriance Rogier. This handsome piece houses an ever-changing collection of books, bibelots and pictures, interspersed with porcelain and glass.

There is nothing heavy-handed about the room. The design and hang of the damask and tartan silk curtains, suggested by decorator Mimmi O'Connell, have an exciting swagger, and the furniture and accessories are arranged with vivacity.

Decoration in detail

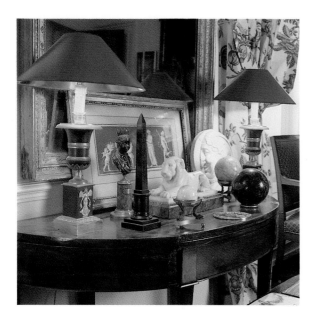

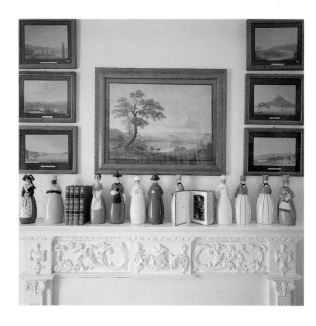

All the objects on this mahogany fold-top table in Etienne Dumont's *appartement* in Paris are connected with antique cultures. Early-nineteenth-century, neoclassical ormolu-and-bronze urns have been converted to lamps which illuminate marble spheres on tripod bases, a marble obelisk and a lion.

A jolly row of early-twentieth-century French bottles by Robj, disporting all manner of colourful garbs, is paraded along a mantelshelf beneath a collection of nineteenth-century views of Naples. Characters ranging from a plump matron to a portly priest are made even more delightful by being shown *en masse*.

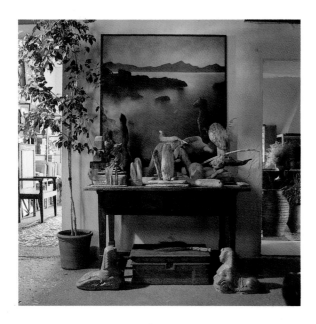

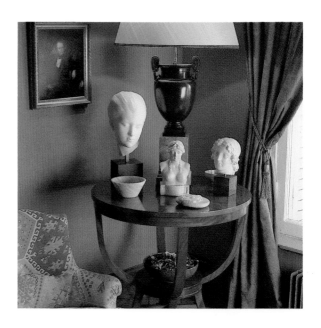

Driftwood worn into surreal shapes makes a sculptural composition on a country table in a house in Majorca. The seascape by Yannick Vú is a particularly apt backdrop, its misty colours and evocative style conveying a poignant, age-old serenity. The setting is the seventeenth-century home of Toni Muntaner.

A circular table is an effective means of filling a corner which would otherwise be a dead space. Here, a table with an unusual 'basket' base displays a trio of marble heads. Their similarity in subject, material and colour counters their difference in scale. (The flat is also shown on pages 56–57.)

Decoration in detail

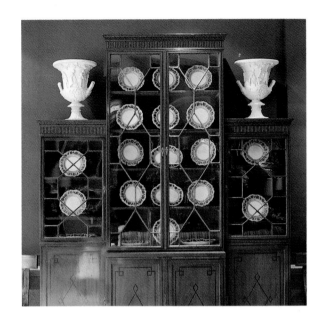

A Regency bookcase has taken on a new role as a display cabinet for Bloor Derby china. The circular plates, attractive in their own right, make a striking geometric pattern when arranged with such regularity. The stepped shape of the cabinet is an ideal platform for a pair of urns. (See, too, pages 180–181.)

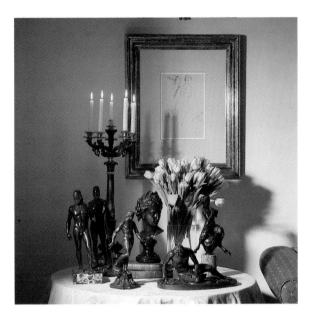

In a flat designed by David Seaton, bronze figures of various styles and periods are assembled beneath a nineteenth-century French candelabrum. The ensemble is especially distinguished because of the lack of extraneous colour. Only the tulips add variety, but even these link with the tawny spectrum.

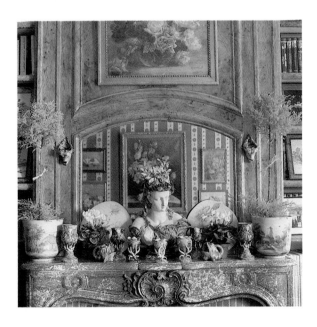

An intriguing collection of nineteenth-century vases with botanical and zoomorphic decoration lines the marble chimneypiece in a room decorated with advice from Sabine Marchal. The bust, with her sensuously draped dress, has much the same character as the vases. The painted overmantel is inset with mirror.

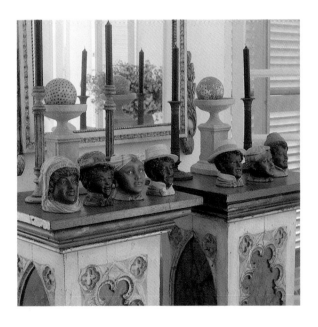

Carved and painted wood is the leitmotif of an eccentric and heady gathering in a house in Majorca interior-designed by Ursula Hubener. The be-hatted countenances rest on a French altar picked out in gold, earthy reds and greens. The candlesticks and *tazze* are painted in harmonizing shades of green.

Decoration in detail

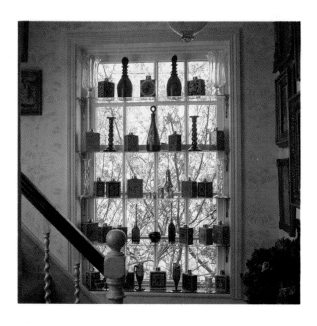

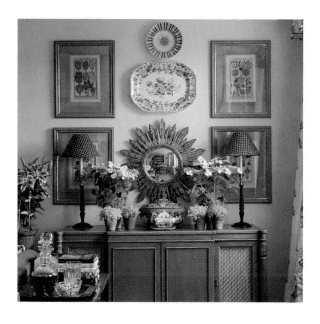

Glass is one of the most difficult of materials to display effectively. To be seen at its best, it needs light from behind, so a window site is excellent. Here, on glass shelves in Stephanie Hoppen's house in London, blue glass is interspersed with blue-and-white oriental tea-caddies and decorative silver bibelots.

Symmetry and surprise are the qualities that make this arrangement especially appealing. In an unlikely mix of the humble and the flamboyant, flowerpots are grouped to either side of a sunburst mirror and a tureen. The busy interplay of shapes and colours suits the cottage setting. (See, too, page 198.)

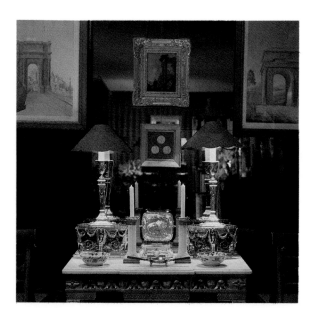

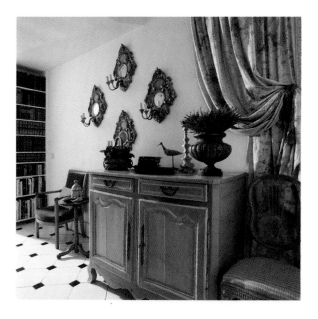

Early-nineteenth-century Elkingon-Mason silver lamp-bases are the most notable features of a monochrome group on an Italian giltwood console. The mirrored wall behind the table reflects the intricacy of the silver and makes an ethereal, lucent surround to architectural pictures. (The flat is also seen on page 216.)

Nineteenth-century Italian wall-sconces, hung more for decoration than function, plus an eighteenth-century French *buffet*, bring a Continental air to an informal assembly in a flat in London. Specialist painter, Lauriance Rogier, has given the *buffet* a charming finish in shades of blue-grey and broken white.

Decoration in detail

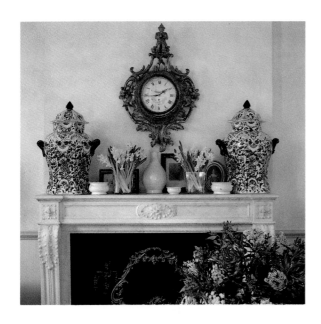

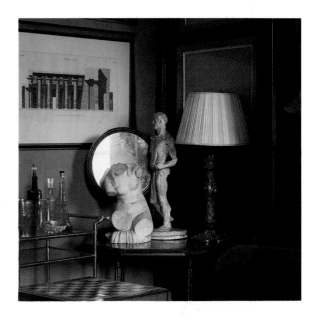

The salient point about this arrangement is the atypical use of scale, the splendidly forthright blue-and-white pots making more conventional levels of chimneypiece decoration seem positively feeble. The tall stance of the pots forms a pyramidal link with the wall-clock. (See, too, pages 218–219.)

A corner is brought alive with a standing figure and torso reflected in a giant shaving-mirror in antique dealer Christopher Hodsoll's flat in London. The distemper background is a dusty-green mixed with burnt ochre for warmth, and all the elements of the arrangement have an esoteric interest.

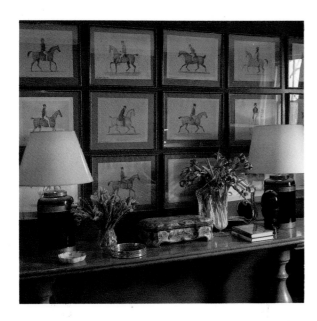

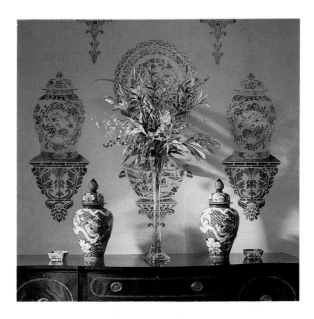

A total of twenty-one prints depicting English horse-riders is hung frame-to-frame above a side-table in a flat decorated by Penny Morrison. The walls have been lacquered red by Lisa Porter to match the picture mounts. Such intensity of colour and repetitious hanging makes an instant impact.

The combination of blue, white and yellow has a freshness which never loses its appeal – as seen in this witty partnership of real and *trompe l'oeil* vases, painted by Verona Stencilling, in a house decorated by Alidad. A spray of flowers in an elegantly attenuated vase continues the colour theme.

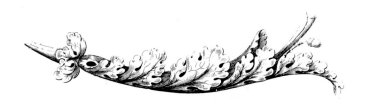

Playing to the gallery

Space is probably the supreme domestic luxury. Although rural cottages and urban attics, with their low ceilings and sloping walls, have a cosy appeal, most people have a yearning, at least occasionally, for a really big room, a room with true largesse of space and air.

Perhaps the most luxurious and costly of all forms of inner space is vertical, especially in contemporary urban settings where, even in quite grand buildings, the ceiling heights are far from heroic. (Surprising, when the average height of the inhabitants of the Western world has appreciably increased over the past century, yet the ceiling heights in modern buildings are less than those in comparable Victorian buildings.) If, however, you are one of the world's true fortunates and have a high ceiling – of sixteen feet or so – there's a lot to be said for having a gallery, which will provide extra floor area and, far from spoiling the room's sense of space, can actually enhance its spatial qualities. A gallery looks interesting from the lower level, and an unexpected viewpoint is opened up from the vantage of the gallery itself. The gallery may be decorated and furnished in unison with the rest of the room or, as in the interior on pages 136–137, it may warrant a different treatment to suit a specific purpose.

The rooms which lend themselves particularly to such split-level arrangements are, traditionally, artists' studios, of which several are featured in this book. But conversions of warehouses and other interesting old commercial buildings seem ready-made for these infiltrations.

(Right) The sitting-room of Vanessa Hoare's mews house in London has a library beneath what was once a roof-terrace and is now a glazed conservatory. Reached by a spiral metal staircase with barley-twist balustrade, the gallery-conservatory lights the room below and gives a refreshing view of plants and sky. A terracotta-tiled floor enhances the conservatory concept, but in the seating-area it is overlaid with a rug to augment the comforts of the day-bed and armchairs.

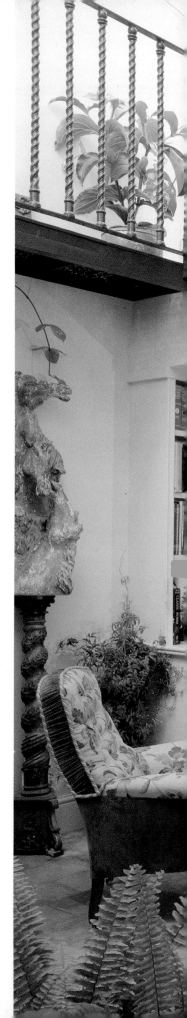

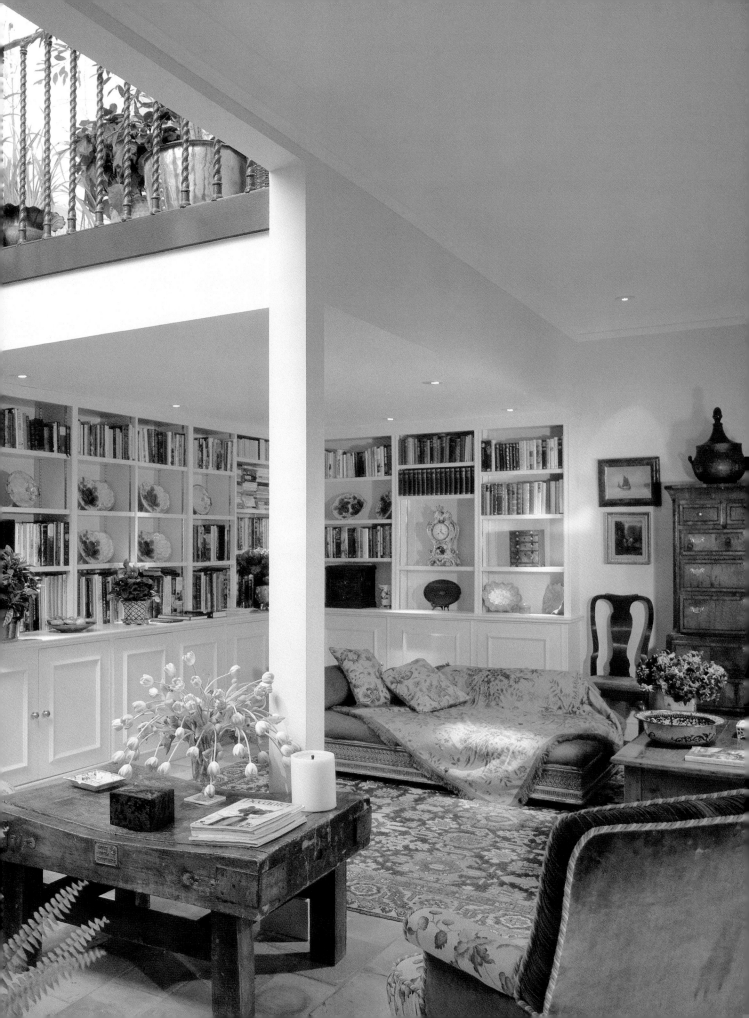

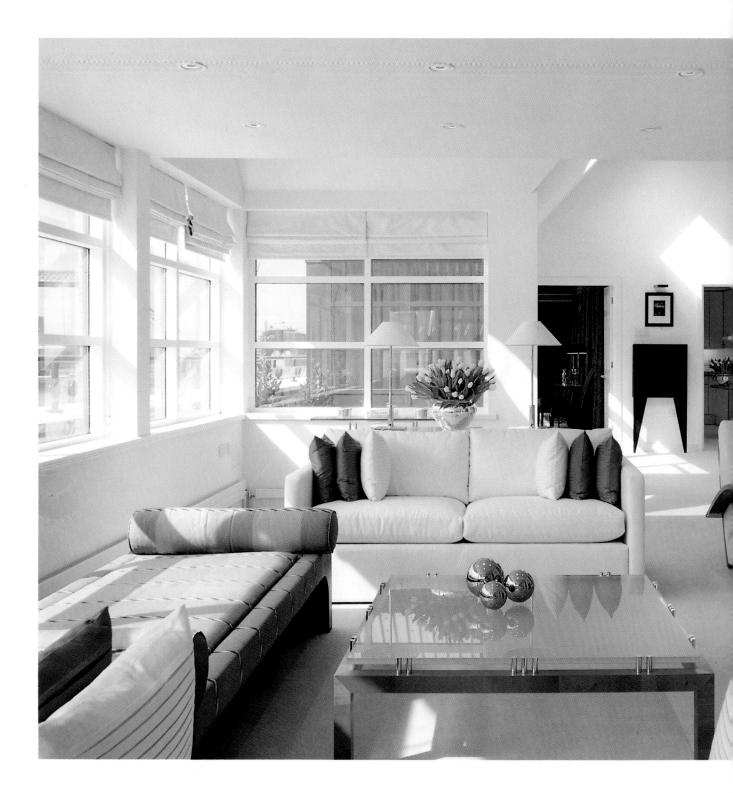

Palest colours in a room with open views

The panoramic view of the River Thames from the huge windows of the penthouse of a converted wharf prompted Kate Govier Wright of Fox Linton Associates to keep the interior 'light, creamy and slightly nautical in feel'. The walls are painted white; the floor is covered in cream carpet; the furniture is simple in shape and limited in colour; plain

Roman blinds are used instead of curtains. The upper level, which serves as a second seating-area and study, also has extensive glazing and continues the light, unconfined theme. This level projects over the main seating-area, like an upper deck, and has a sand-blasted glass balustrade, specially designed to maintain the sense of openness.

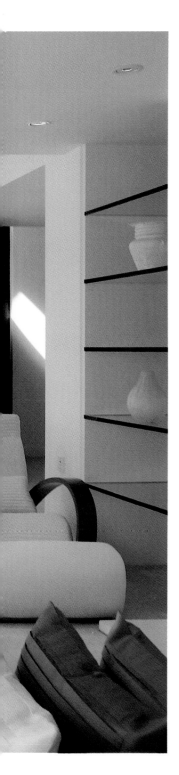

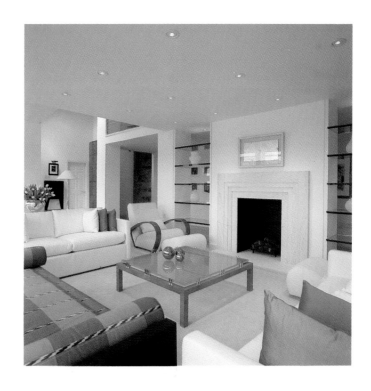

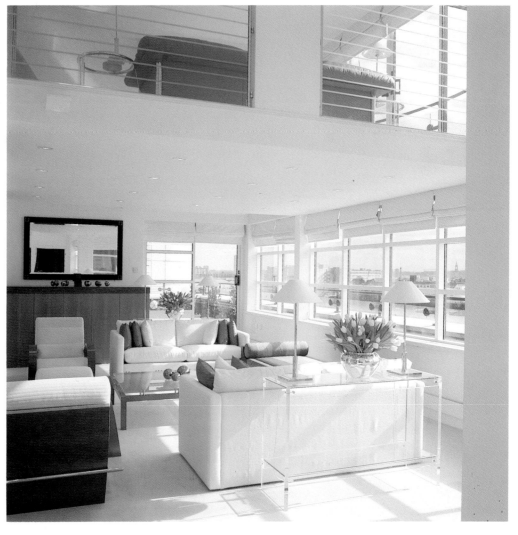

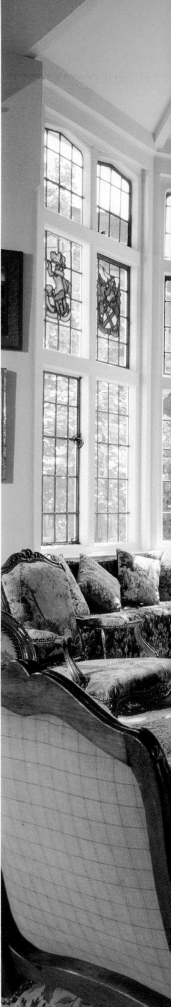

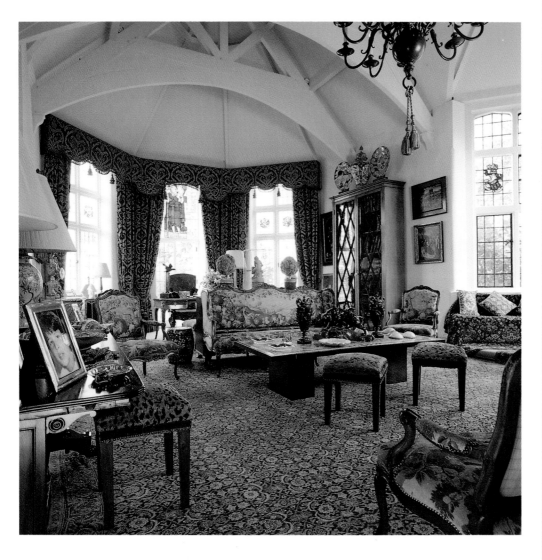

Arranged in several parts

This late-nineteenth-century interior is hard to place. The extensive garden outlook hints at somewhere in the country, perhaps on the outskirts of a Cotswolds village, but in fact the room is in the heart of Chelsea, and it is as surprising in its situation as it is inventive in its decoration.

One part of the room is double-height, with exposed beams and a gallery, while the other part has a low, flat ceiling with enriched plasterwork. The owner, who comes from Paris, felt that the unconventional proportions and character demanded an equally unconventional style of furnishing. The result is an eclectic interpretation of the English, artistic tradition of mixing patterns and unusual, even eccentric, pieces of furniture. The room is a very personal assembly, full of vibrancy and visual stimulation. The original stained-glass windows create shafts of coloured light, emphasizing the >

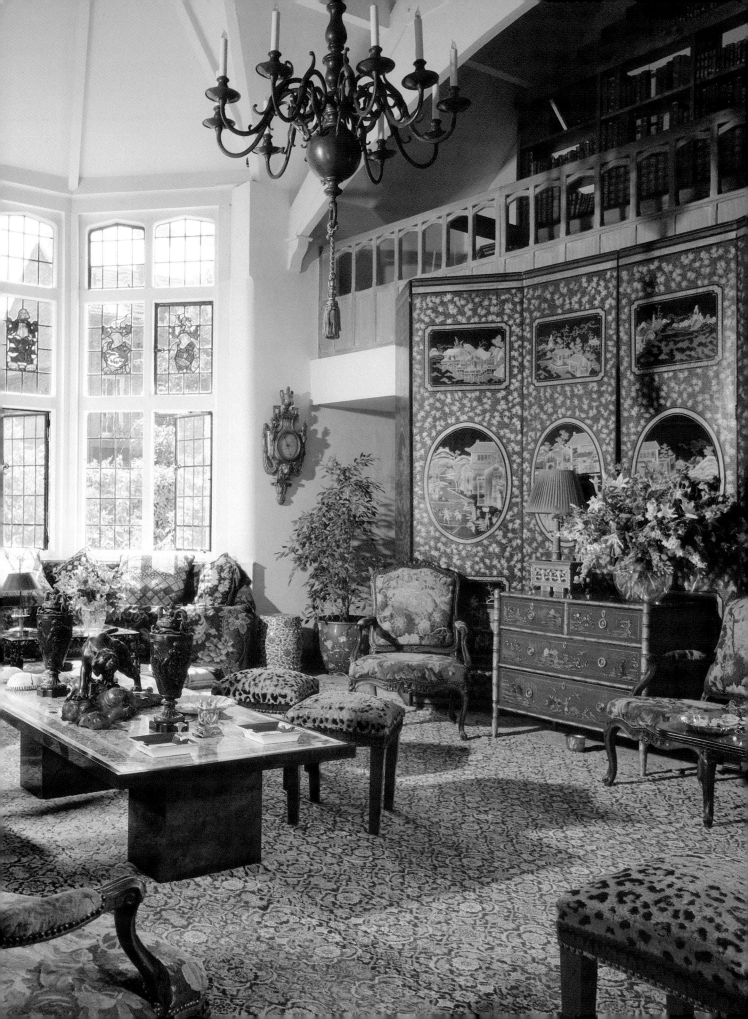

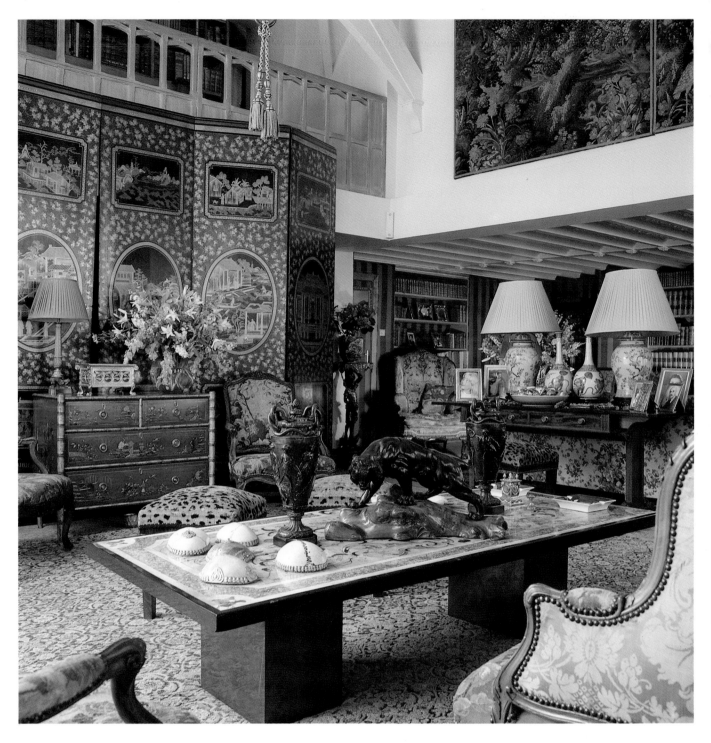

< panoply of textures and curiosities displayed throughout. Indian jewellery is clustered on the table behind the sofa; decorated shells and bronzes are arranged on a coffee-table with an inlaid top of coloured Italian marble; oriental porcelain sits atop a tall cabinet.

One of the most spectacular items in the room is the magnificent Chinese black-and-gold lacquered screen. This is more than a work of art; it also serves the practical purpose of

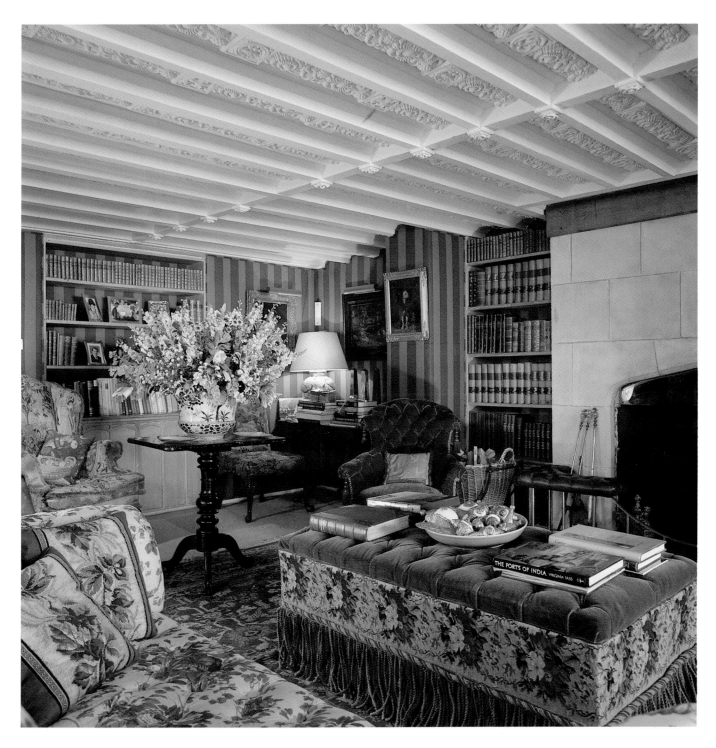

concealing a stairway to the gallery and guest room. In front of this glorious piece is another reference to the Orient: a bamboo-framed, red-and-gold lacquered Japanese chest.

The room's dual ceiling heights have been played up to the maximum. At the tall, vaulted end of the room, the walls and ceiling are painted ivory-white, giving maximum contrast with the low-ceilinged fireplace area which is lined with bold, self-striped red fabric to enhance the sense of cosiness.

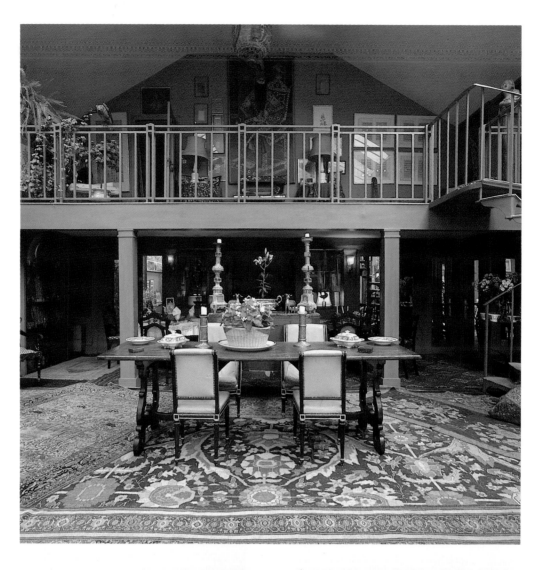

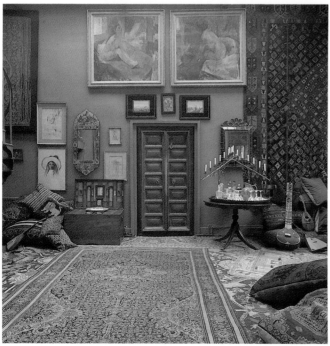

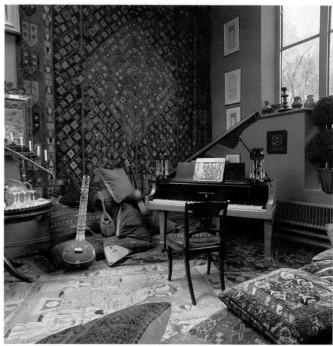

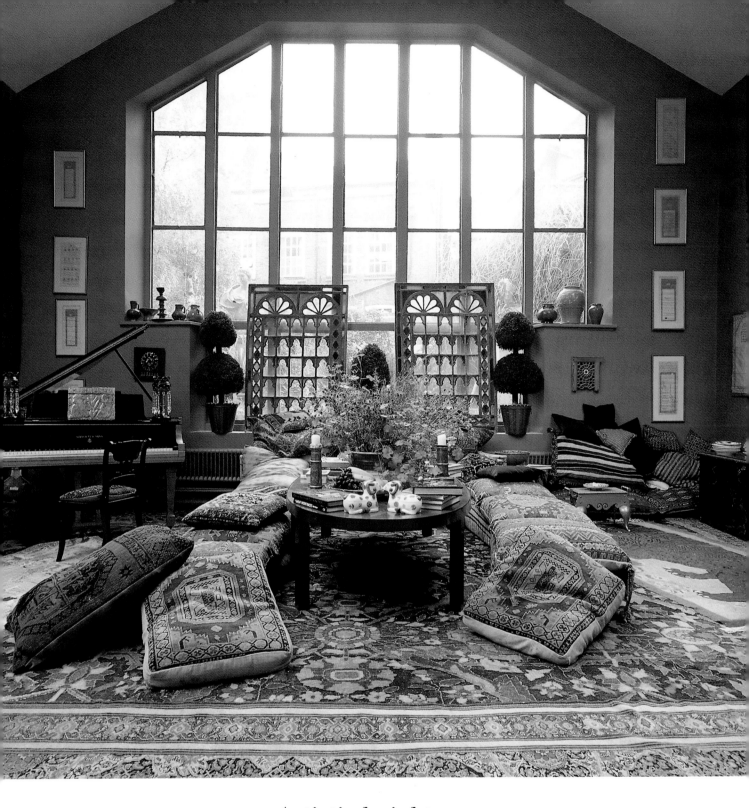

Artistic heights

In an artist's studio in Chelsea, layers of Persian carpets and piles of cushions on the floor are reminiscent of a nineteenth-century orientalist interior. The pillow seating, covered in ancient Persian textiles, and the musical instruments and intriguing array of objects suit the room's unusual architecture and bohemian associations, while the terracotta-and-blue colour scheme, adapted from the rugs, intensifies the Victorian ambience. Opposite the studio window an open gallery gives access to the bedrooms.

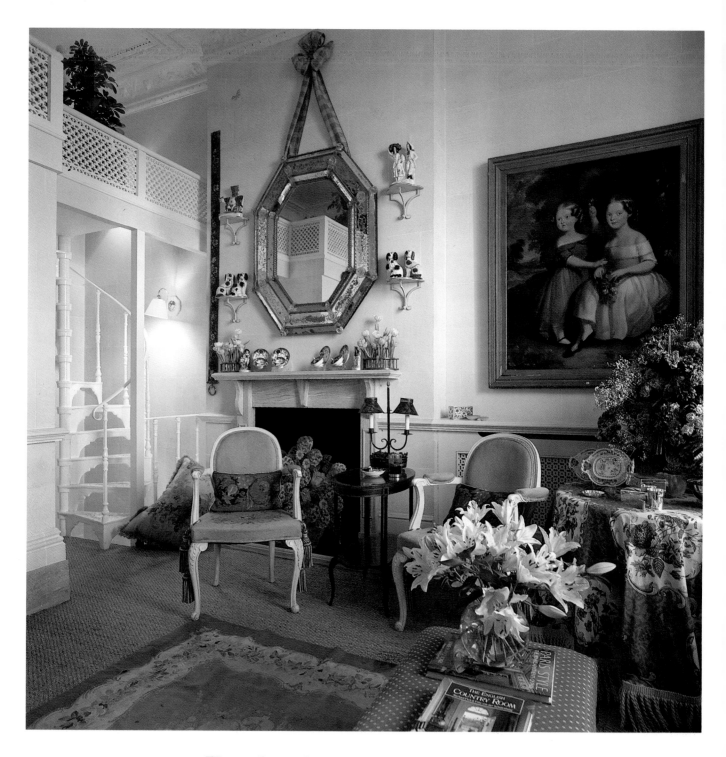

Two levels, two generations

This drawing-room was designed by Sisi Edmiston to suit two generations. The upright elegance of the lower, parental level is conjured by wood-framed armchairs and a fine marquetry cabinet, whereas the upper level, a gallery reached by a metal spiral staircase, is fitted out for teenage lounging.

Downstairs, the colours are soft and pretty, with dusky pinks, lilacs, blues and greens, looking romantically faded against ivory-and-blue curtains and creamy walls. Upstairs, Japanese-style floor cushions are recessed within wall shelving, and a boldly patterned oriental rug reinforces the casual ambience.

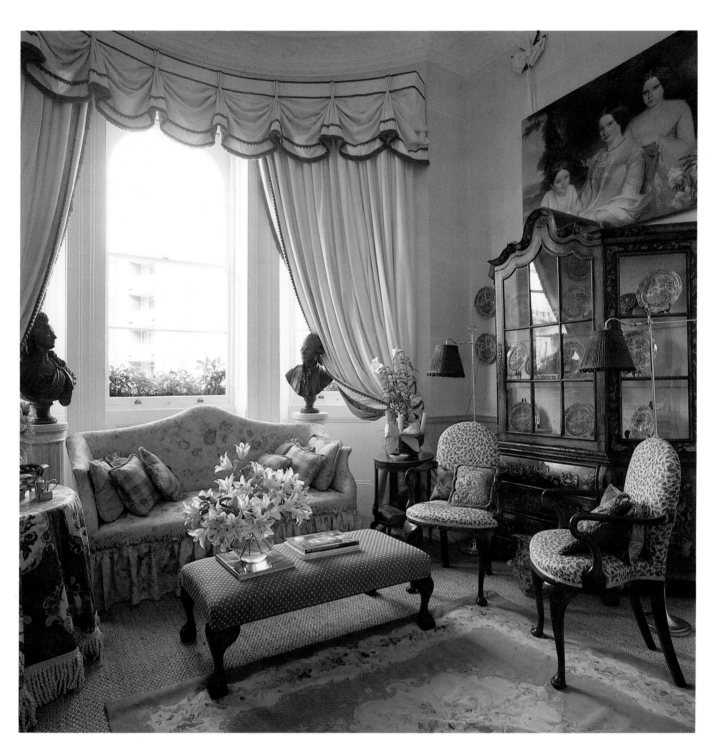

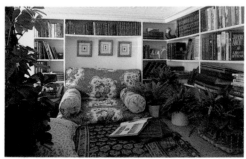

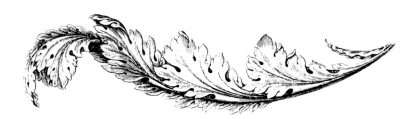

Decoration in high places

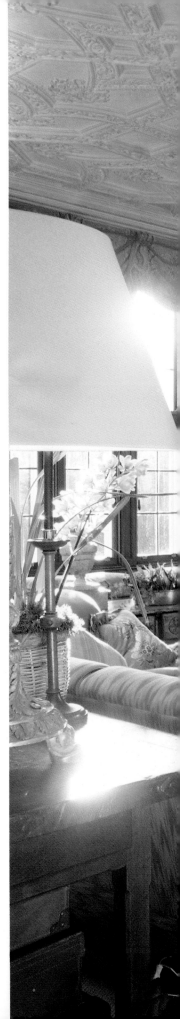

The ceiling is the pariah of present-day interior decoration. Every room has a ceiling, yet while all the other architectural surfaces in a room are embellished with colour and pattern, the ceiling is invariably left unadorned. For some people, a plain white expanse overhead is a positive choice, but, for many, white is a negative solution, arrived at more by apathy and indecision than by intent. Contrary to practice in past eras, today's ceilings are rarely given a second thought, which is especially curious in an age when we like to think we are so highly design-conscious and when there is a widespread vogue for enriched styles of interior design. Strange, too, how we accept impressive decoration and clutter on the sides and floor of our rooms but see nothing unbalanced in leaving the top part bare.

It is no coincidence, perhaps, that some of the most imaginative and visually rewarding rooms in this book are also those where the ceiling has been decorated. The design of these rooms has a wholeheartedness, authority and integration that outstrips other settings. They are clearly the work of designers who have gone right back to square one and have a more comprehensive view of interior decoration.

But, even if a room's ceiling is left plain, what about the top part of the walls? Isn't there something to be said for embellishing this part to balance the lower part? A giant cornice and frieze, or a broad band of colourful stencilling, for example, both provide high-level visual interest and a link with the furnishing.

(Right) Redolent of baronial Scotland, this Highland drawing-room conveys an established air of protectiveness. The oak-panelled walls, carved stone chimneypiece and, above all, the magnificent Jacobean-style ceiling are reassuringly dateless and provide a warm framework for a colourful furnishing scheme by Sylvia Lawson Johnston. The elaborate plaster ceiling, decorated with interwoven strapwork, bosses and pendants, has a plain cornice abutting the carved wooden frieze.

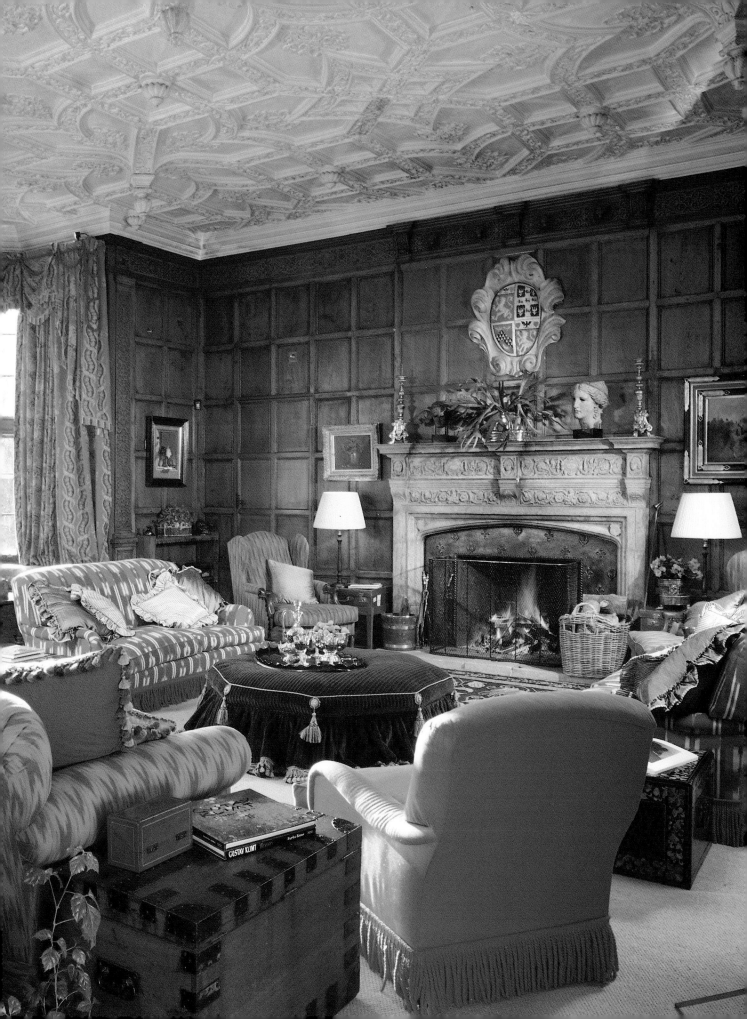

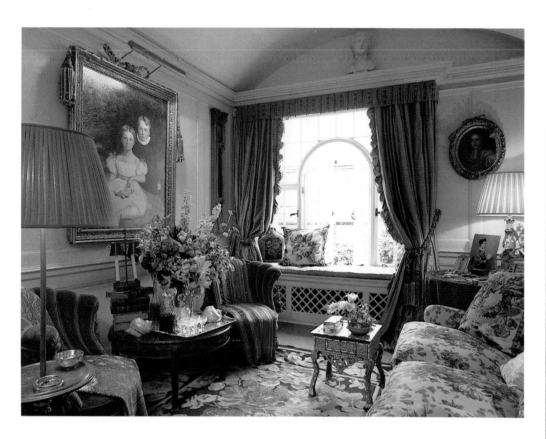

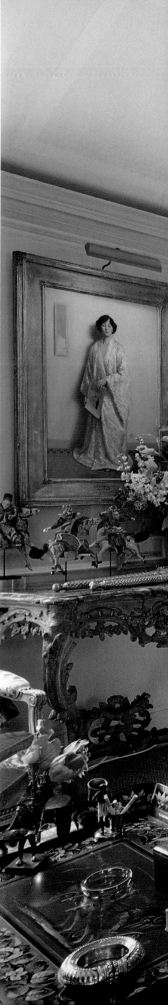

Archetypal arches

The ceiling here is barrel-vaulted, with compartments painted in the Italian manner. The compartmentalization is very underplayed but draws attention, almost subliminally, to the unusual ceiling form, and the colouring harmonizes with the dusty-salmon-pink paint used on the wall panelling.

There are two seating-areas in the room: one, at the fireplace end, is grouped on a vivid Ziegler rug; the other, more intimate, has a large sofa and buttoned chairs arrayed on a nineteenth-century Bessarabian rug. The room was decorated with advice from Anthony Ormiston.

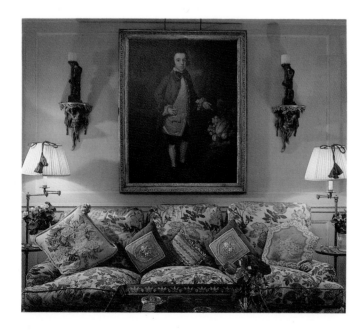

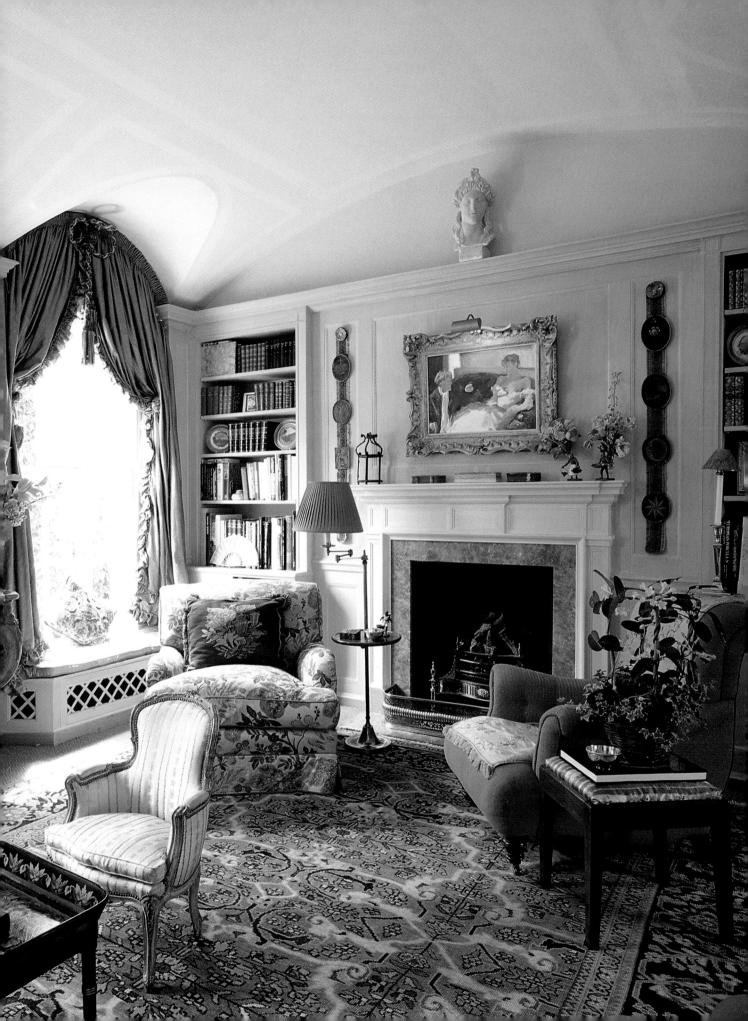

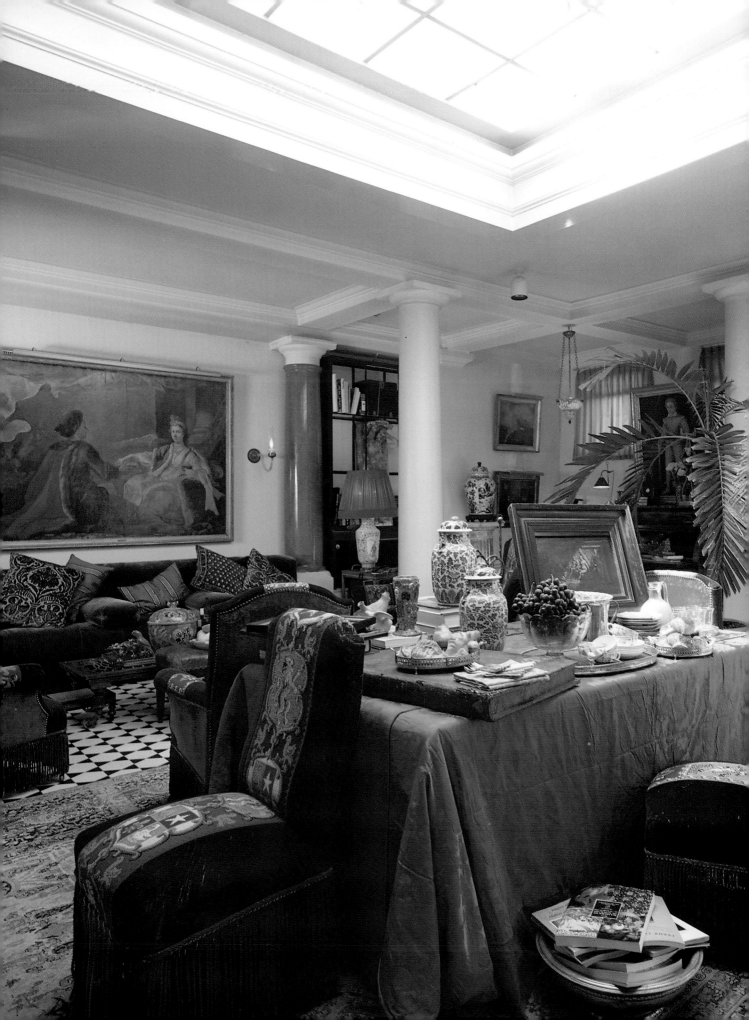

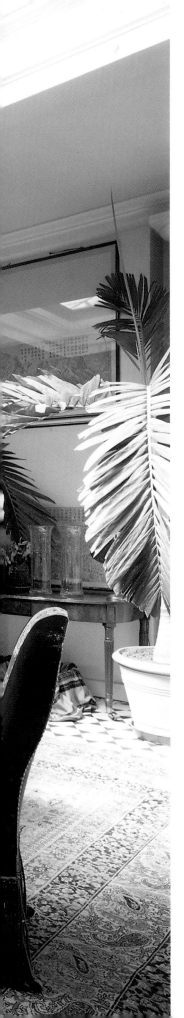

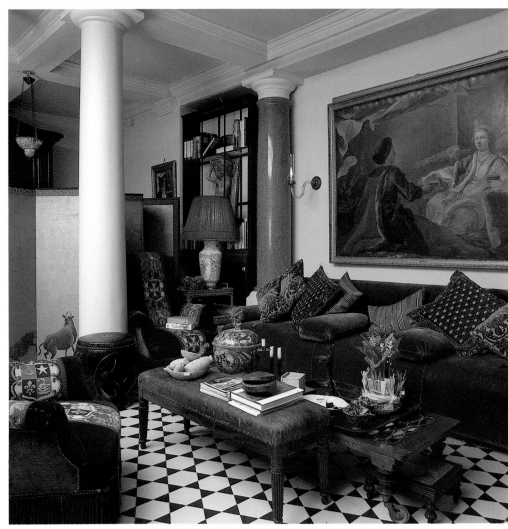

In a one-time ballroom

Formerly a hotel ballroom, now home to antiques dealer
Maroun Salloum, this room on the Left Bank in Paris is lit by a
huge skylight and imparts much of the feeling of a stage-set.
Maroun Salloum likes to keep the basic elements of furniture –
the capacious green sofa, for instance – in situ, but he changes
the smaller pieces, the props, according to mood and need.
The sofa is covered in 1940s velvet from Italy, its jewel-like
colour and sheen making a vivid contrast with the black-and-
white floor. Above the sofa hangs an eighteenth-century
Turkish scene depicting two figures in gorgeous costumes.
The sumptuousness of their robes is emulated by the silken
finery of the room, especially by the red damask on the table,
which is set with an eclectic array of objects in the manner of a
seventeenth-century still-life painting.

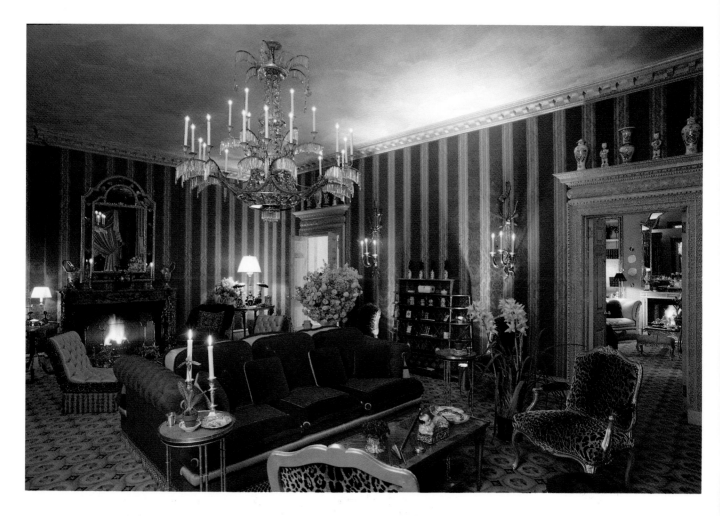

Life after twilight

Contrary to first impressions, this *tour de force* in elaborate French style is not in a nineteenth-century mansion in Europe but in a 1920s Art Deco building high above Fifth Avenue in New York. The interior is the work of the renowned Parisian designer, Alberto Pinto, who was commissioned by American clients to indulge their fascination with *fin de siècle* France, at the same time taking into account a sophisticated lifestyle in a dynamic city. Alberto Pinto designed the red-and-gold striped wall fabric and the carpet, based on Directoire originals, while the deeply-upholstered chairs and sofas are his versions of Napoleon III models. The back-to-back sofa establishes two seating areas, one facing the chimneypiece and the other completed by a

pair of giltwood armchairs covered in simulated leopardskin. The clients' request for 'Scarlet O'Hara' curtains resulted in the extravagant ruching and draping of triple-layered blue and yellow silk suspended from blue poles with gilt finials.

The whole point of the scheme is its opulent splendour, guaranteed by wonderful textures, gorgeous colours and insistent luxury. Masses of sparkle radiates from the magnificent Russian chandelier and furniture – a mix of Russian, French and English – and from the ornaments. Above all this splendour, the celestial ceiling has been painted to project a twilight mood, a fitting treatment for a room which is perfectly contrived for luxurious evening entertaining.

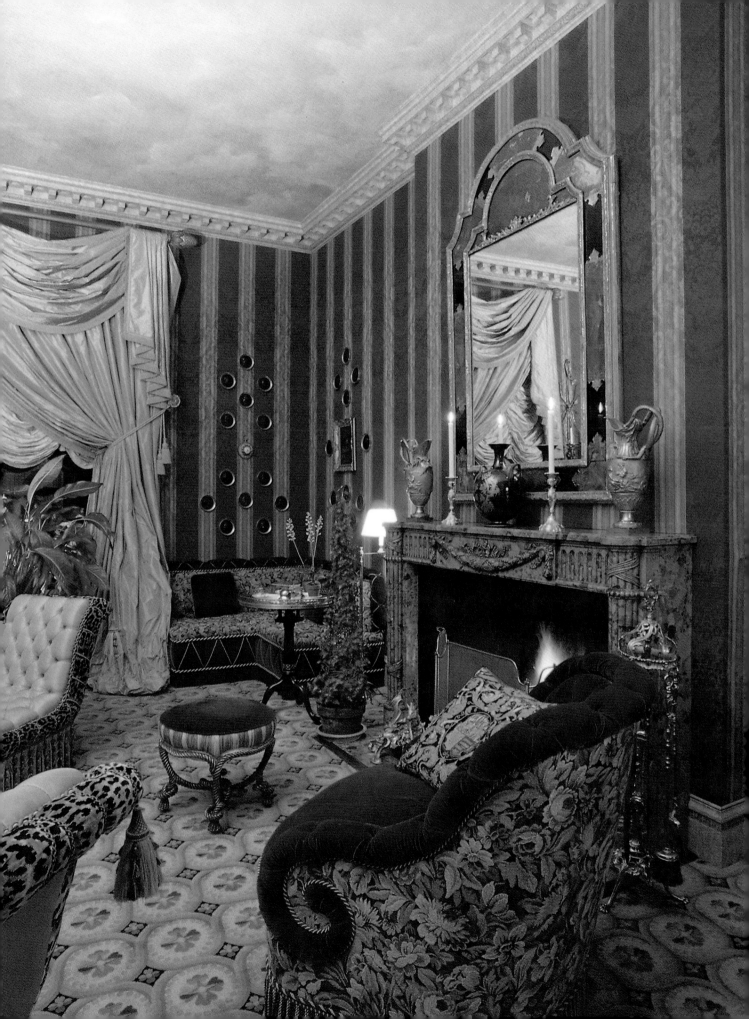

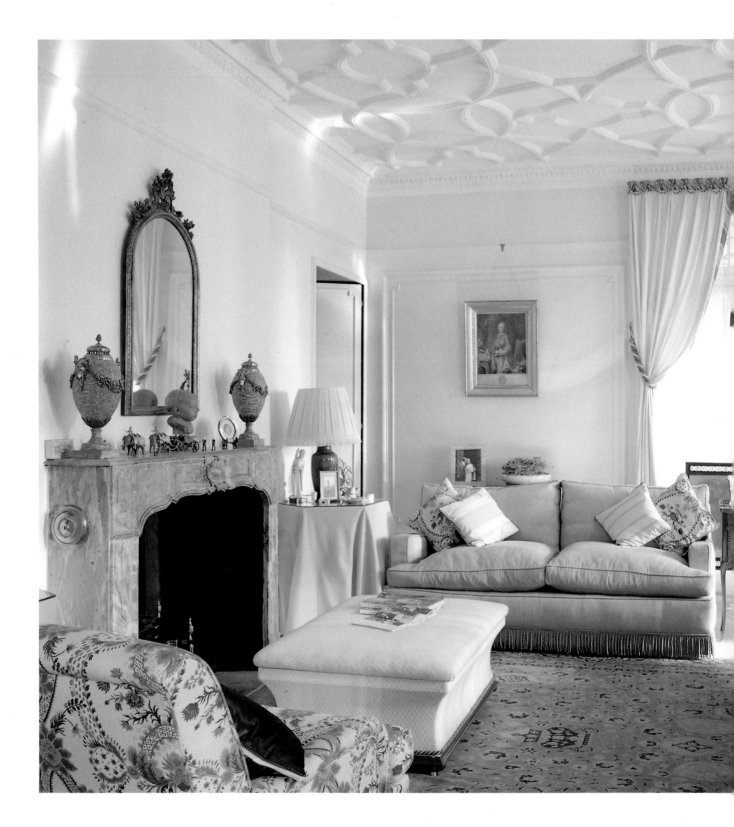

No frills, no frippery, no chintz

Sometimes, less means more. In this case – a first-floor flat in central London – the brief from the Swiss owners to Liz Smithers of Sloane Decorators was quite specific: no chintz, no frills. The resulting scheme is airy and inspiriting, with clear colours, well spaced furniture and delicately detailed curtains. Above this understated scheme is an elaborate gothic-style ceiling. Its plain white treatment panders to the restrained character of the room's furnishings but the fluent mouldings have a subtly cosifying effect.

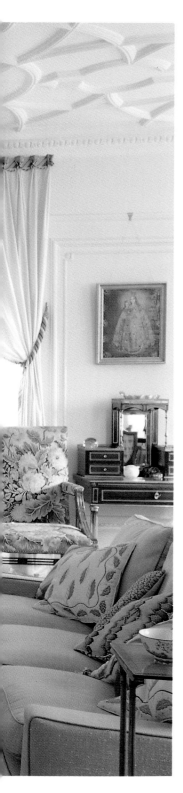

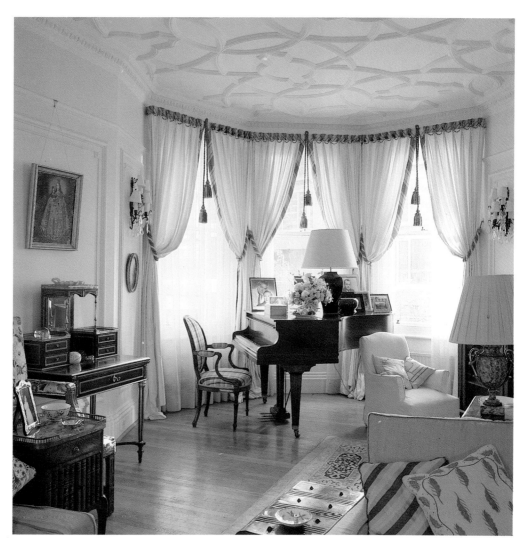

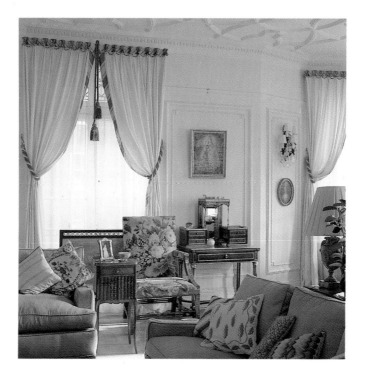

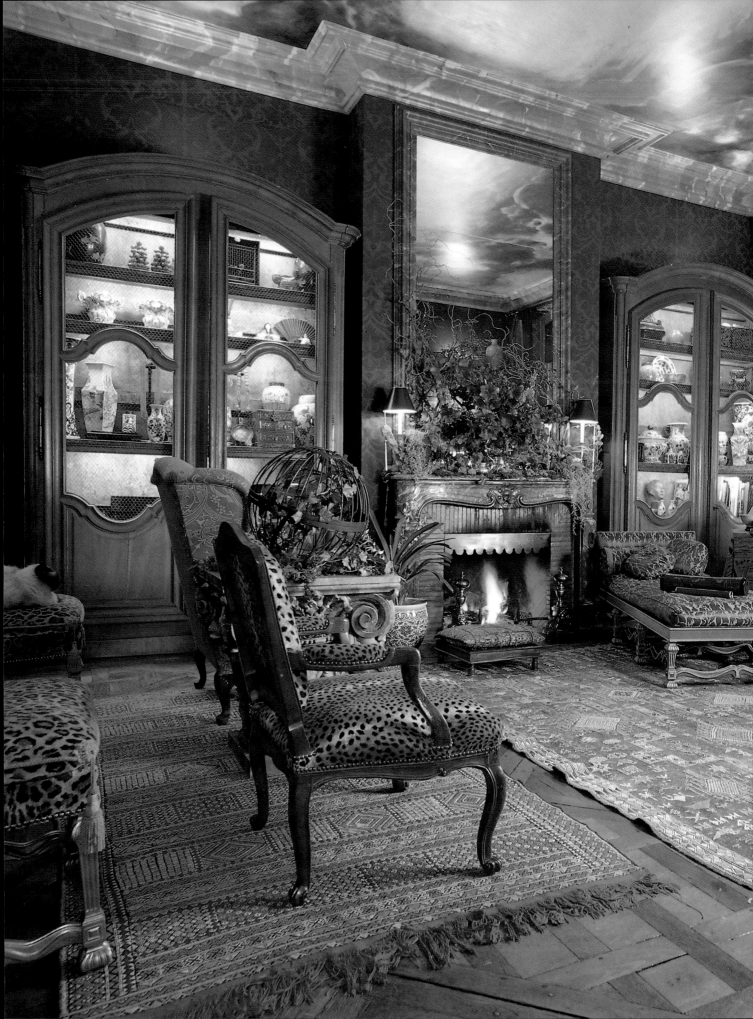

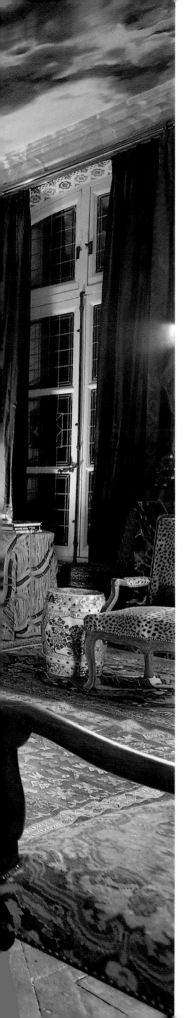

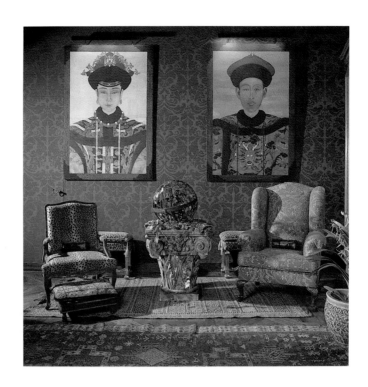

Every cloud . . .

The placing of the furniture in Monique and Laurent Normand's grandly proportioned room in Paris, decorated in collaboration with Yves Taralon, is dignified and exact. The two wire-mesh-fronted *armoires*, displaying a collection of blue-and-white china, have an imposing presence, and the pair of Chinese imperial portraits makes an equally potent contribution. To give 'movement' to this powerful alignment, the ceiling has been painted with scudding, nocturnal clouds by Legrand-Tardiff. A massive cornice divides the sky from the walls, which are covered in blue damask. Flowers and plants are arranged like living sculpture, spilling over the entire chimneypiece and acquiring an even more attenuated, surreal effect by being reflected in the mirror behind.

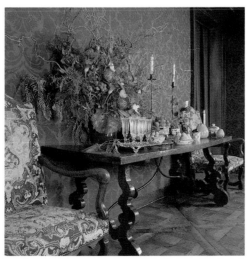

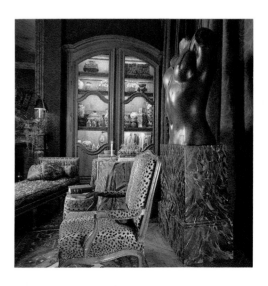

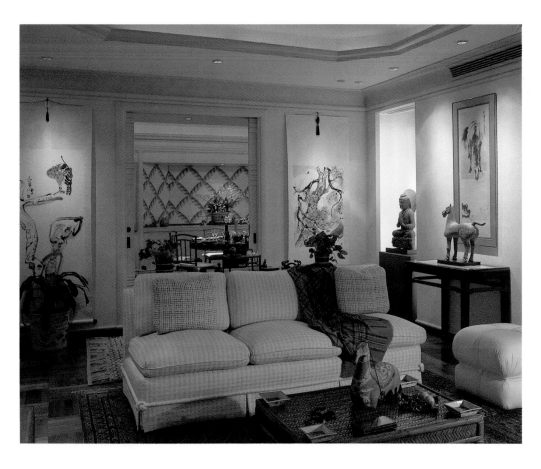

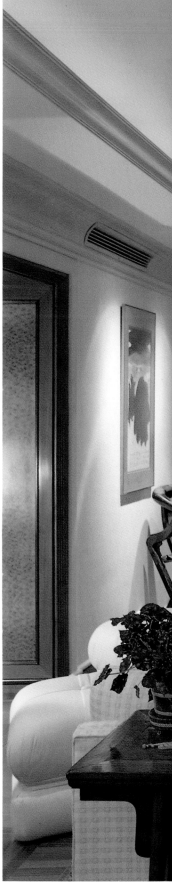

Sophisticated and soothing

A cut-away ceiling improves the definition of a room in a modern block in Hong Kong and houses an ingenious lighting system, designed by Tina Stolle of Architects Hawaii for jewellery designer Kai-Yin Lo. The system casts a band of illumination upwards on to the upper ceiling as well as pools of light downwards on to specific objects.

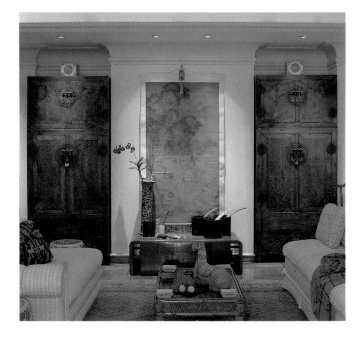

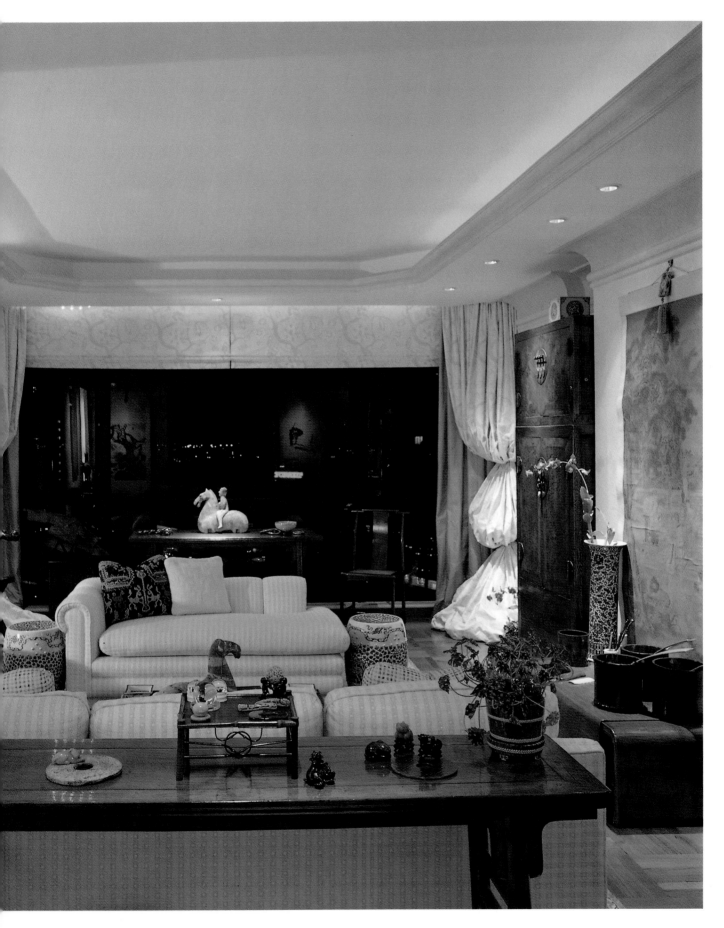

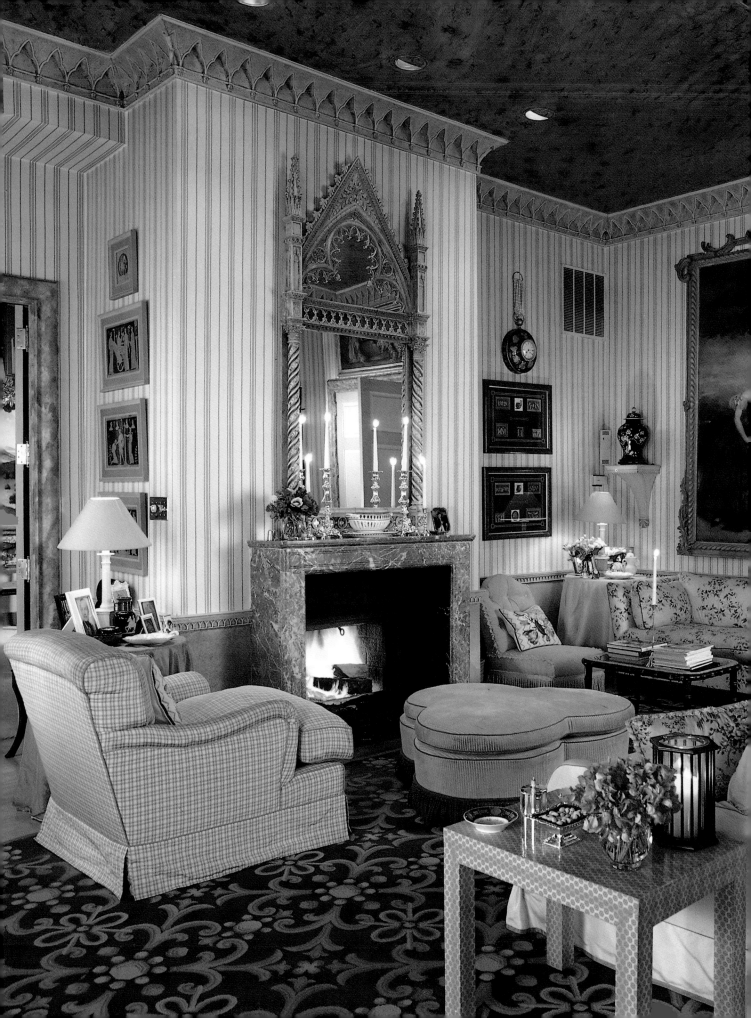

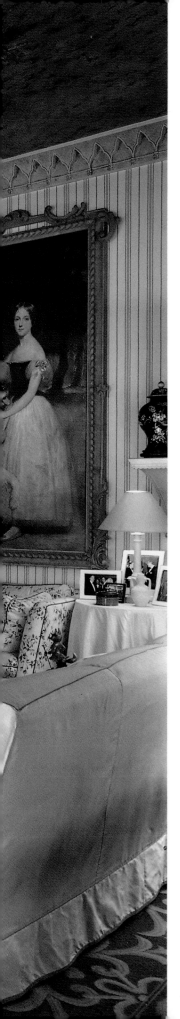

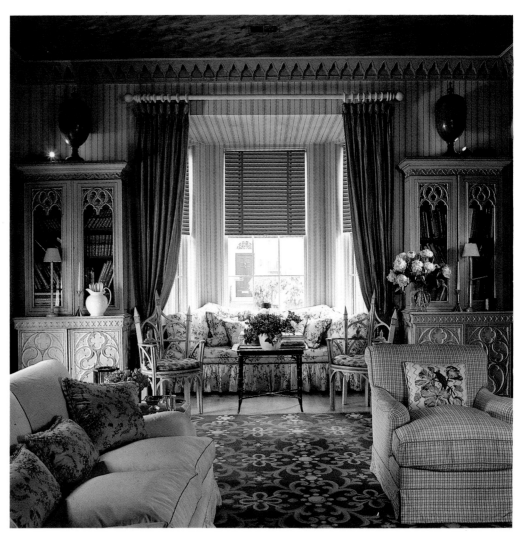

All-encompassing palette

Disliking the idea of a plain white ceiling in a room decorated with a rich build-up of textures, Anthony Browne opted for *faux* tortoiseshell overhead in his house in Washington. It is a novel and astonishingly realistic foil for the room's skilfully integrated patterns and colours. The latter form an harmonious palette of beiges, siennas and orchres, which extends even to the collection of Etruscan prints. The setting is deliberately 'silky', rather than chintzy, and has some enviable examples of gothick exuberance. The intricacy and convolutions of the two chairs, cabinets and mirror are echoed in the gothick arches of the cornice. The room is masterfully designed for year-round enjoyment: for evenings and winter, there is capacious seating centred on the marble chimneypiece; for daytime and summer, there is an amply-cushioned window seat.

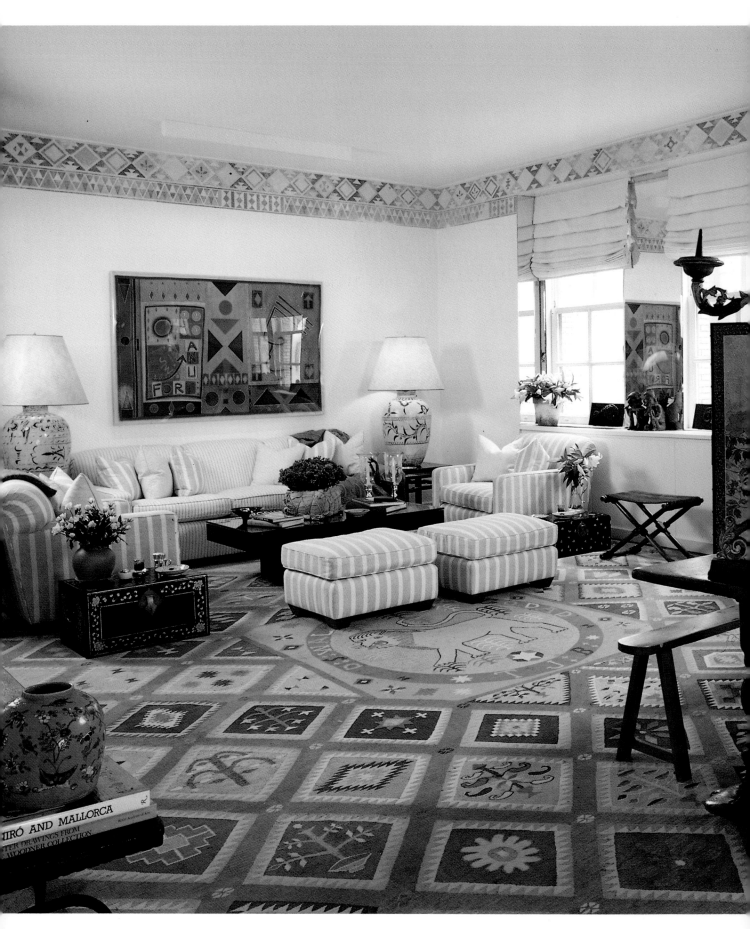

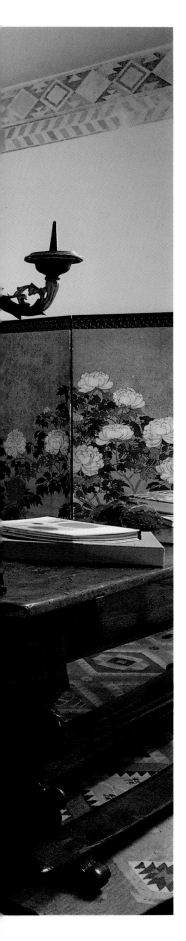

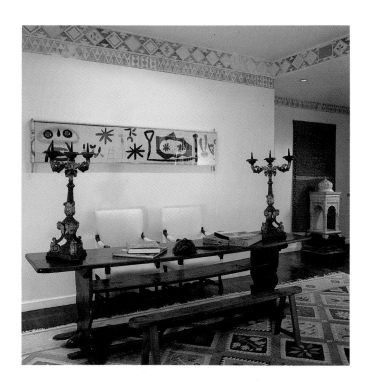

A colourful geometry

The vibrancy and geometry of a room in New York designed by Lyn Rothman, with architectural assistance from Adam Tihany and Robert Couturier, is refreshingly individual. The pictures are bold, graphic and colourful, fortuitously relating to the Indian dhurrie on the floor. An Indian connection is also apparent in the coffee-table, made from an antique Indian door, and in the nineteenth-century, miniature, marble temple. The simple lines of the refectory table and benches are echoed by those of the side-table, while an oriental screen relates to the lacquered trunks by the striped armchairs. In a room with so much colour and visual interest at low level, the geometric frieze, painted by Philippe Lauro-Baranes, provides a crucial counterbalance.

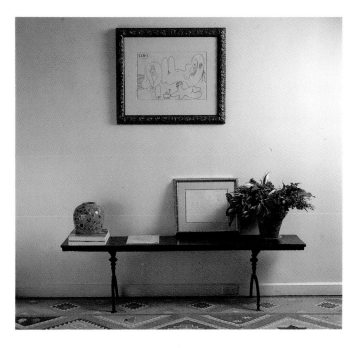

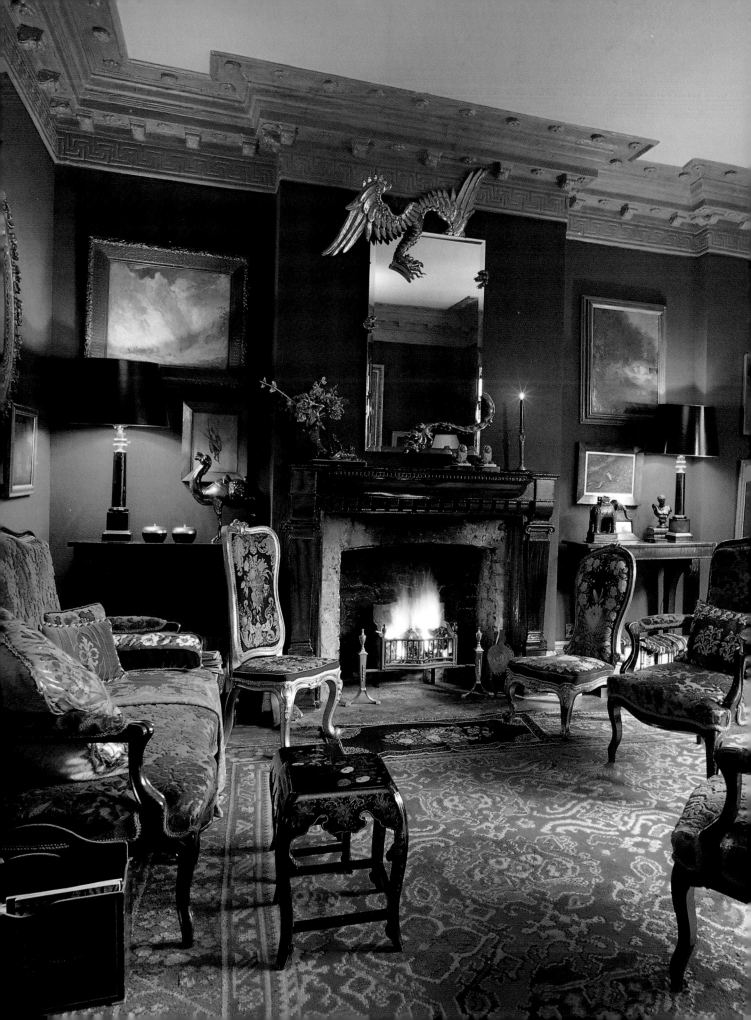

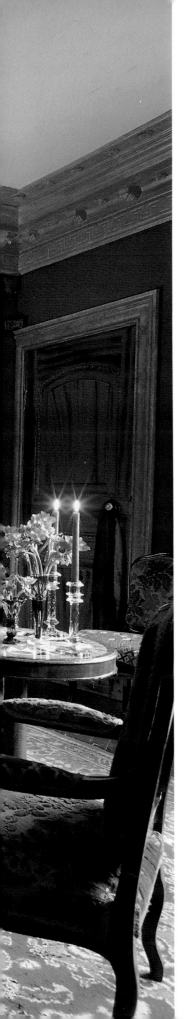

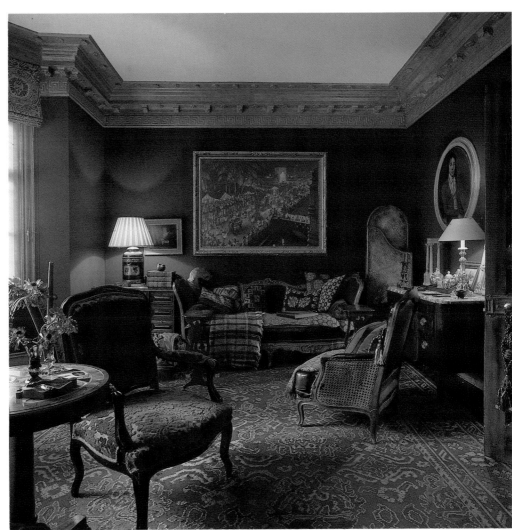

A winter retreat

The decoration by Christophe Gollut of a room in a late-Victorian building in West Kensington is a dramatic, assured scheme conceived as a background for a collection of ebonized furniture upholstered in nineteenth-century gauffraged velvet. The furniture suggested the idea of a winter retreat, enhanced by deep-red linen on the walls and mahogany wood-graining on the doors and chimneypiece. The shadowy richness, perfectly attuned to the style of furnishing and to after-dark hours, seems a natural habitat for the strange beasts that spring from behind the mirror and perch on the consoles. There is something reminiscent of a theatre-set here, manipulating time, place and atmosphere, with one of the most theatrical elements undoubtedly being the over-scaled cornice and frieze, a huge band of classical motifs emphasized by strong colour.

Decoration in detail

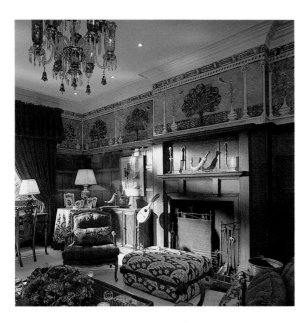

In an Edwardian house in Hampstead, the wall-space between the original panelling and ceiling inspired interior designer, Alidad, to carry out a long-held ambition to reproduce the frieze from the Palazzo Davanzzati in Florence. Painted by Simon Brady, it is a near-exact copy providing high-level visual interest.

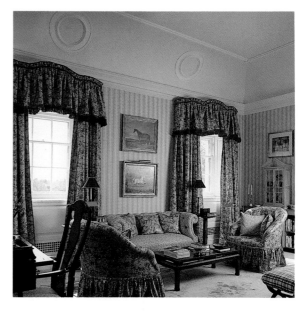

The ceiling of this room in a neo-Palladian house in Kentucky, designed by Quinlan Terry for Josephine Abercrombie, has a handsome architectural presence. The deep cove is embellished with roundels, and the various planes are picked out in different colours echoing the rest of the interior decoration.

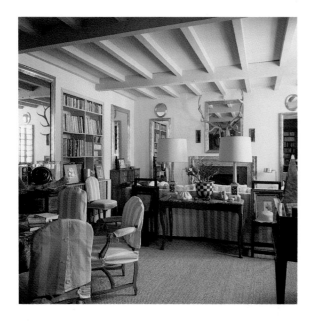

Beams create interesting shadow effects even when painted white to match the plaster infill. Here, in a sitting-room in Provence designed by Dick Dumas, the ceiling is totally integrated yet plays a noticeable part in the overall scheme. There is a nice balance between worldly chic and rural casualness.

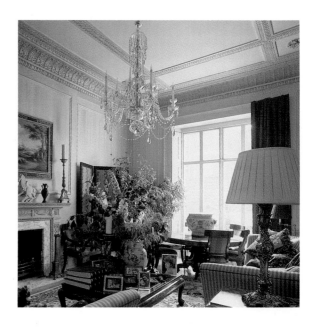

The ceiling in this flat decorated by Margaret Tiffin is not over-ornate but it does have a pleasing degree of embellishment to balance the lush style of furnishing. The decorated bands which divide the ceiling into compartments are painted in the same warm beige as the walls. (See, too, pages 102–103.)

Decoration in detail

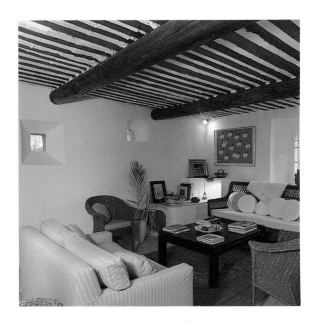

In Peter and Jenny Mayle's house in the South of France, small windows and thick walls conjure that special, timeless, rural quality which is so appealing in an age of instant, urban building. But the most strikingly rural feature of all, the one which literally dominates everything, is the massively beamed, sloping ceiling.

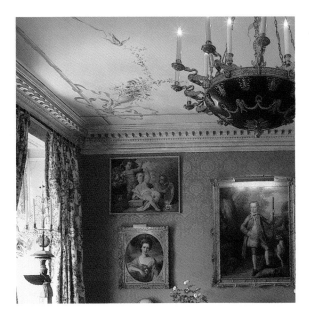

Painted by Bob Denning, this deliciously delicate ceiling, strewn with ribbons, birds and garlands of flowers against a softly lit sky, is in the New York apartment of Carroll and Milton Petrie. It is a celestial fantasy which pulls together the various elements and colours in a virtuoso scheme evolved by David Easton.

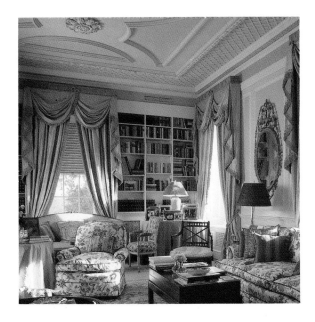

The furnishing of this recently built, neo-Palladian drawing-room in Kentucky (also shown on page 6) is harmonious without being so exact that the result is claustrophobic. The ceiling, designed by Quinlan Terry, is especially remarkable, with vigorous mouldings and panels painted in unison with the walls.

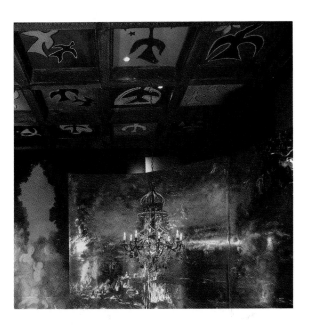

With its stylized bird motifs, Elizabeth Reber's painted ceiling in a room designed by Nicholas Glover recalls the works of Braque. It is a highly decorative element in an eclectic scheme which allies modern finishes with numerous historical influences, including sixteenth-century Italy and nineteenth-century France.

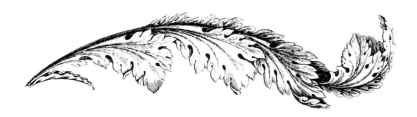

Windows revealed

In a perfect, arranged world, suitable for the most sensitive of householders, every window would be of the right proportions, of elegant shape and in the right place, shedding exquisite light into the room exactly when needed, and overlooking captivating views. Such windows would be so beautiful that either they needed no further embellishments, or they inspired effortless and instantly successful curtain treatments. Alas, few windows are so obliging. Most need a little help to ensure that they make a positive contribution to the room's attractions.

First and foremost, the decision to play up or play down the window must be made. Should the window be the most dominant feature in the room, reason enough for a decorative exercise in curtaining which will stun by its sheer flamboyance? Or is the shape of the window so pleasing that it would be a pity to obscure it? Is the window merely a source of light, to be treated as decorously as possible but not made a focal-point?

The design of curtains and pelmets is constantly undergoing subtle changes in fashion. Currently, softly draped pelmets seem more in favour than flat box-pelmets, and fringes and tassels are added with enthusiasm, but there are no hard-and-fast rules. When mistakes are made, they are usually more to do with proportion and scale than with the choice of fabrics and trim-mings. Very basically, sill-length curtains are rarely pleasing in town houses with vertical windows, and floor-length curtains look wrong against horizontal, cottage-type windows. These are simplistic guidelines but, with the return to a more classic style of decoration, they are all the more relevant. You may, of course, make a bold decision and dispense with curtains altogether. Some of the most striking rooms in this chapter have very exciting window treatments achieved without a single yard of fabric!

(Right) There is nothing intrinsically special about this window in New York, but its incorporation within a scheme which considers the window-wall as a single entity has resulted in an articulate and handsome focal-point. The pedimented bookcases have a striking classicism; the classical bronze is dramatically silhouetted against the skyline. The room was designed by Paula Perlini and Alan Tanksley.

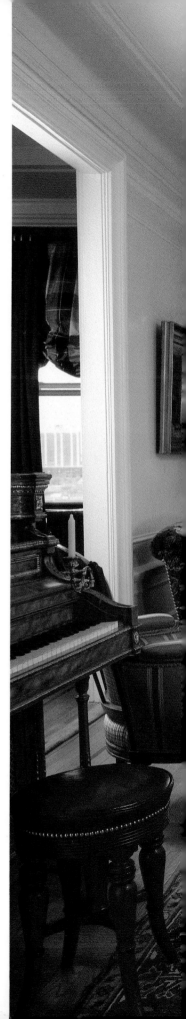

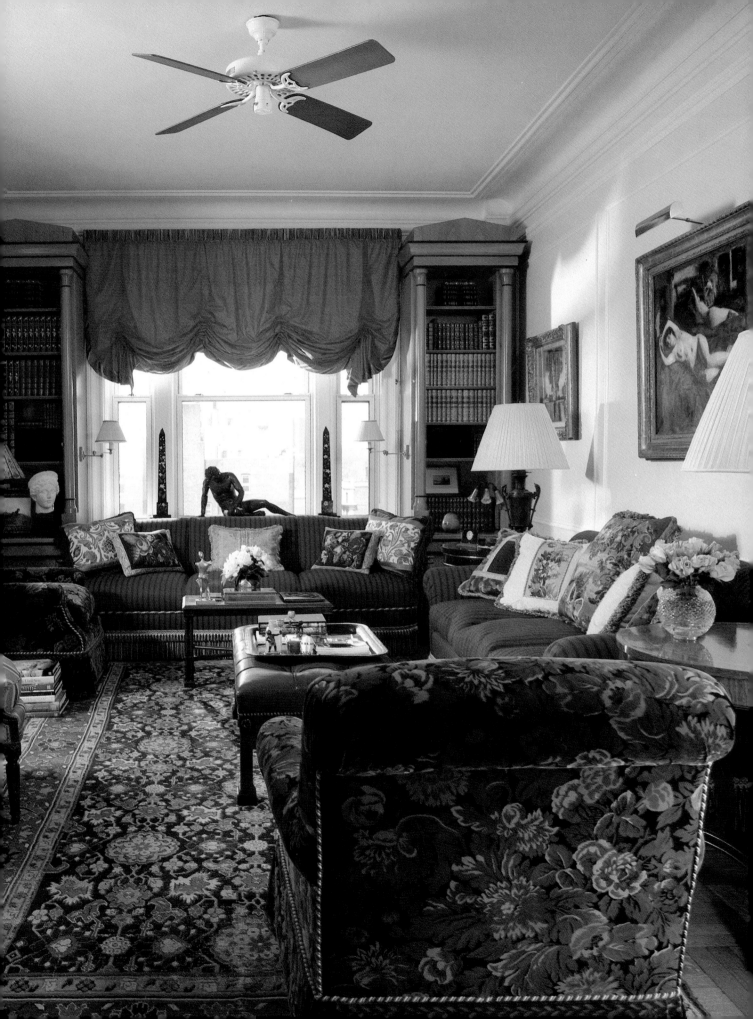

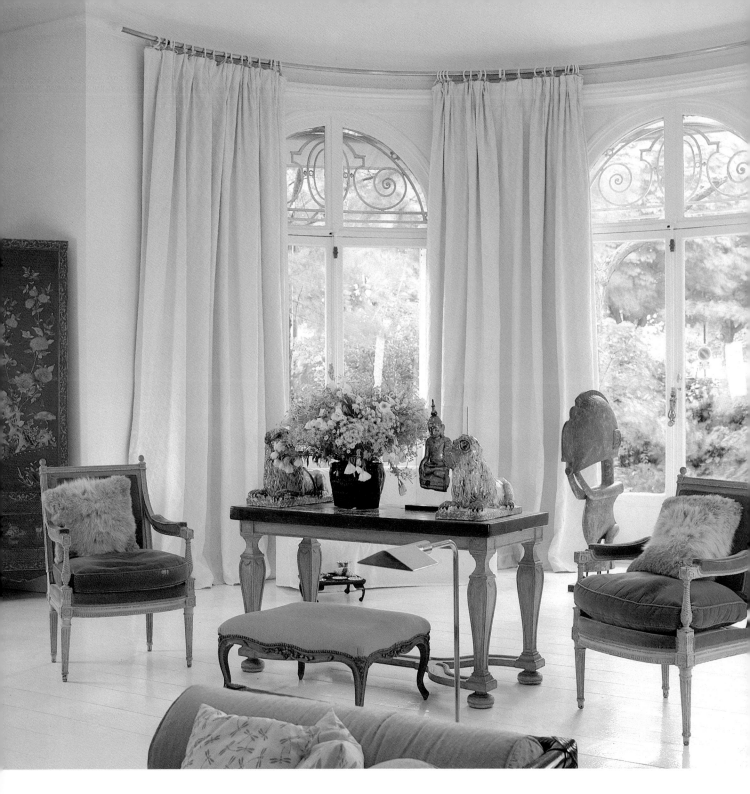

Whiter than white

Dreda Melé's favourite colour for interior decoration is white. In her very large, very stylized sitting-room in Paris, she has whited out the entire space, so that furniture and objects appear to float in mid-air. The whiteness is made even more pronounced by the superabundance of light from the triple French doors, which are hung with simple white piqué curtains. Against this ultimately colourless backdrop, she has used various shades of peach and coral, accented by sculptural green plantlife.

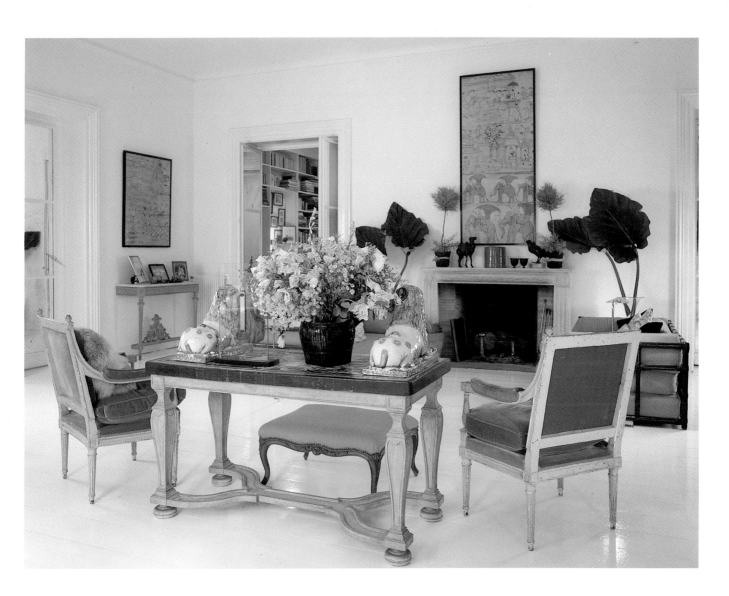

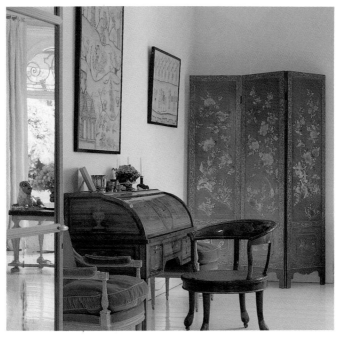

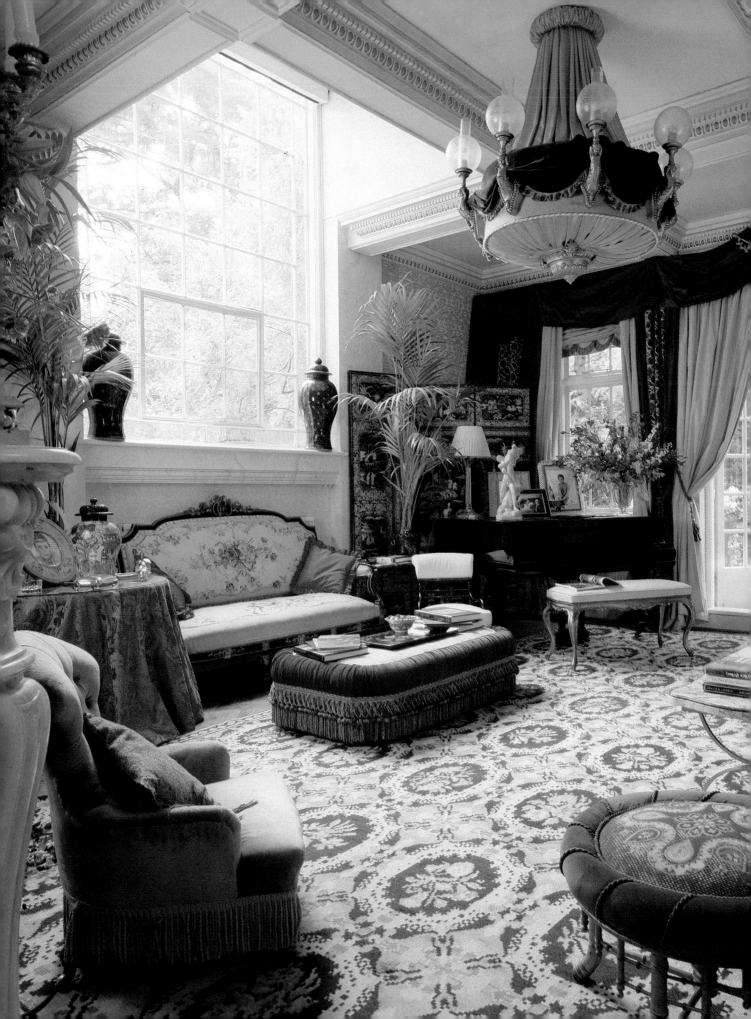

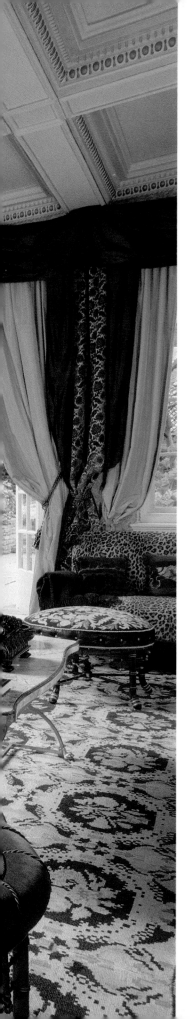

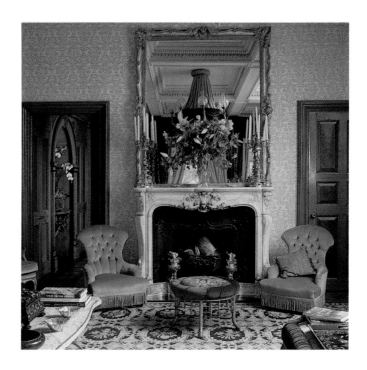

Continental ingenuity

Astonishingly, this vast studio room, built in 1900, is in the centre of London, attached to a Queen Anne house. Reflecting the continental connections of Sylvia Serra di Cassano, who devised the present scheme of decoration, the room has a Napoleon III ambience, realized with sumptuous colours, lavish textiles, heavy fringes and tall plants. There are no curtains to obscure the impressive studio window, but the glazed doors and windows overlooking the garden have continuous drapery and blinds in yellow and burgundy silk. The nostalgic style of furnishing is enriching and warming in a space which is lit predominantly from the north. An ingenious touch is the chandelier which is draped with velvet to conceal a film projector. A screen can be lowered in front of the studio window.

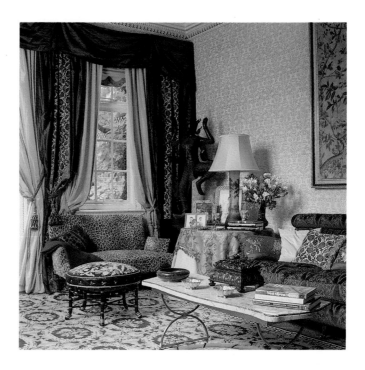

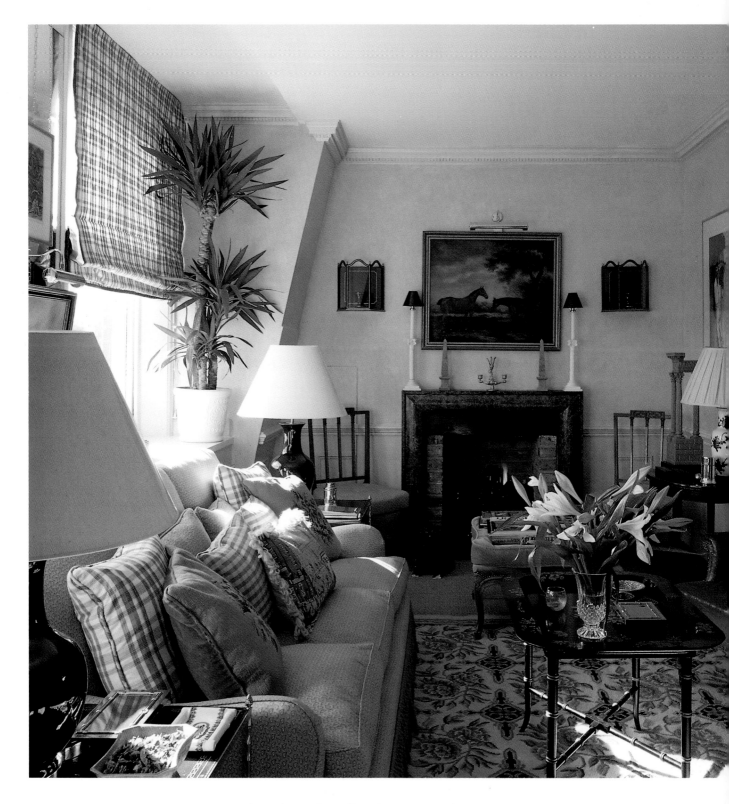

A checked alternative

In spite of the narrow, awkward proportions, this attic sitting-room, decorated by Brian Juhos, has been imbued with elegance. The wall facing the windows is mirrored to reflect the sky and to increase the room's apparent width. Checked blinds filter the strong, southerly light and are a neat, tailored alternative to curtains.

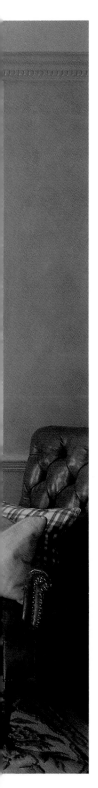

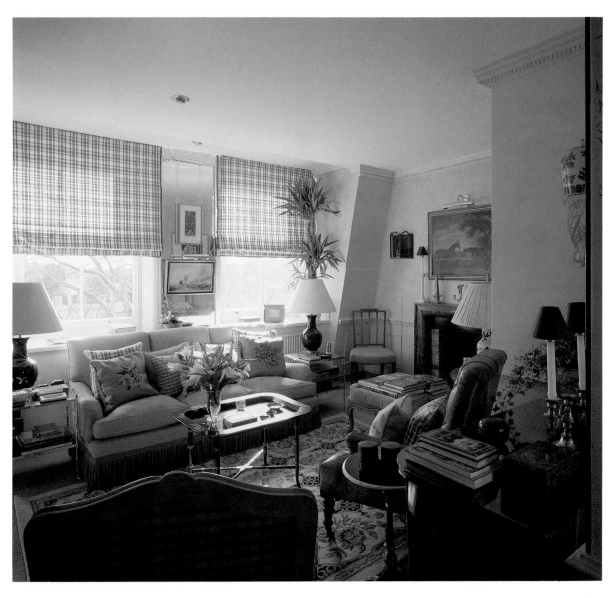

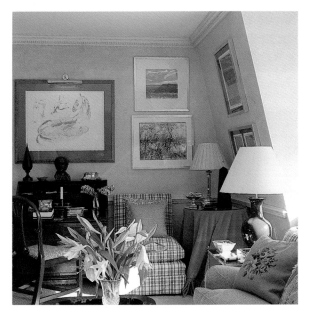

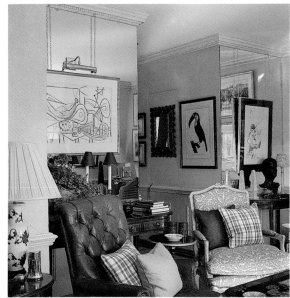

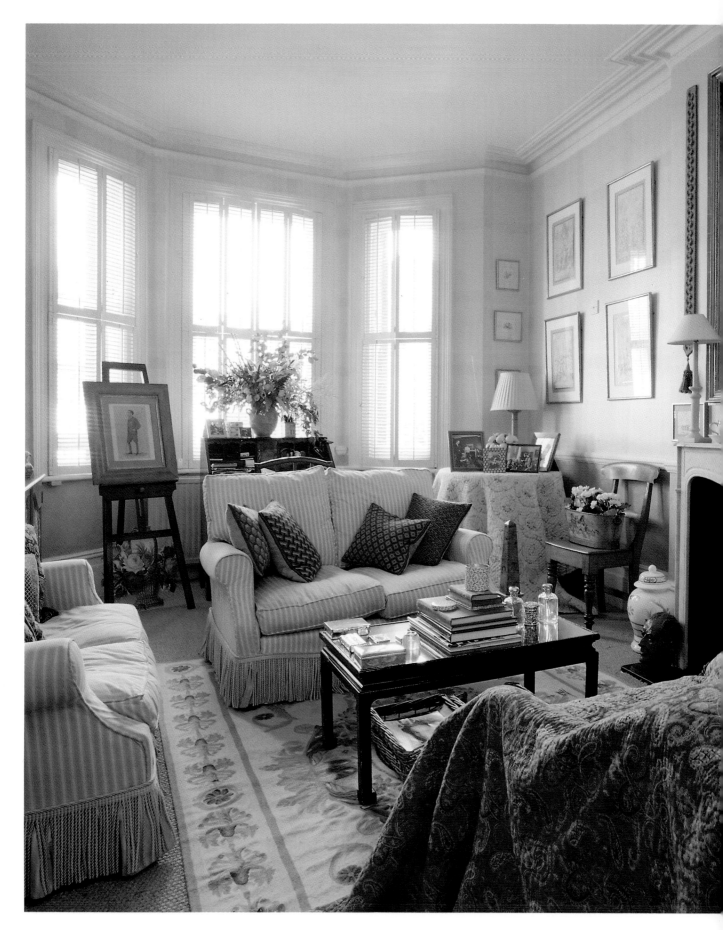

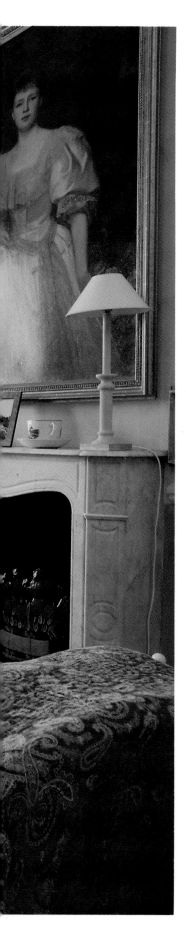

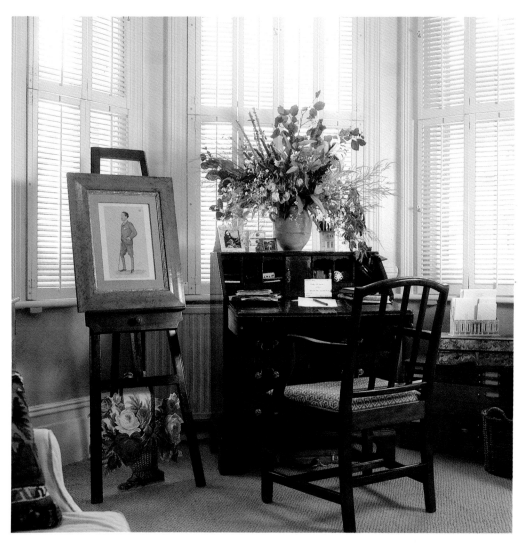

Recessive and space-enhancing

When paint-effect artist, Harry Lendrum, and his wife, Wendy, decorated their small flat in a central London mansion block, their first priority was to create an impression of space. Their choice of harmonious colours and subtle paint finishes – a faded linen-effect print above the dado rail and a soft terracotta stucco-effect below – is recessive without being bland. Equally recessive and space-enhancing is the treatment of the window bay. Instead of predictable curtains, there are louvred shutters, all of which can be opened independently, and the louvres can be angled up or down as required. Although the room feels totally unified, there is no sense of rigid co-ordination or laboured perfectionism.

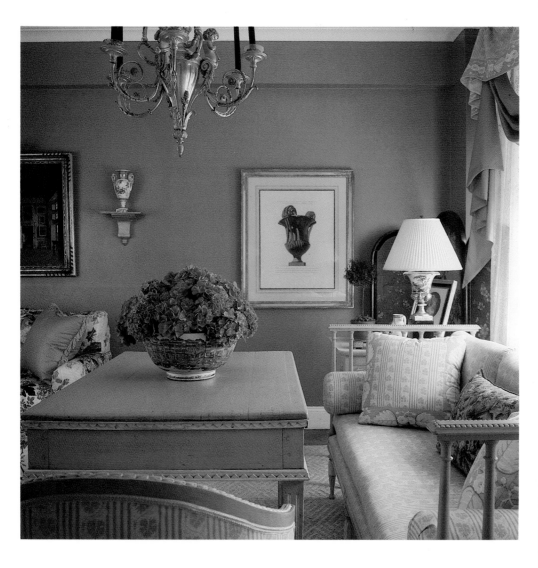

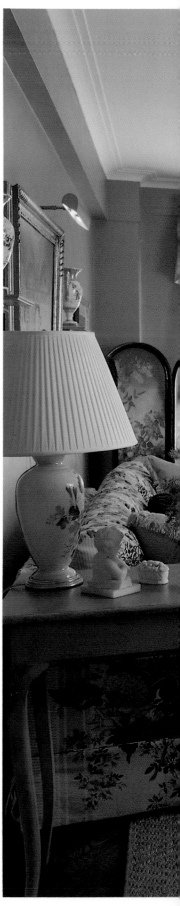

Scandinavian influences

The Swedish-American owners of a New York *pied à terre*, decorated by Dennis Rolland, wanted it to be kept simple and to have a Scandinavian inflection – hence the grey-white painted cot sofa, the two chairs in the same group, and the bench in front of the fire, all made in Sweden circa 1800. The table is also Swedish, and was made about the same time, but its sturdy profiles have a more countrified character. The window spans almost the entire width of the room and was previously hung simply with lace curtains and a pelmet, again showing a Scandinavian influence, but this seemed too severe in New York, so swags were added to match the Venetian-red walls without spoiling the modest charm of the original scheme. The effect is a dexterous translation of the Swedish talent for handling daylight in interior decoration.

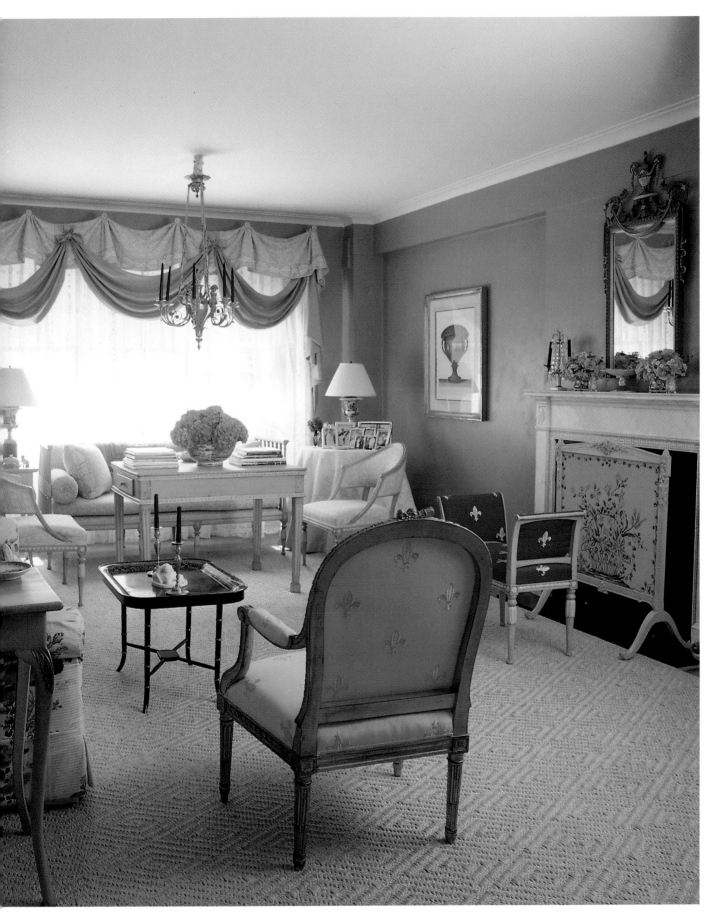

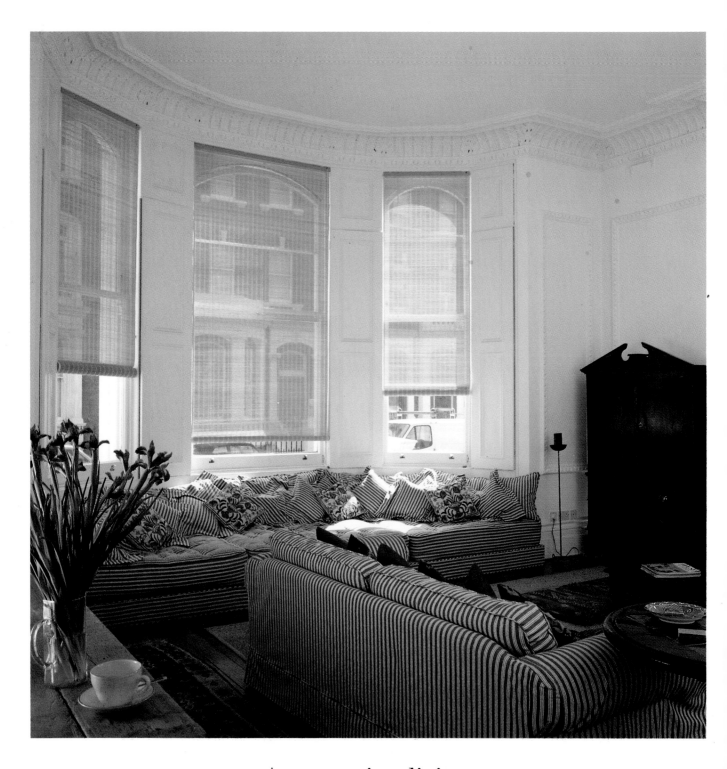

A smart simplicity

Richard Hudson's clear-cut views on interior design are ably expressed in the sitting-room of his London *pied à terre*. Measuring twenty-three feet square, and embellished with original mouldings, the room retains its traditional character but the pure white paintwork, simple blinds and smart, unfussy stripes have, if anything, given the architecture greater distinction. The bay, some twelve feet wide and three feet deep, is filled with a massive window seat, an idea suggested by decorator Mimmi O'Connell. The antique furniture is of mixed provenance but is linked by a country informality.

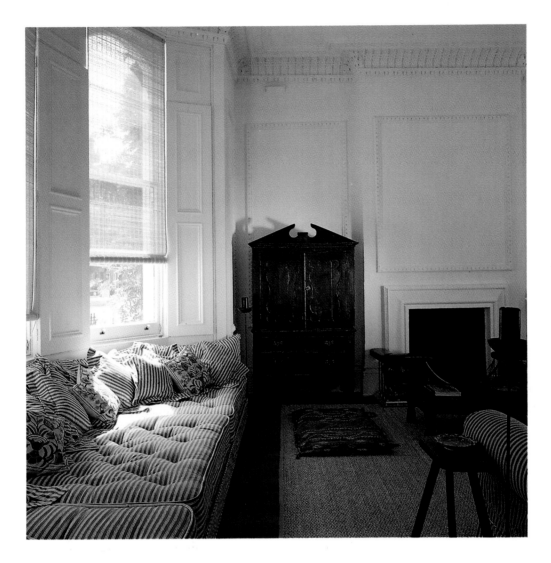

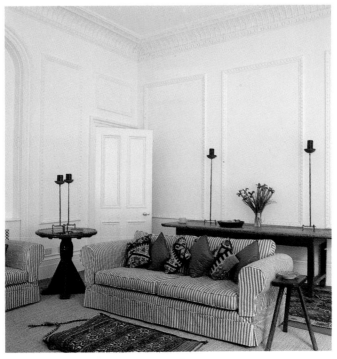

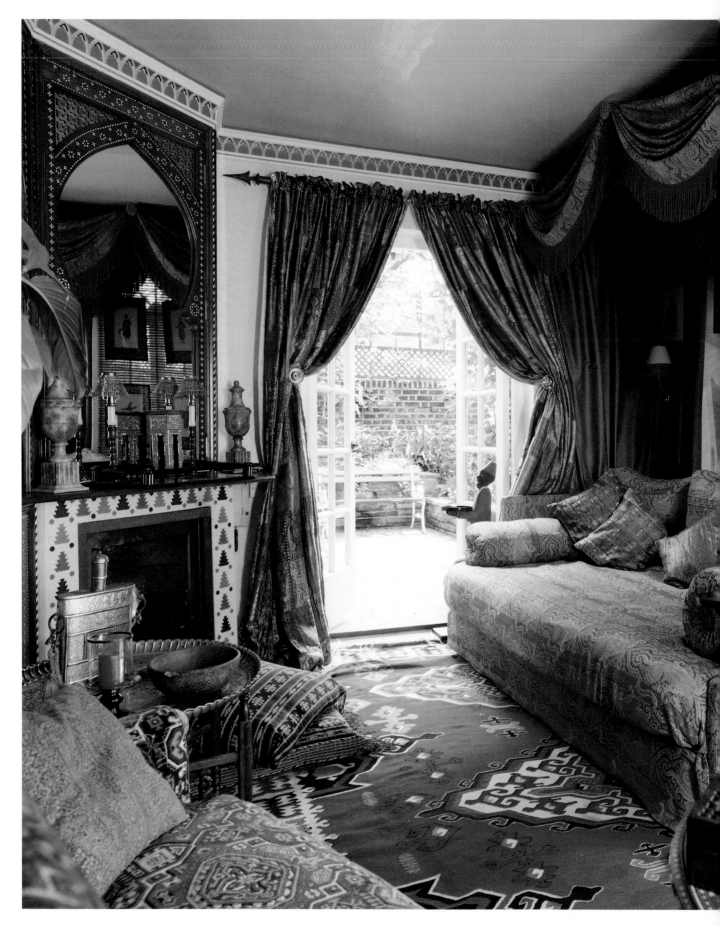

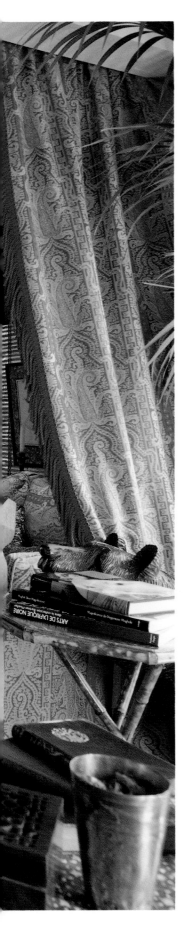

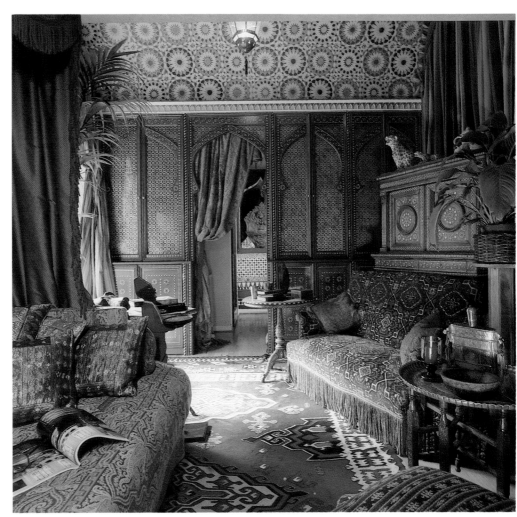

Turkish delight

This garden-room in Chelsea, decorated by Sylvia Serra di Cassano, is used mainly as a bedroom but it has all the attributes and cushioned comforts of an oriental sitting-room. The cornice, fire surround and fretwork cupboards are painted with Islamic motifs; there is an uninhibited use of textiles; and there is a tent-like sense of enclosure. The large area of glazing is a bonus during the day, especially in summer, but at night this could have made the room seem too exposed. The problem has been overcome by exotic curtaining tightly gathered on a pole across the French doors, and by narrow-slatted blinds against the window behind the bed. Unusually, and very decoratively, pictures are hung on the blinds.

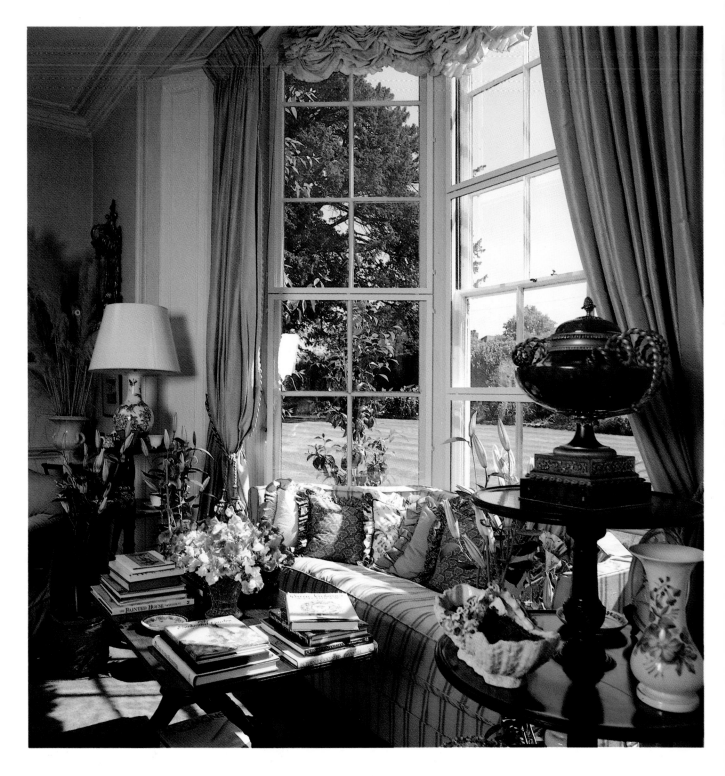

A cheerful coexistence

Sky-blue is the felicitous, apt choice of colour for the walls of Jane Stevens' country sitting-room which basks in light from large windows overlooking a mature garden. Everything about the room is summed up by the summery, nonchalant treatment of the bay window. Nothing is too obviously organized, nor too matched, yet all the elements are cheerfully cohesive. The Venetian mirror and German porcelain lamps look perfectly at ease with the piles of books and loose-covered sofas and armchairs.

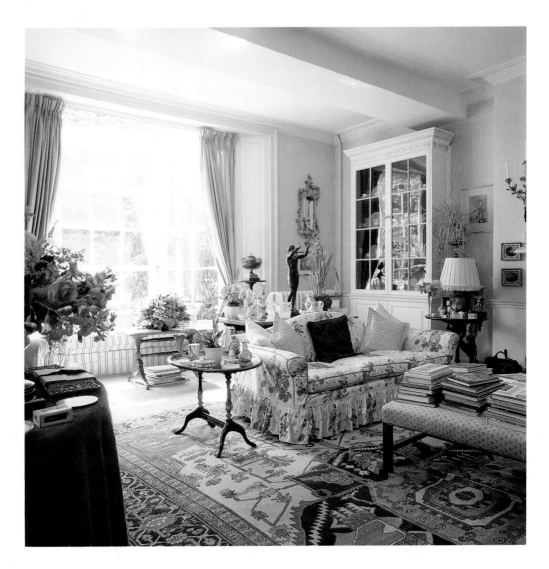

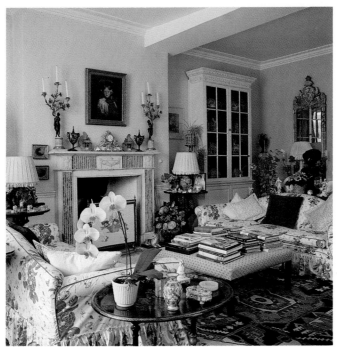

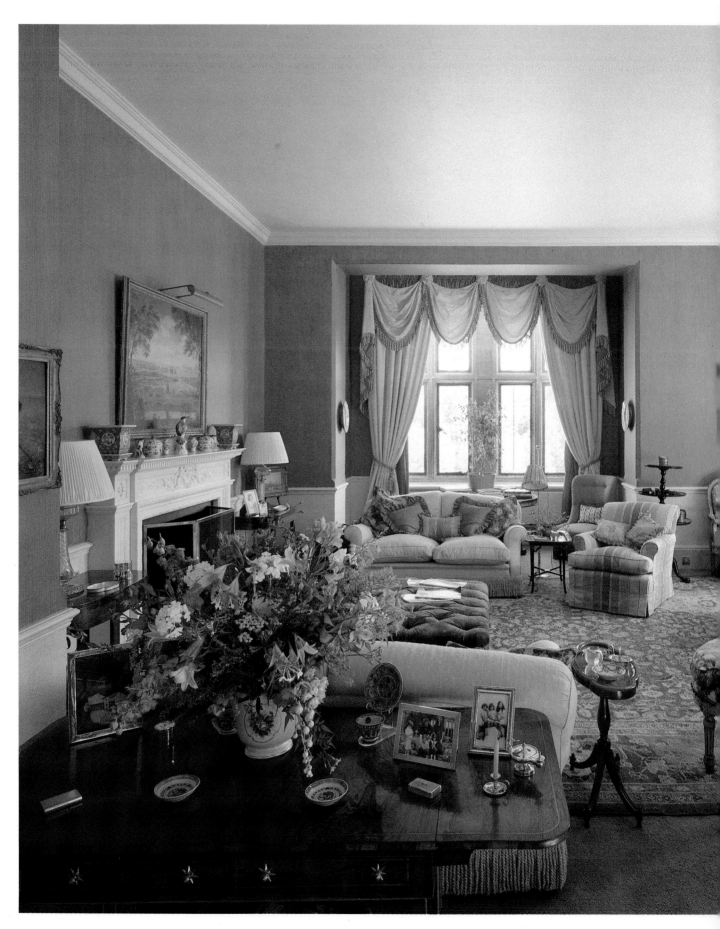

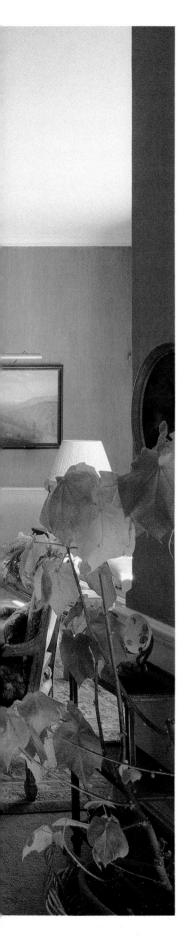

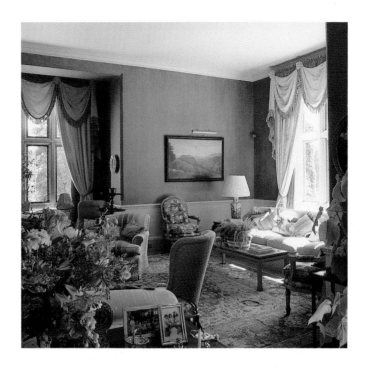

A colourful serenity

The deeply swagged pelmet treatment, suggested by Nina Campbell for a distinctly English room in Dorset, softens the architecture and links the disparate windows and glazed gothick door to the garden. It also enhances the generous, comfortable nature of the seating which is pleasingly mixed and has lots of cushions. The room's cheerful colour scheme has some emphatic contrasts but the general effect is serene.

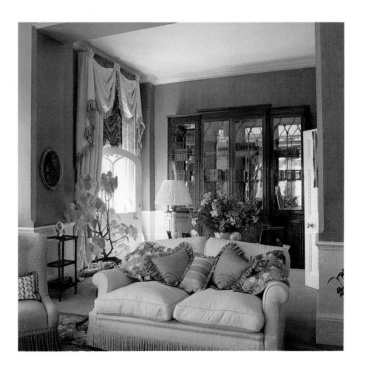

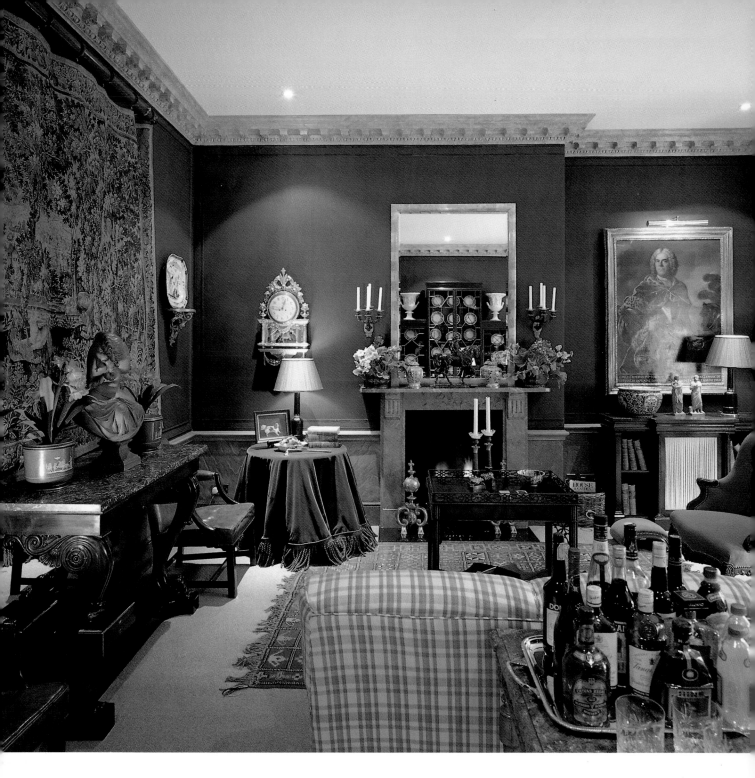

Masculine comfort

Although the colours and style of decoration are essentially masculine, the stress here is on comfort. Soft textures are all-important in creating an agreeable and discreet sense of indulgence. The walls are lined with forest-green fabric; a heavy-fringed velvet cloth covers the table to the left of the fire; a French tapestry hangs opposite the bay window; the fitted carpet is enlivened by a Saharan rug. In contrast, the treatment of the window bay is unexpectedly simple – but wholly successful. Plain sailcloth blinds amidst such lush furnishings make a far more telling foil for the handsome neoclassical statue than elaborate curtains. The interior was designed by Brian Juhos.

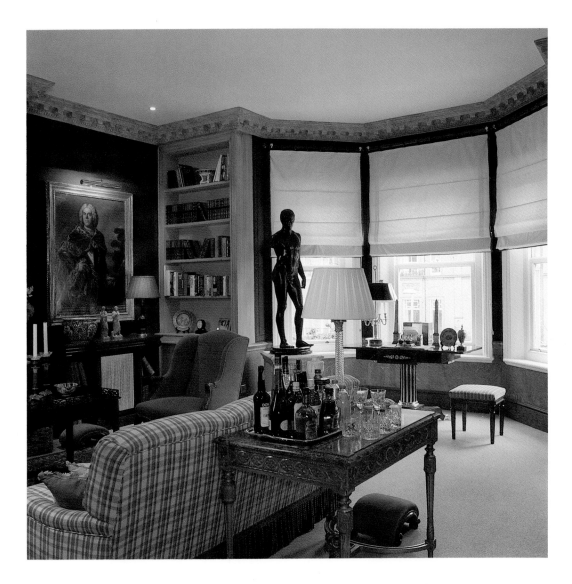

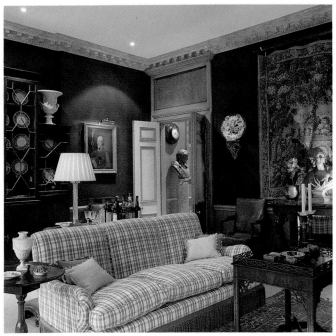

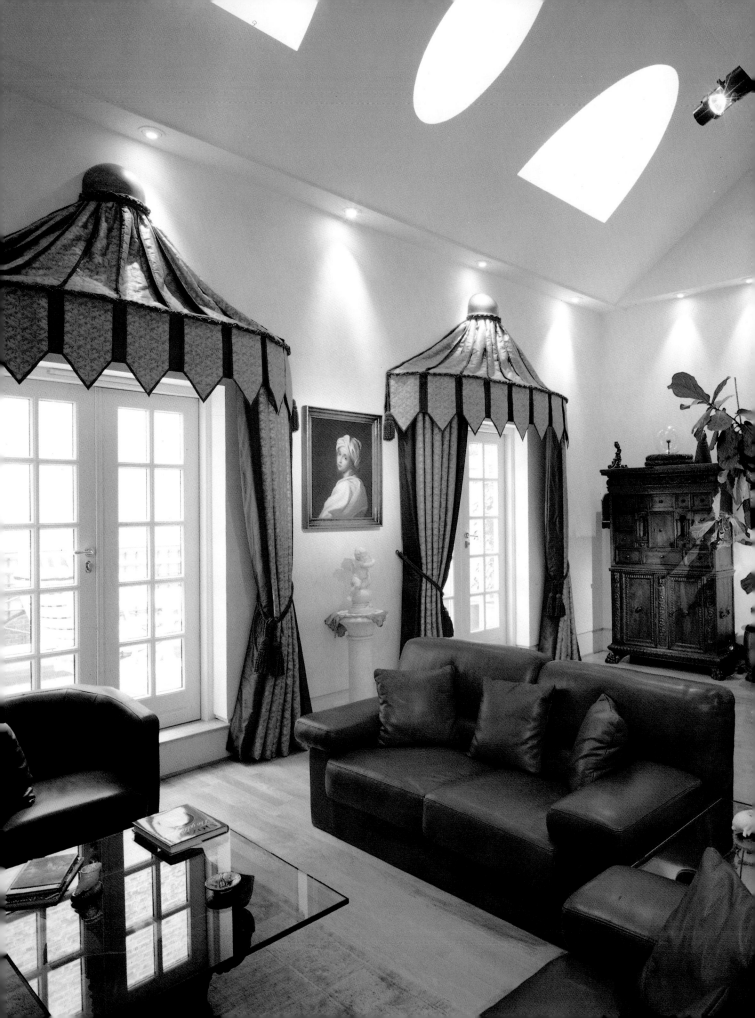

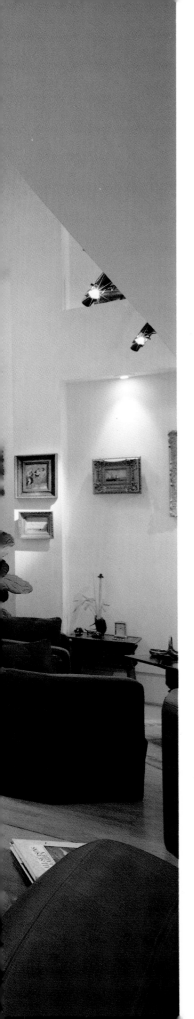

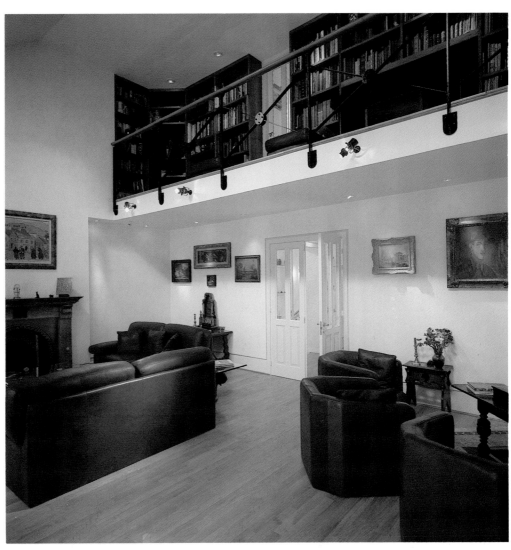

Modern medievalism

This sitting-room in a London mews house has been designed by Andrea Cenci with originality and practicality. The insertion of a library gallery makes good use of the double-height space, while the shape of the room, with large windows piercing the sloping ceiling, is full of visual interest. Traditional mouldings have been eschewed in favour of a lighting system which outlines the room's architecture and creates dramatic shapes within a variety of textures. Beneath the ceiling windows are French doors leading on to a balcony terrace. The curtains have been designed with humour to resemble jousting tents, their medieval connection reiterated in the sixteenth-century Florentine cabinet.

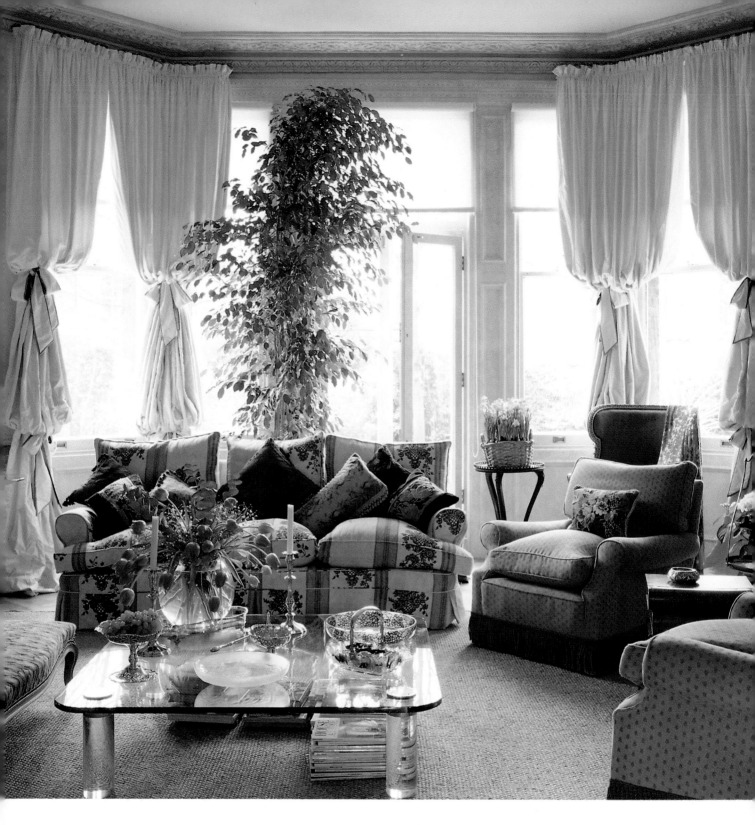

A leafy outlook

What first attracted interior decorator, Jenny Phillips, to her London flat was the exceptional drawing-room with French windows opening on to a secluded garden. In order not to hide the view, the creamy chintz curtains, with fine blue edging, are permanently tied back at high and low levels. The room's parchment-and-pink palette is prettily echoed in the painted Provençal door panel leaning, casually, against the wall.

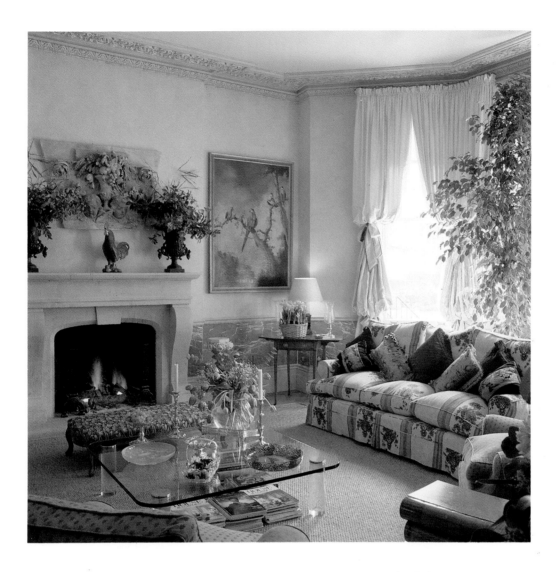

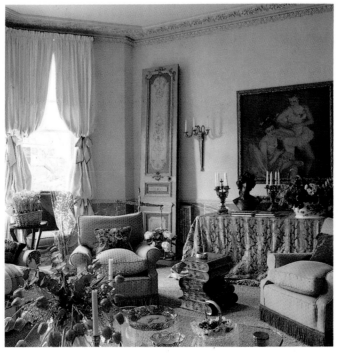

Decoration in detail

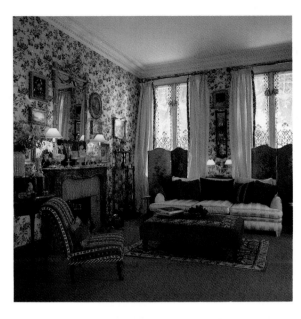

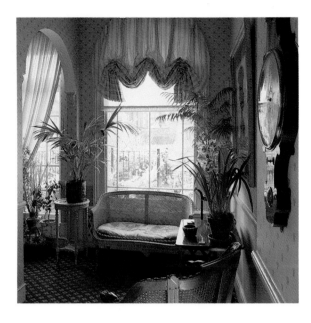

Embroidered voile panels screen the upper part of these full-height windows in a Parisian sitting-room, devised with advice from Sabine Marchal. Folding screens ensure daytime privacy at a lower level, while vivid yellow silk curtains give a sunny aspect to the urban interior, even on dull days.

Traditional, Georgian-style, arch-headed windows have such agreeable shapes that it is a pity to hide them with conventional curtains and pelmet. Here, in a house in London decorated by Christophe Gollut, the architectural form remains unimpaired, thanks to a specially curved festoon blind with pleated heading.

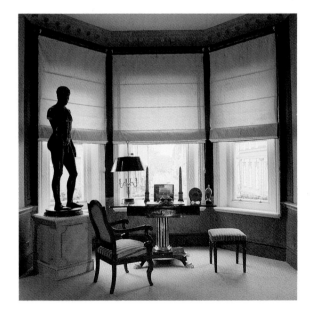

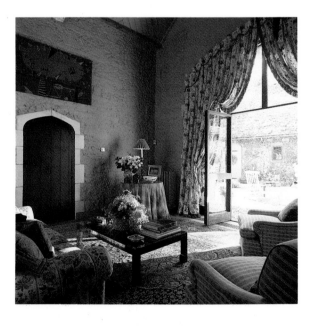

The tripartite bay window of a nineteenth-century flat in Belgravia, designed by Brian Juhos, has ultra-simple Roman blinds made of natural-coloured sailcloth. As a backdrop for carefully poised furniture and an imposing statue, the plain treatment is dramatically effective. (See, too, pages 180–181.)

The family sitting-room of a converted coach-house in Salisbury, decorated by Karen Armstrong of Pavilion Designs, is dominated by a vast window with doors opening on to an inner courtyard. Trimmed with blue fringe and cord, the curtains of the archway are reefed back at two levels, softening the expanse of glazing.

Decoration in detail

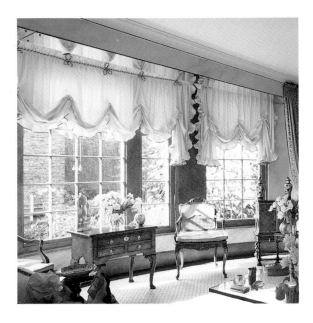

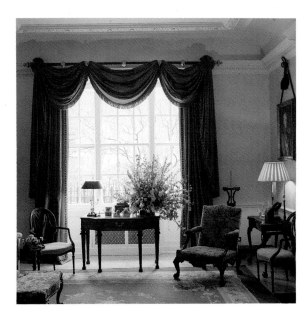

The wide, shallow proportions of this bay window present problems for curtaining, but the charmingly light confections at the windows, combined with dress curtains hung from the beam, are ideal solutions. The ceiling of the bay is faced with mirror to reflect more light and to suggest greater height.

This curtain treatment in a house in London, decorated by Bob Perkins, is Regency-inspired. The generously swagged pelmet, attached to the mahogany pole by brass fittings, has long tails falling from buttoned rosettes. The curtains are made of the same raspberry-pink fabric and trimmed with narrow braid.

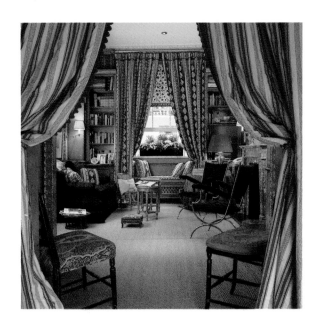

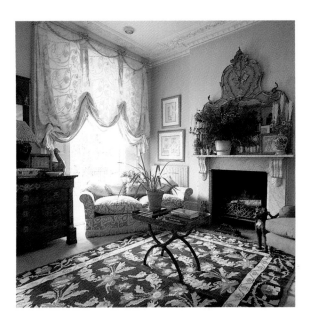

The doorway of a library/sitting-room by Monika Apponyi is theatrically curtained with striped silk. Beyond, the window has a double arrangement of curtains and blind in contrasting patterns. The curtains are caught back to frame a window seat, with cushions of the same fabric, and a window-box.

Made of vibrant yellow fabric printed with tassels and cord, these curtains are gathered up at wide-spaced intervals and decorated, wittily and prettily, with real cord. They are kept well back from the window, disclosing original shutters and, even more importantly in central London, an unusually leafy view.

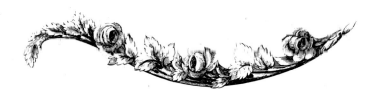

Country sophistication

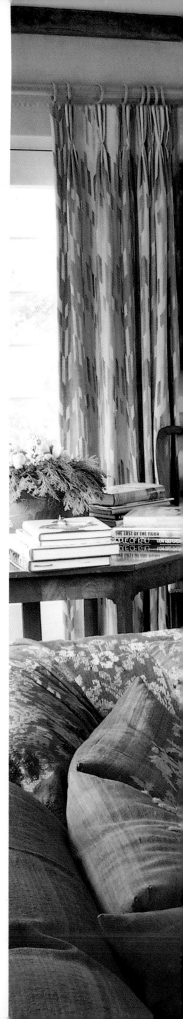

Many a town-dweller indulges a rural fantasy extending way beyond wearing a waxed green jacket in Fulham or driving a Range Rover in Mayfair. We see the fantasy being played out all around us, especially in interior decoration, with far more of the 'English country house' look in London than in all the shires of Britain put together. But the town-and-country fantasy is not entirely one-sided. Country-dwellers often show a preference for mild urbanization in their homes, using furnishing with a metropolitan suavity which is chic and consciously fashionable.

Part of the reason for this cross-fertilization is undoubtedly the emergence of the second home. When weekends in a tiny, primitive cottage turned out to be less comfortable than weekdays in the city, extra comforts were added and there was a general grading-up of all the rural furnishings. Back in town, however, home suddenly began to feel less satisfying, lacking the 'character' of cottage life, so the rooms were countrified, just a bit, with rugged paint effects, rustic furniture, unpretentious sisal matting. The combination might seem mildly artificial but the practical and visual advantages are many. Now we can experience many different cultural associations, from rough-hewn beams to fine antique furniture, all within the same setting.

Only a few of the rooms in this chapter represent the English chintz look, simply because that theme permeates many of the chapters. Here, settings tend to have a more bucolic, more rustic emphasis, with exposed beams, big open fireplaces, echoes of Provence. Some are prestigious but others are in cottages decorated with heightened style and a touch of grandeur.

(Right) The decorative elements of this drawing-room are entirely foreign to an English rural setting, yet they have taken up residence in a seventeenth-century house in Wiltshire with the utmost ease. They combine the early sophistication of a Roman bust with the more ethnic patterns of the Cretan tapestries on the sofa. Above the Louis XV settle is a seventeenth-century Dutch painting framed by a Turkish embroidery.

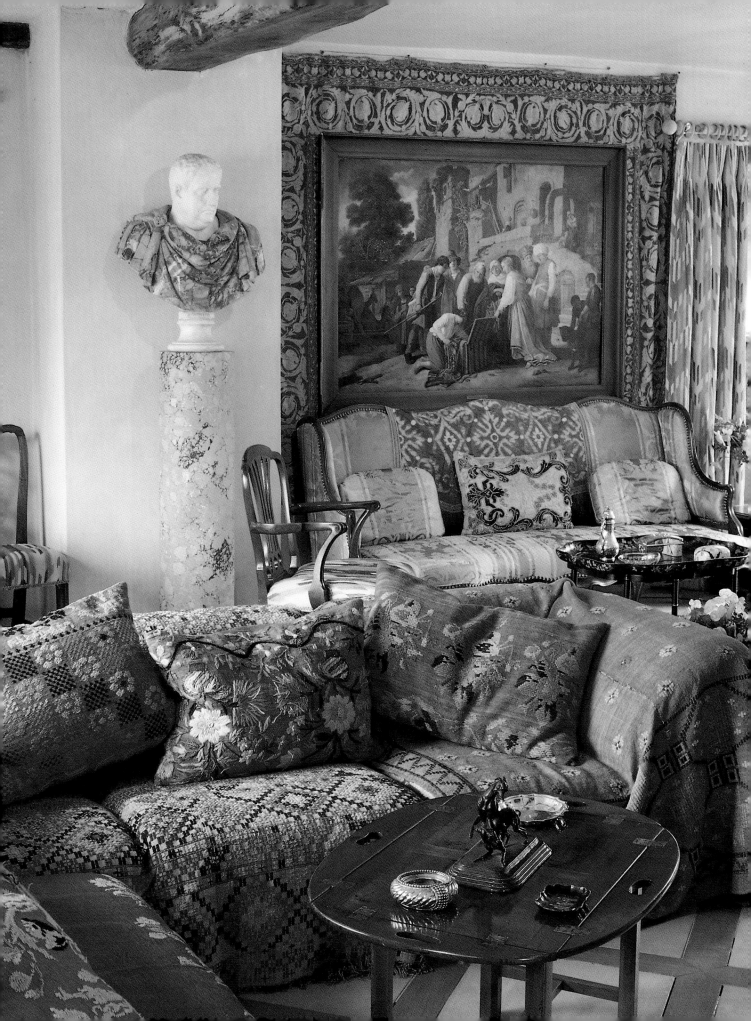

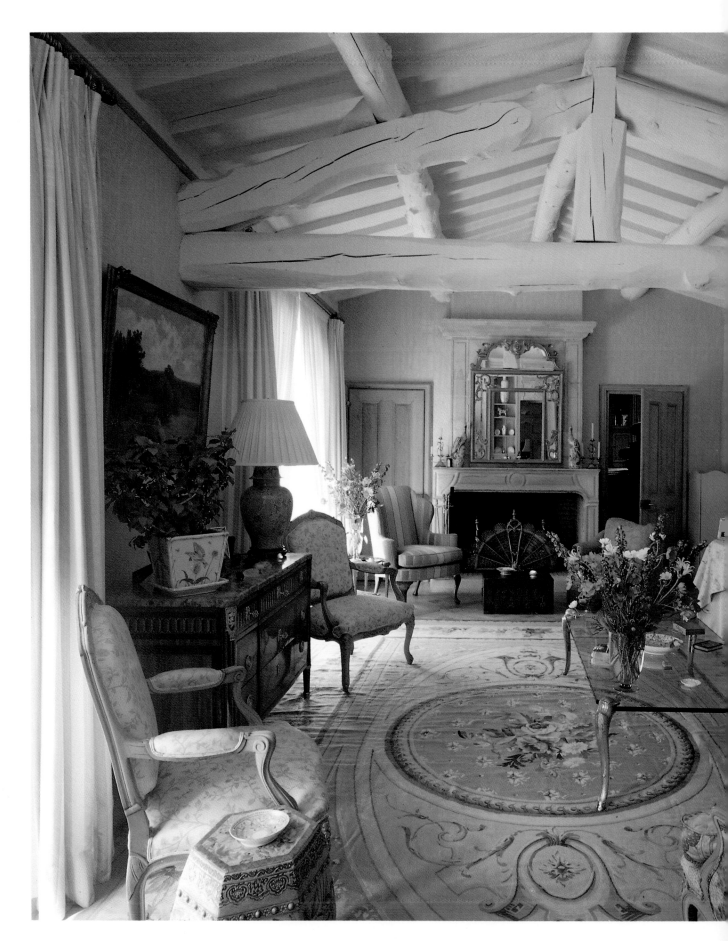

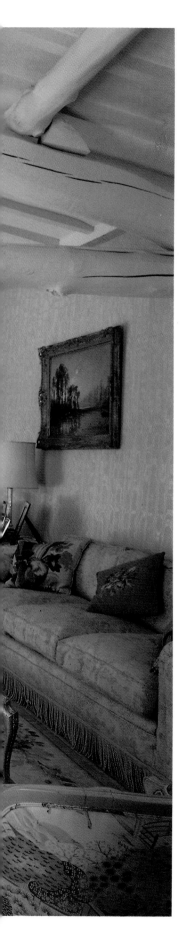

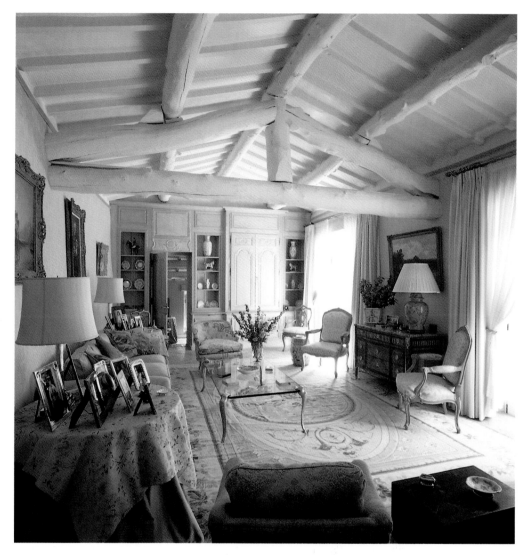

From New York to Provence

The location is Provence and the roof is unmistakably that of
an ancient building in the country, but the furniture is
sophisticated and highly finished, with notable examples of
eighteenth-century craftsmanship. The handsome commode
and carved *fauteuils* are part of a collection of antiques which
was brought by James and Patricia Campbell from their
previous home in the city of New York, and which now looks
uncommonly effective in a totally different, totally rural,
environment. The roof has been painted white for greater
lightness, but the rugged timbers are nevertheless a surprising
juxtaposition with such fine furniture, paintings and Aubusson
carpet. Another surprise is the moiré wall-covering.

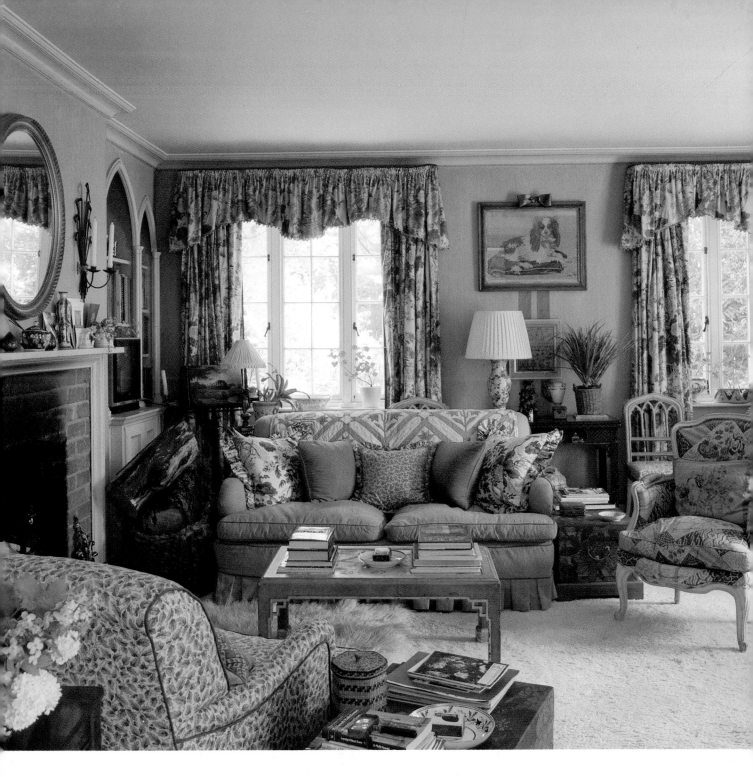

A decorative fusion

The arched form of the bookcases in this cottage sitting-room was inspired by the architectural style of the building. In a picturesque gothick folly, built in 1776, Elizabeth Hanley has made a room of appropriate simplicity and freshness, cleverly fused with comfort and finesse. Green and pink are the main colours, recurring on the painted furniture as well as in the patterned fabrics. Beyond the wide arch is the dining-hall, where the tracery of the chair-backs continues the gothick theme. When not in use, the chairs are placed against the walls which are painted with *trompe l'oeil* panels.

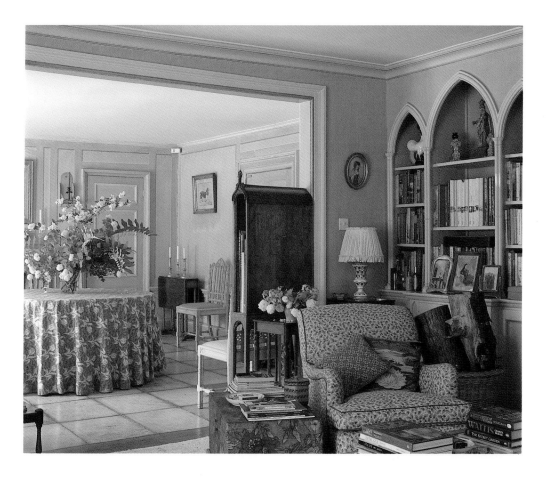

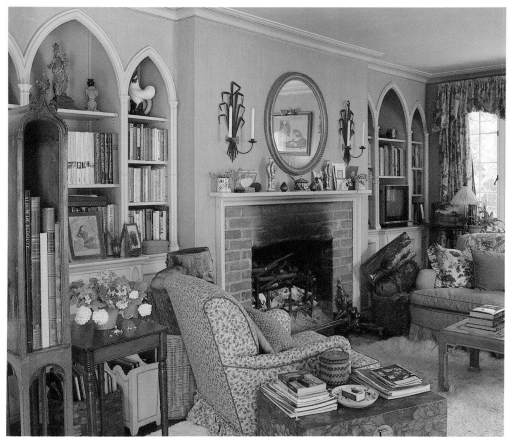

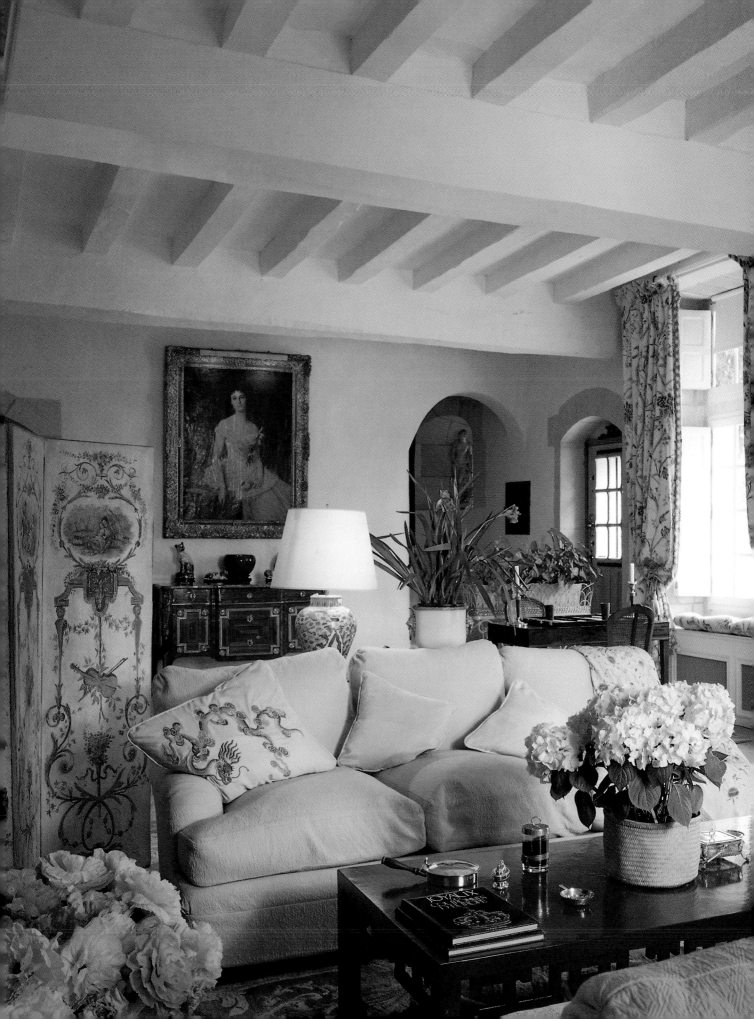

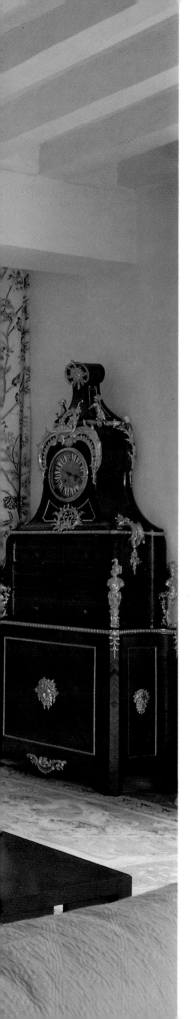

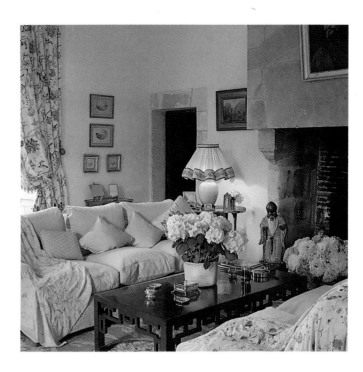

Behind a fortified façade

Massive beams and thick walls testify to the seventeenth-century origins of this room in a fortified *manoir* in the Loire Valley, but the monumentality and rural nature of the building have not been allowed to dominate the style of decoration. The furniture is certainly not rustic – the Louis XVI clock between the windows is a particularly impressive piece – and nor are the colours and textures. Delicate and refined, they were chosen by the Duchesse de Caraman to brighten the rather brooding architecture, especially the massive stone chimneypiece. The background of the exquisite floral silk curtains established the ivory and cream tones used for the walls and upholstery. The stone-flagged floor is overlaid with fine, pastel-coloured rugs.

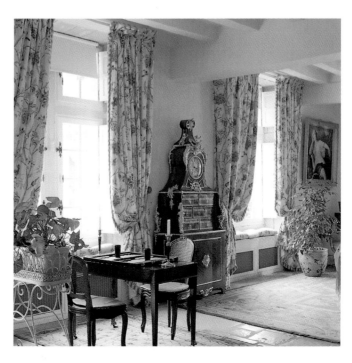

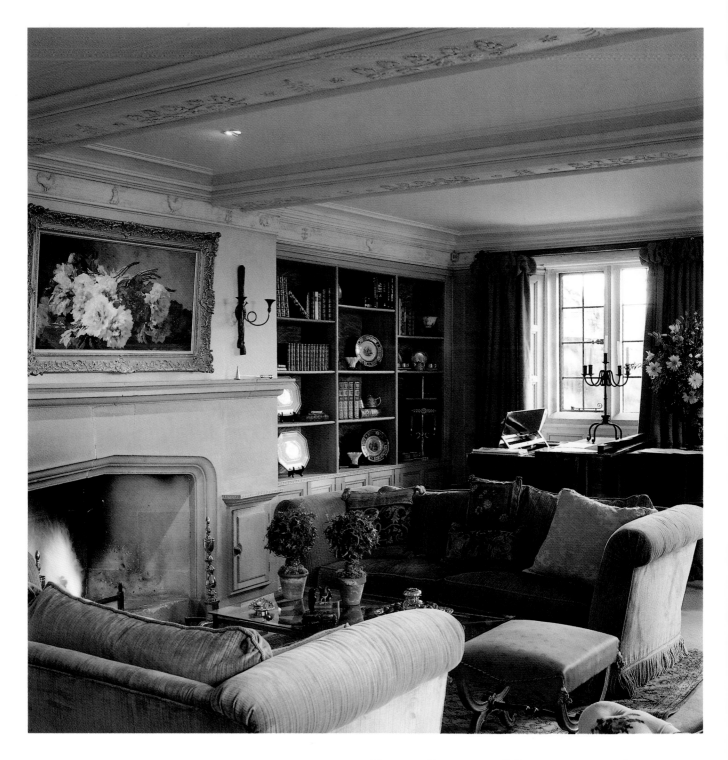

In a Cotswolds manor-house

Enchanting images of animals and birds characterize the cornice in this drawing-room, a 1920s addition to a mellow Cotswolds manor-house with a reassuring and unaffected style of decoration. The room is used frequently for entertaining, so seating for at least eighteen people was a prime specification in the brief to Woodstock Designs. The scheme, which strikes a

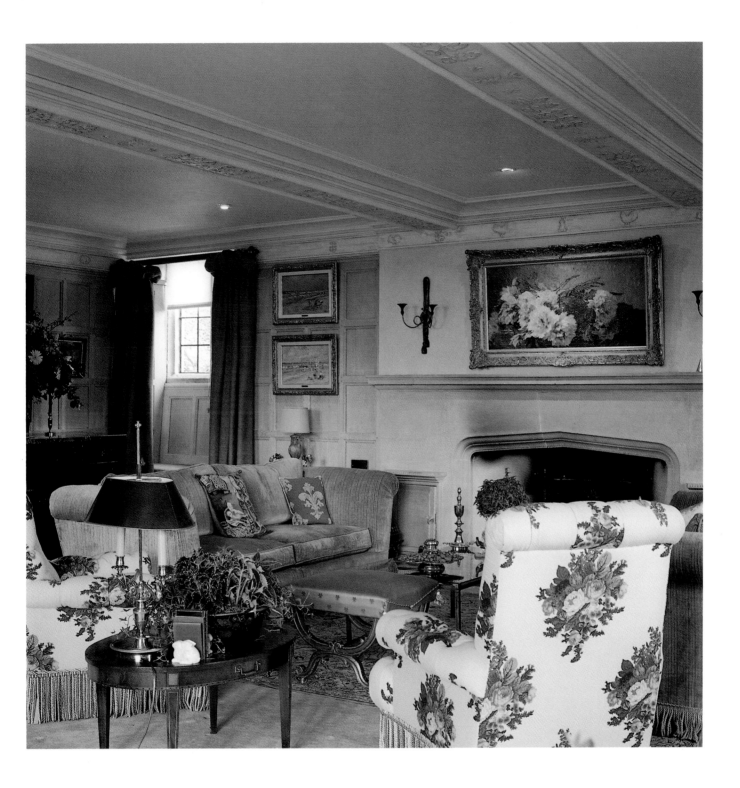

fine balance between rural casualness and urbane composure, copes effortlessly with this number and also finds space for a piano. The limed oak panelling and stone chimneypiece contrast happily with ruched silk curtains, embroidered cushions and velvet upholstery, their colours chosen to complement the painting above the chimneypiece.

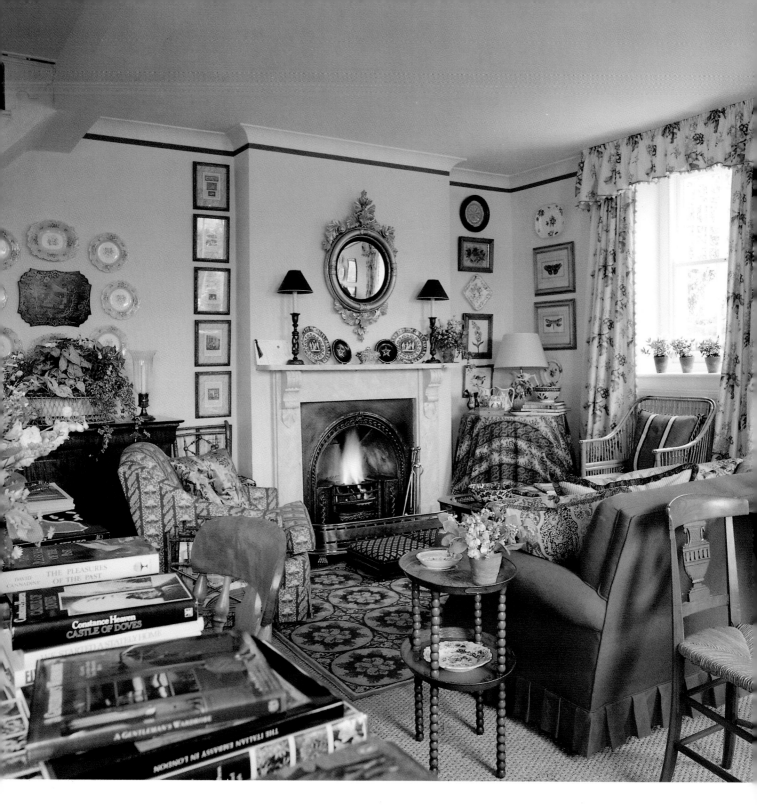

A wayward naturalness

Bright yellow walls emphasize the sunny aspect of this sitting-room in a cottage in Wales. The mood is bright and relaxed, engendered by exuberant patterns and decorative objects, displayed in a lively, informal manner. Pine furniture and terracotta flowerpots heighten the rural theme, but these more rustic elements are unpredictably partnered by gilded mirrors and other sophisticated pieces. The room, which has a natural, wayward charm, was decorated with advice from Jo Robinson.

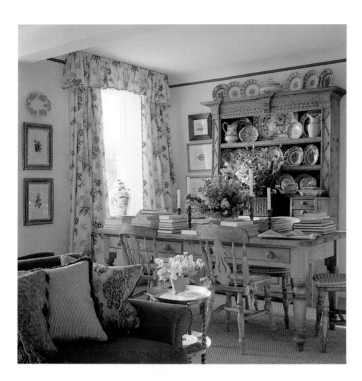

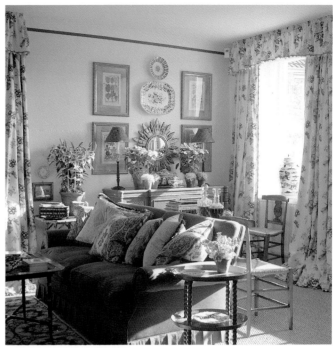

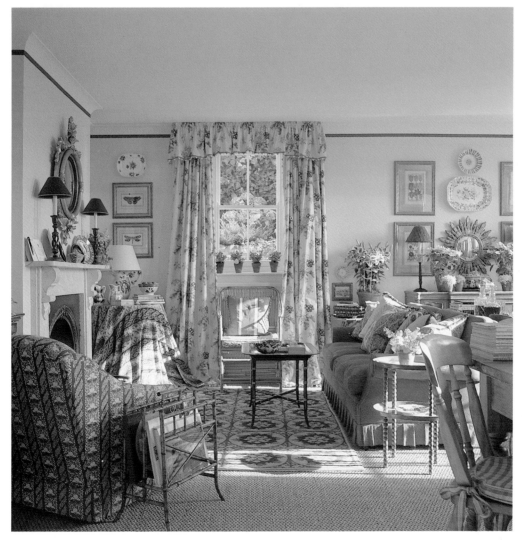

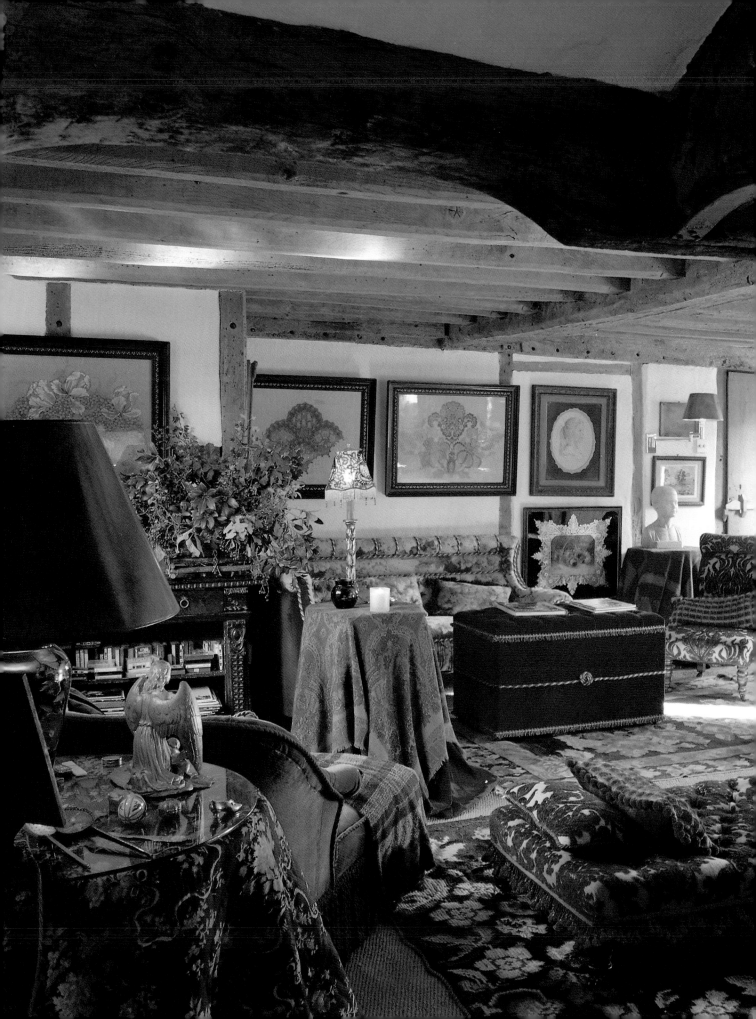

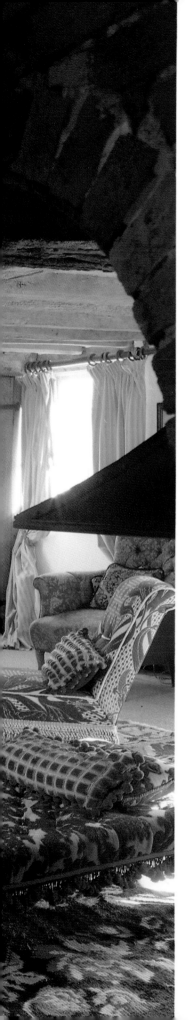

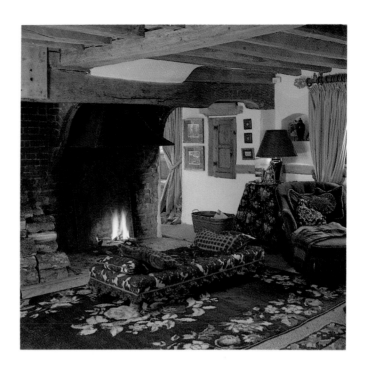

Seasonal contrasts

Charged with rich colours and fabrics, this is obviously a room for winter. Intimacy and invitation are the major characteristics, effected by deep-buttoned upholstery and a multitude of textures and patterns. All have been selected to create visual warmth and to offer a seasonal contrast to the adjoining summer drawing-room, shown on pages 202–203. The confident medley combines grandeur with rusticity, while reflecting Andrea de Montal's enthusiasm for Victorian furniture. She has covered the sofas, armchairs and ottomans with nineteenth-century textiles in sumptuous reds, golds, blues and greens, edged with fringes, tassels and cording. Above this profusion, gigantic beams hark back to a more rudimentary time when the room formed part of a monastery.

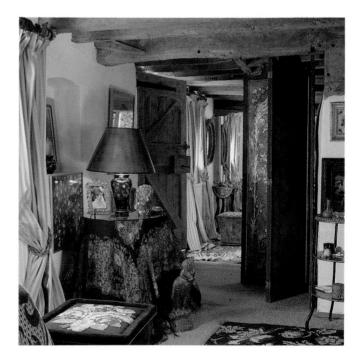

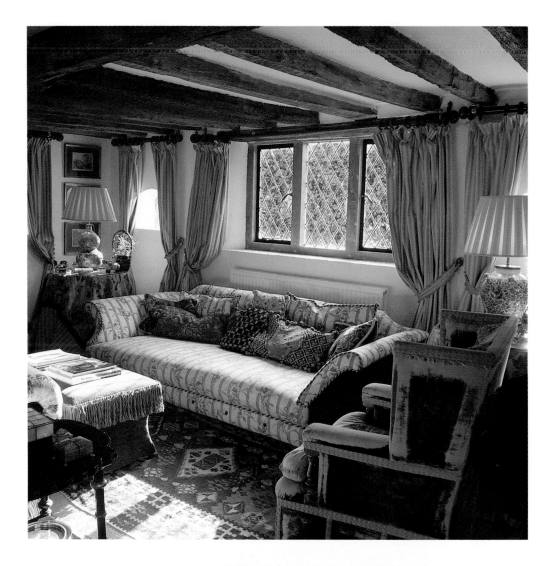

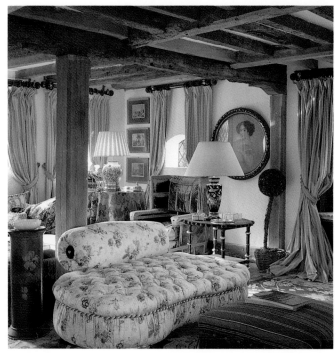

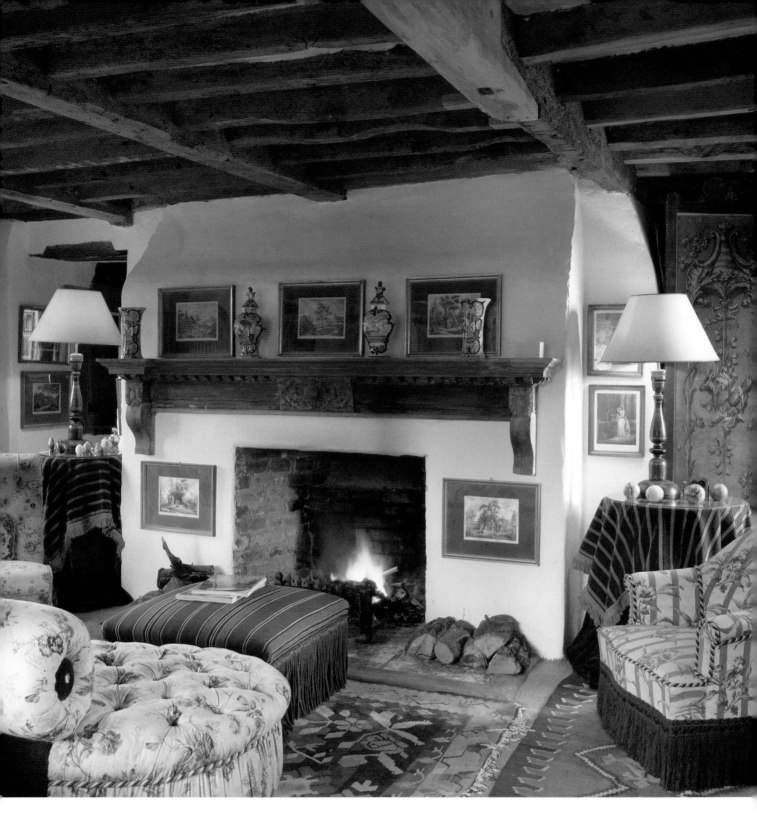

Beams and posts

Within a rustic framework, Andrea de Montal has made a drawing-room which is light and pretty, orchestrated for use in summer. A vast Edwardian foyer seat faces the fireplace and semi-divides the room into two seating-areas.

The second area concentrates on a long, splayed-arm sofa. The pastel colours of the fabrics are in deliberate counterpoint to the deep tones in the adjoining winter sitting-room, illustrated on pages 200–201.

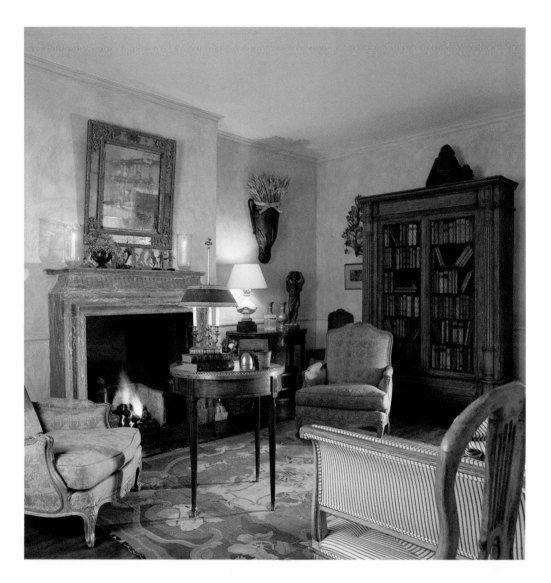

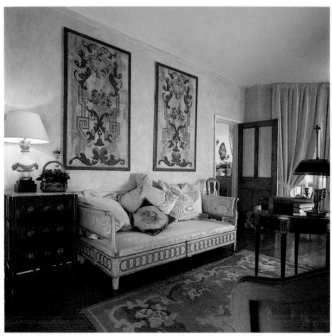

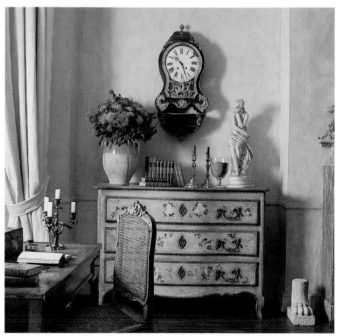

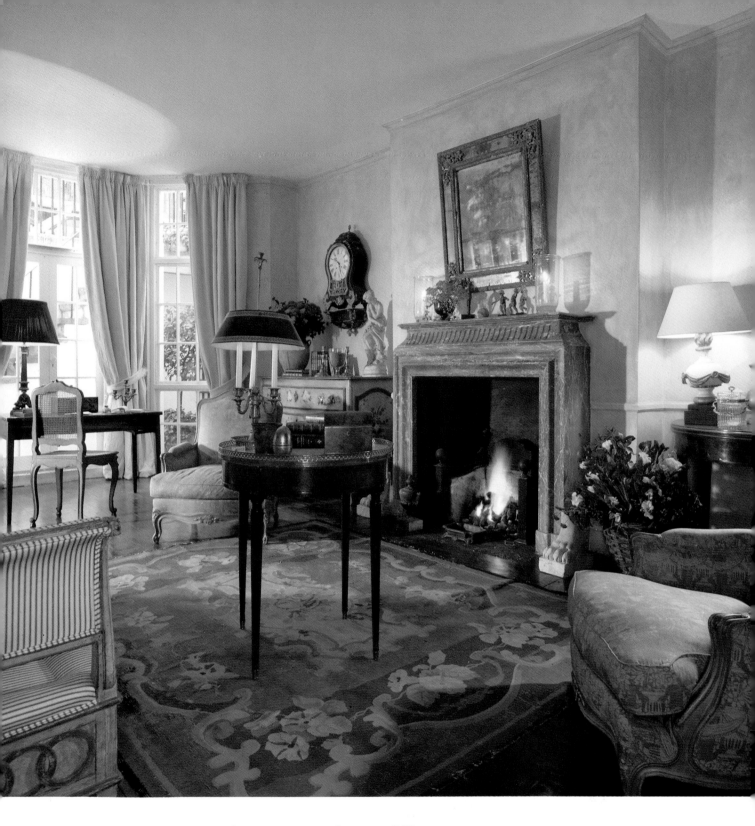

An evocation of Provence

Lauriance Rogier is a brilliant exponent of the art of painting furniture, and her sitting-room in London contains many examples of her work as well as allusions to her native Provence. The imposing *armoire* has *trompe l'oeil* panels of books; the Provençal chest of drawers is charmingly flowered; and the painted Swedish bed has a frieze of decorative roundels. The walls were given several coats of heavy emulsion, then 'pulled' with a large brush to create the pleasing irregularity seen in old Mediterranean farmhouses. The room evokes a rural ideal but is decidedly chic.

Decoration in detail

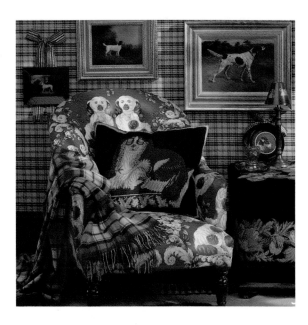

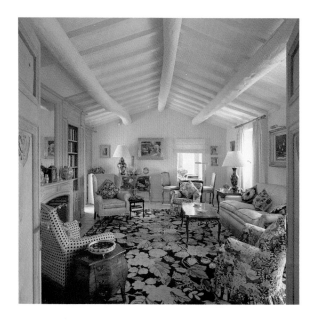

Inextricably linked with country living, dogs are the decorative theme in this setting by Anne Hardy. These dogs, however, would adapt equally well to city living and make no demands on their owners. Some of the representations may be naïve, but their presence in interior decoration is decidedly sophisticated.

In a sitting-room in Provence, James and Patricia Campbell have chosen an accomplished style of interior decoration for a rugged form of building. The two styles work well together, creating an interesting interior far removed from the stereotype *style rustique* seen in so many houses in the French countryside.

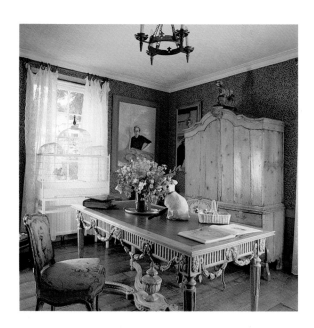

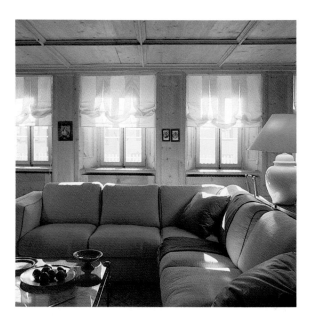

This room in the home of artists Elizabeth Organ and Eugene Fisk shows an agreeably artistic disdain of convention. The furniture is a maverick mix of styles, a simple country *armoire* contrasting with an elaborately carved table. 1980s portraits by Eugene Fisk hang against 1890s wallpaper by William Morris.

The stylish character and informal sophistication of this sitting-room in an alpine chalet, designed by Gerard Bach, refutes the clichéd Swiss images of stuffiness and cuckoo clocks. The natural colour and texture of the upholstery is an appropriate, unpretentious choice against natural wood panelling.

Decoration in detail

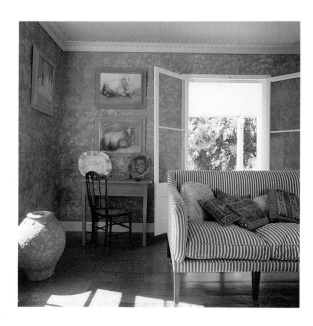

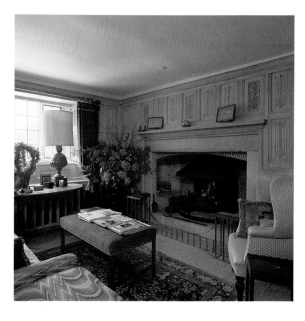

Walls coloured to match the copper beech outside are the background for sheep pastels by Susan Milne in the sitting-room of Elizabeth Organ and Eugene Fisk. The impression is countrified but not in a predictable way. Its charm derives from simplicity and openness, plus a hint of bohemianism.

Liming has brought out the soft honey tones of the panelling in this setting in a Cotswolds manor-house. The vast fireplace is the ultimate country emblem but the room, decorated with advice from Woodstock Designs, avoids the chintzy fussiness often associated with country-house decoration.

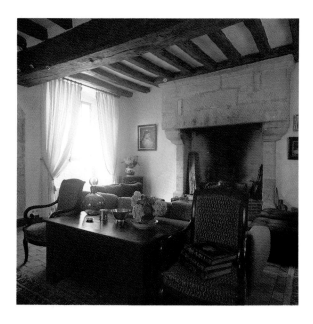

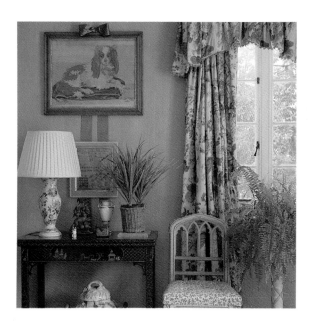

In the Loire Valley home of Patrice Mauny, chestnut beams, a tiled floor and massive stone chimneypiece epitomize the French country idyll. The sitting-room is furnished very simply but very precisely. Upholstered seating is ranged, U-shape, in front of the fire, and a pair of armchairs flanks an antique chest.

This glimpse of Elizabeth Hanley's drawing-room in her gothick folly in Essex (also shown on page 192) reveals a true understanding of traditional English decoration. There is a happy, unaffected eclecticism, marrying a needlework portrait of a spaniel with a gothick chair and decalcomania lamp.

Deep-buttoned comfort

The nineteenth century was the great era for deep-buttoned upholstery. Along with endless folds of curtains and pelmets, massive fringes and elaborate tassels, deep-buttoning reflected the high-Victorian and Second Empire French taste for highly elaborate, over-stuffed and occasionally overpowering interiors. Now, in the late twentieth century, perhaps in reaction to hard-edged modern design, there has been a noticeable resurgence of interest in these extravagant and, admittedly, extremely comfortable decorative addenda.

As with all revivals, the current interpretation is subtly different from the original manner, though there are some obvious parallels, psychological as well as manifest. Deep-buttoned, or *capitonné*, upholstery satisfies the recurring wish for a room to look, as well as be, comfortable. Its lushness is deeply gratifying visually and has the built-in bonus of being supportive and cosseting physically. But whereas most of the deep-buttoned sofas and chairs shown in this chapter are authentic nineteenth-century examples, and many are covered in textiles of the period, several of the rooms in which they feature are light and colourful, quite unlike the sort of interiors favoured by our Victorian forebears. There is an eclectic juxtaposition of deep-buttoning and other forms of seating within settings which look traditional but evoke no particular period in history. These rooms are full of visual interest and range from the robust interpretation of the English country-house genre on pages 210–211 to the exceptionally pretty *pied à terre* on pages 212–213.

(Right) The perception of comfort has as much to do with appearance as with substance. Everything seen here conspires to generate a visual and actual warmth: the walls are lined with a gloriously patterned damask, the seat furniture is covered with soft velvets, and the colours throughout have a Titian glow. Deep-buttoning and cording emphasize the generous upholstery. The room was designed by Nancy Stoddart Huang.

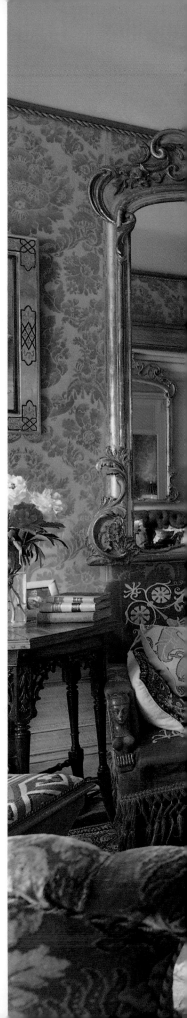

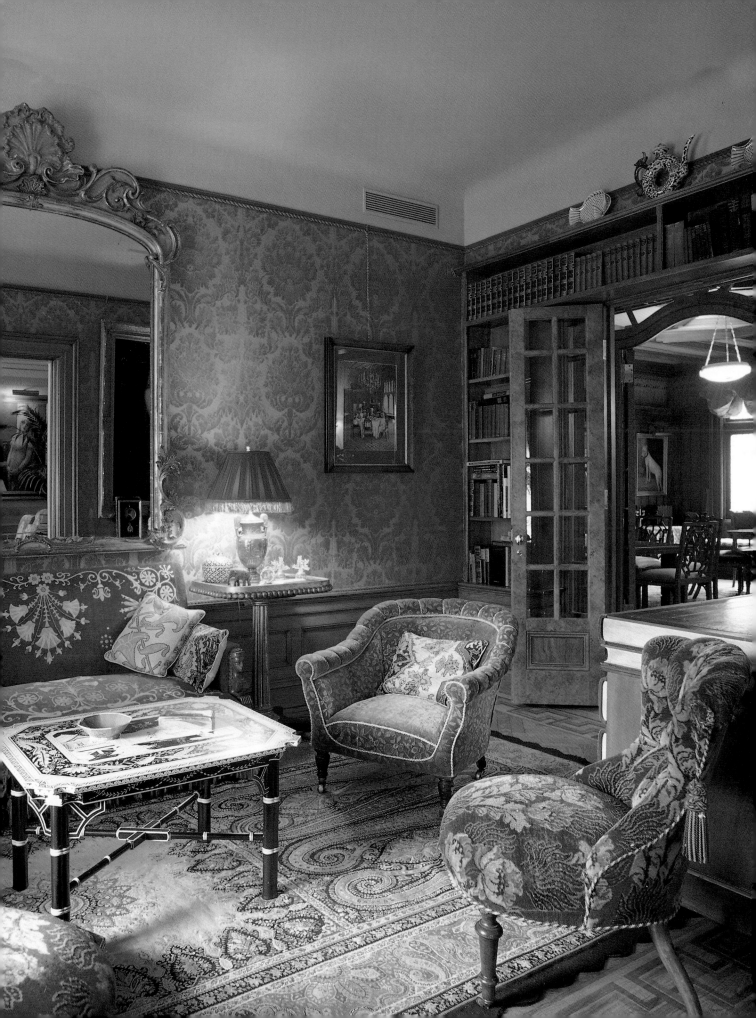

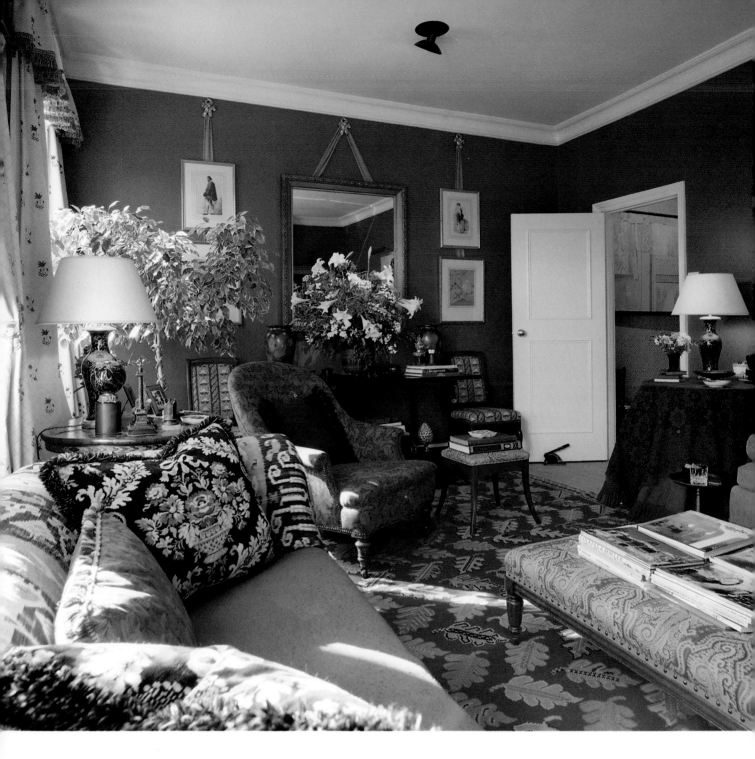

More and more red

Interior designer, Nelson Morrow, has decked out the sitting-room of his London flat in a crescendo of reds. His style manifests a country-house vocabulary, but there is a robust, masculine edge in the overall use of strong colour, which he feels is particularly enhancing to period furniture. He also likes to introduce an interesting dissonance by adding occasional touches of 'odd' colour. Here, the 'odd' colour is turquoise, represented by the chenille-upholstered sofa and silk picture ribbons. The arrangement of the room combines symmetry with casualness: bookcases are matched to either side of the chimneypiece, but the deep-buttoned armchair is pulled into the centre of the room to give a less rigid complexion. Plants defuse the strength of colour and pattern.

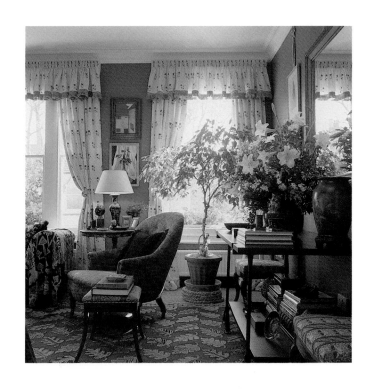

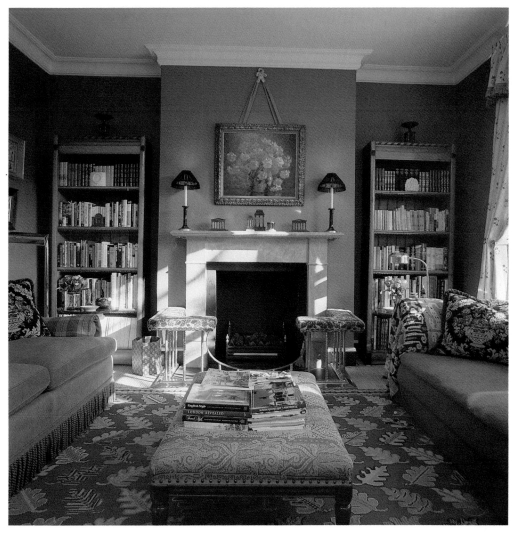

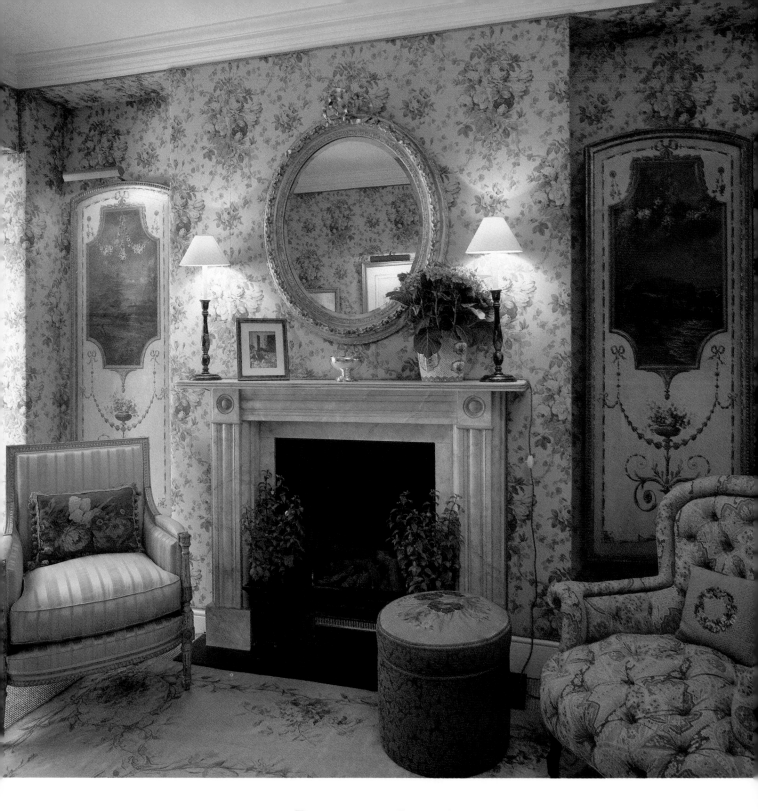

Pretty and petite

The London *pied à terre* of transatlantic decorator, Donna Ward, is very small, very pretty and very practical. Lined with a beautiful, faded-looking fabric printed with bouquets of roses, the drawing-room has several different styles of seating, chosen for comfort and shape, focused on a *faux* marble chimneypiece painted by Malcolm Connell. The floor is covered with sisal, a reticent background for the fine Aubusson rug in front of the fireplace. The decoration of the room was co-ordinated by Bellhouse & Co.

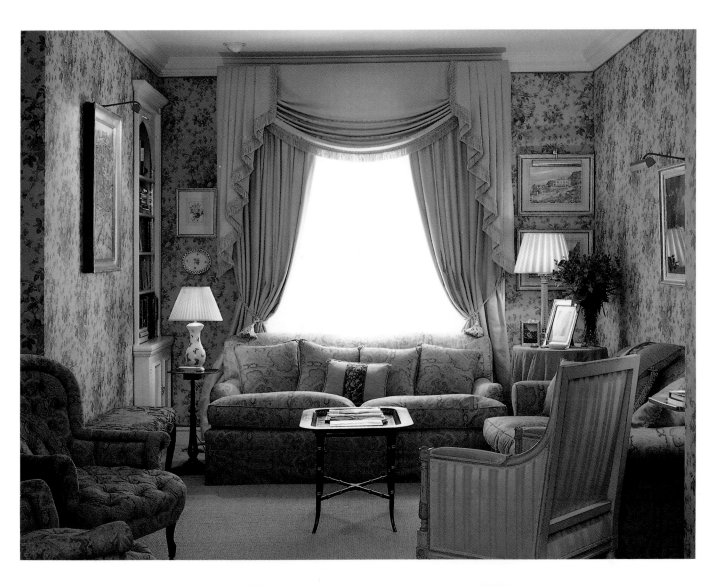

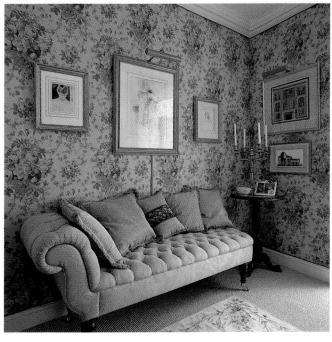

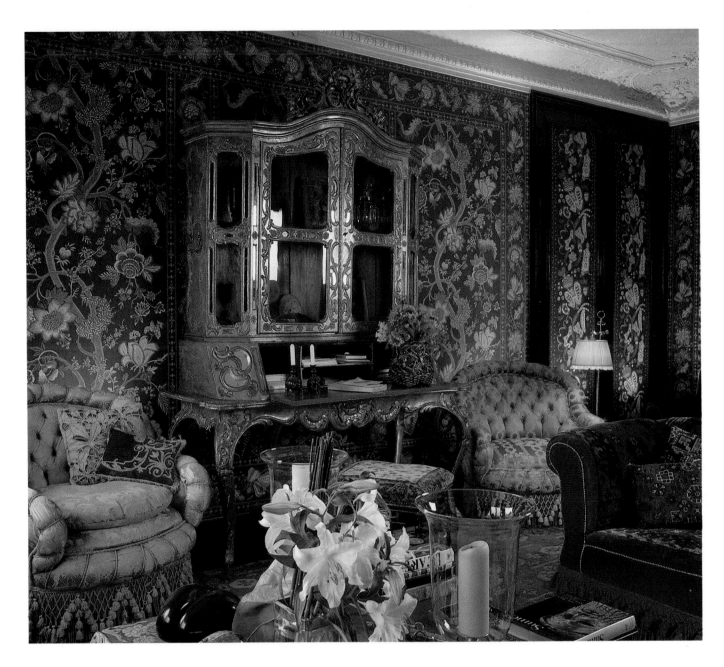

More pattern, more harmony

These interconnecting sitting-rooms display
resolution and confidence in the handling of
their decoration. There is no fear of mixing
patterns; no playing safe. The fabric on the
walls in both areas is busy, and the furniture
is elaborate, yet a harmony of 'weight' locks
the jigsaw together. Apart from the *capitonné*
chairs and deeply upholstered sofas, which
are mainly covered with antique textiles, the
most important pieces of furniture in the
larger room (above) are the carved giltwood
console and Italian cabinet. The fabric on the
walls was given an additional dip in a
specially-mixed solution to darken the
colours; then it was cut and stitched together
to form borders and panels. In the adjoining
room (opposite, below), the black
backgrounds of the wall fabric and kilim rug
have a unifying effect. This room leads, in
turn, to the dining-room, a stunning contrast
in shades of pale blue and grey with gold and
white highlights. The enfilade, leading from
dark to light, from intense pattern to pure
white, is a daringly successful scheme with a
singular Frenchness. The darker areas are
especially evocative of Napoleon III.

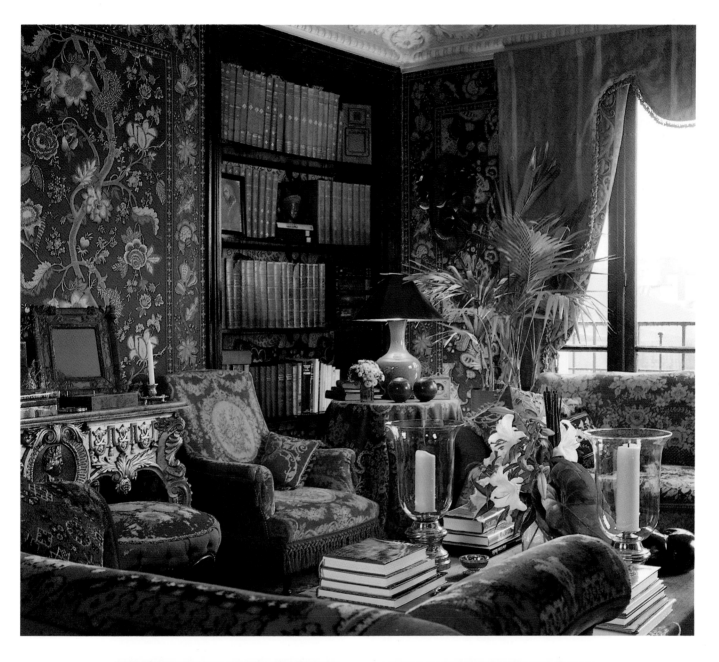

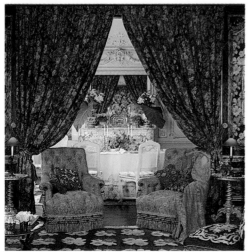

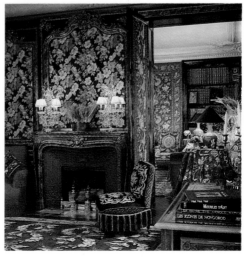

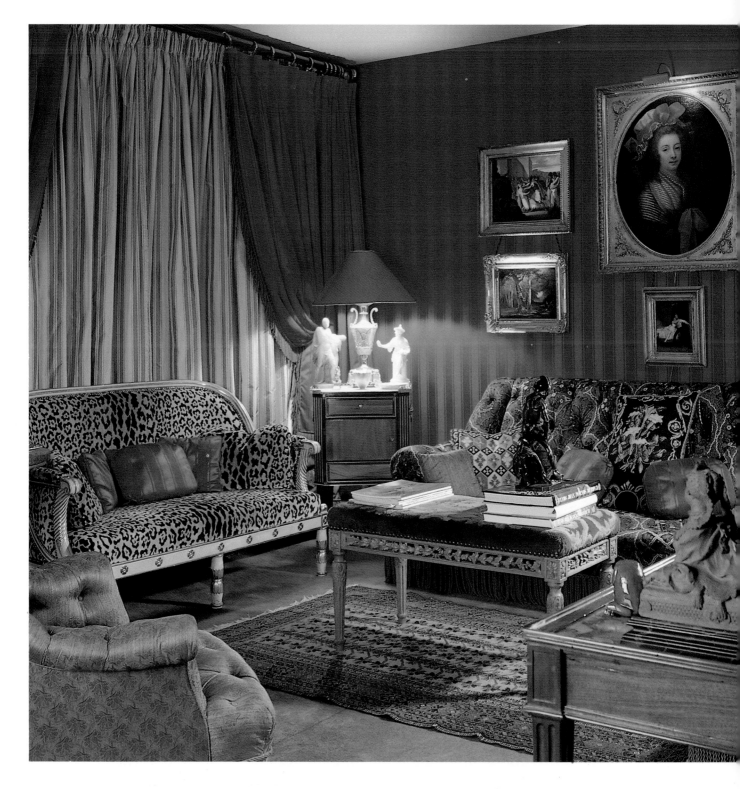

The ultimate bed-sitting room

Dominique Le Marquier's decoration of a one-room apartment in Paris comes fully into its own in the evenings when strategic lighting creates a dramatic chiaroscuro against a richly textured backdrop. Buttoned chairs face two sofas, one covered in silk 'leopardskin'. At the far end, to the left of the bureau, is a semi-open bedroom. The different functional areas are linked by the continuous decorative treatment.

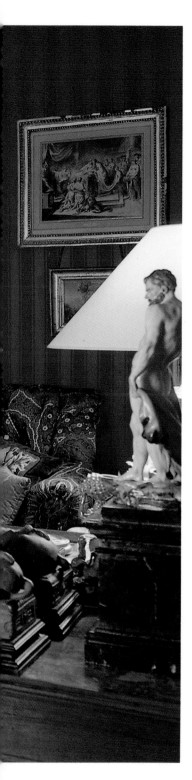

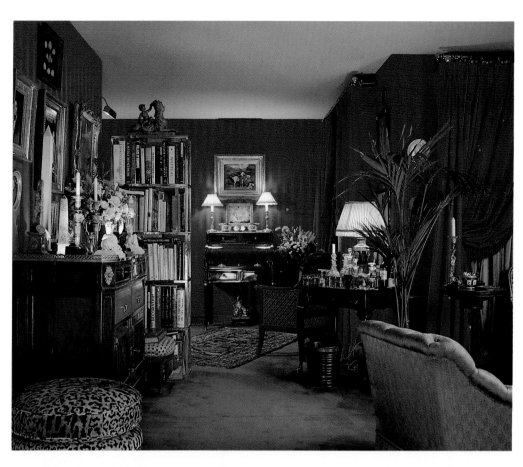

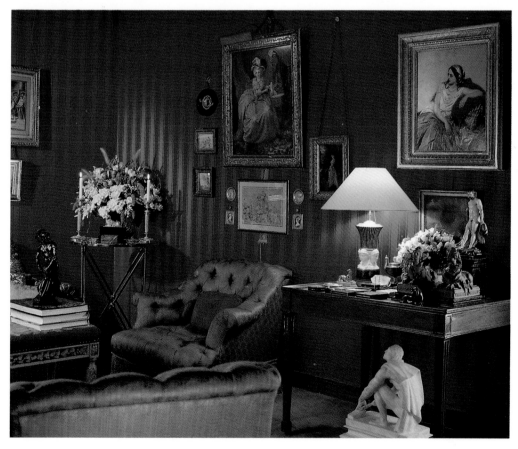

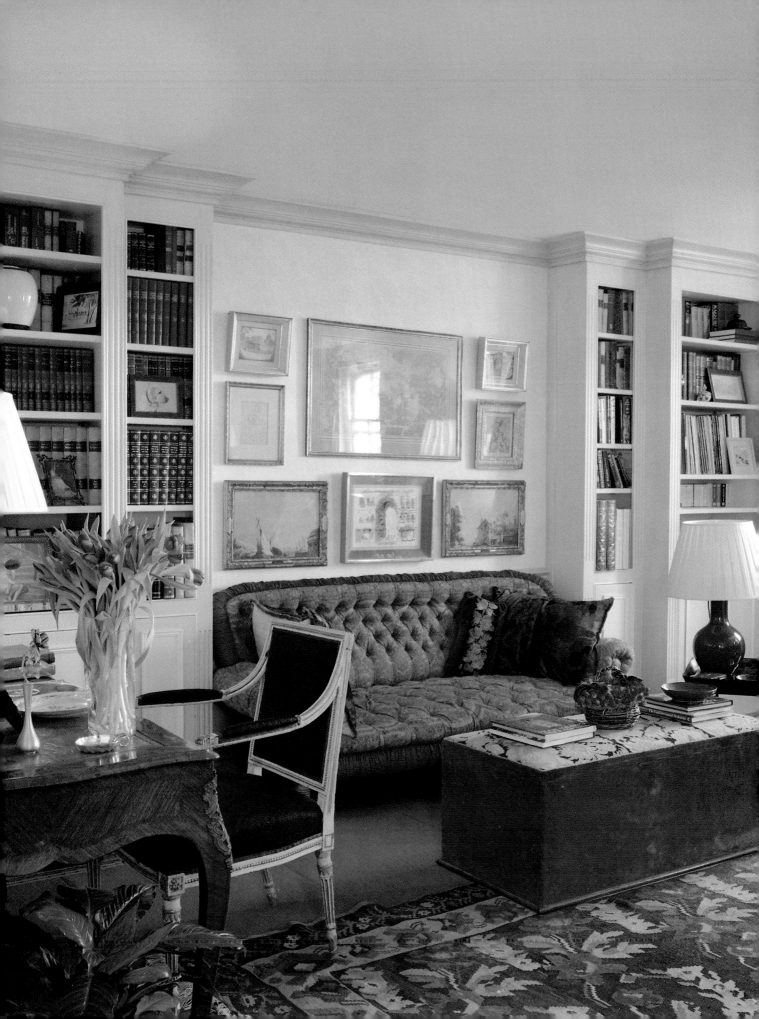

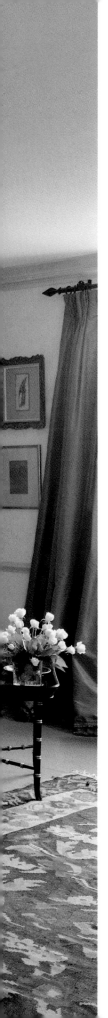

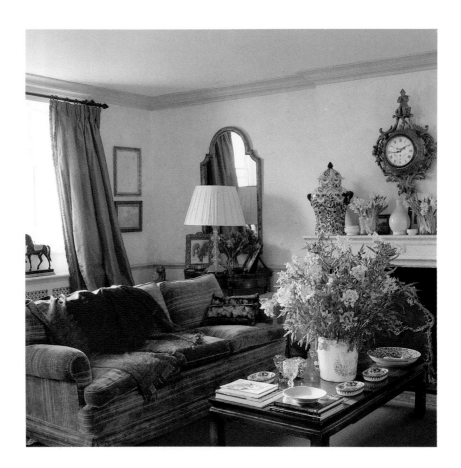

For greater interest and comfort

The long wall opposite the fireplace in this drawing-room in London, decorated by Penny Morrison for Maria Grazia Cameli, has been skilfully broken up to give a sense of movement and interest. The formation of two built-in, break-front bookcases has created a shallow alcove for a deep-buttoned sofa and an ordered array of pictures. In the traditional Italian manner, a clock is hung on the wall above the chimneypiece.

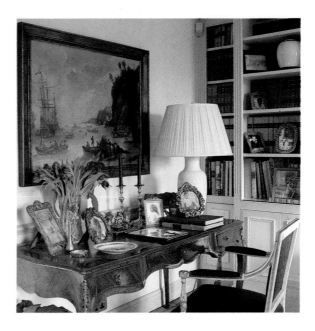

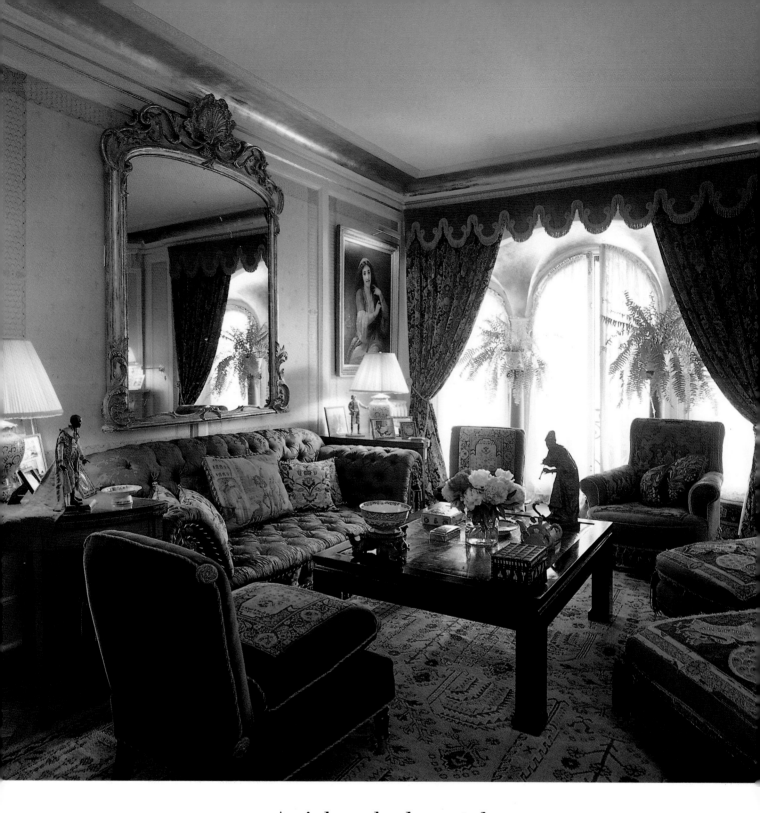

A richer, lusher style

Nancy Stoddart Huang, the owner-decorator of this room in New York, grew up in an environment where the furnishings were plain, stiff and formal. Her own style is a total reaction to this: everything is lush, comfortable and soothing. Here, the walls are stencilled with fleurs de lys within painted borders, accentuated with gold to echo the gilding of the cornice. There

is a nineteenth-century amplitude in the character of the seating, especially in the deep-buttoned sofa and pair of ottomans, upholstered respectively in richly patterned silk damask and velvets, all trimmed with silk ropes and tassels. The floor is covered with a large Turkish rug, bringing further enrichment to the setting.

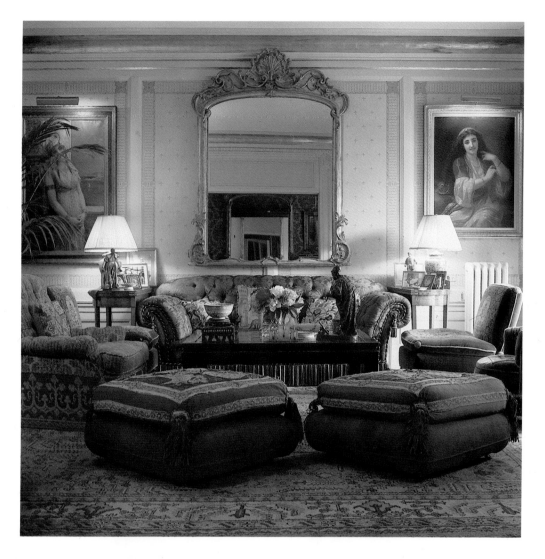

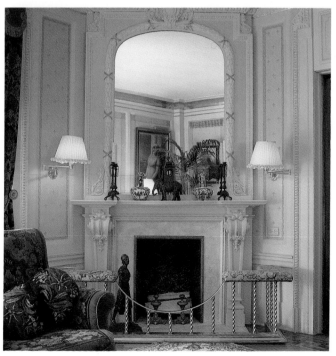

Decoration in detail

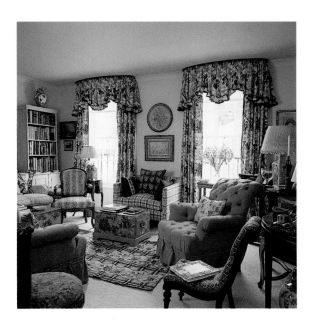

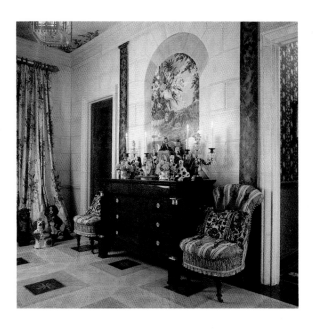

Elizabeth Hanley has turned what was previously a box-like flat into a comfortable home with much to satisfy the eye. The seating is especially important in conveying a sense of well-being. Two scroll-backed, deep-buttoned armchairs form part of a variegated group, with painted chests substituting for coffee-tables.

Side chairs, like hall chairs, are usually upright and wood-framed, but in Anne Le Coney's New York apartment, with *trompe l'oeil* by Robert Warshaw, a pair of nineteenth-century buttoned chairs, upholstered in striped silk, looks far more exciting than plain wooden ones. Note, too, the stencilled floor.

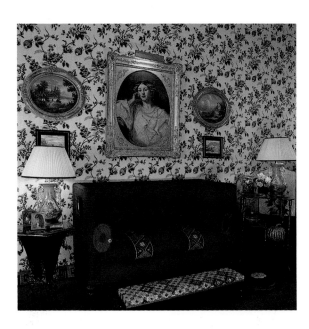

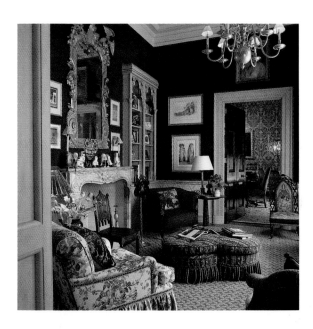

The upholstery of this high-backed, high-sided sofa in a sitting-room in Paris is an unorthodox combination of colours and fabrics. The ends of the bolsters are covered in bright mauve silk to match the buttoned support along the back, and bands of lozenge-patterned embroidery divide the seat into panels.

A trefoil-shaped pouffe, with a heavy fringe and buttoned cushion, takes centre-stage in a room designed by Nancy Kirwan Taylor. The walls are lined with red linen above a dado of fake gothic tracery painted by Emily Todhunter. Gothic bookcases, painted by Giles Gibb, continue the same aesthetic vocabulary.

Decoration in detail

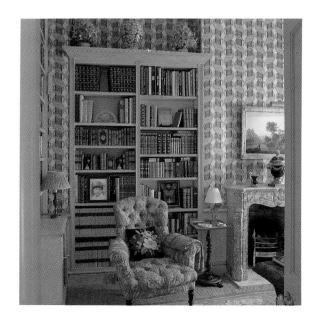

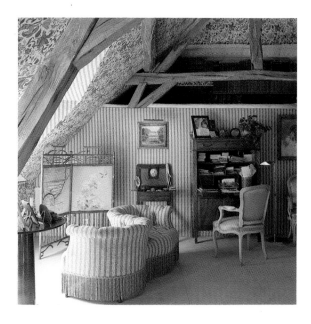

The buttoned armchair in this library/sitting-room in London, designed by Christophe Gollut, has a comfortable character without being cumbersome. The bookcase is recessed in an alcove formed by the chimneybreast and has been painted by Corinne Peers to simulate bird's eye maple.

A buttoned and striped conversation seat gives views in two directions in an attic sitting-area in a French chateau decorated by Elga de Caraman. Lit by a mansard window, the room uses patterns with a country informality, in keeping with the rural building. Just seen above the bureau is a small gallery library.

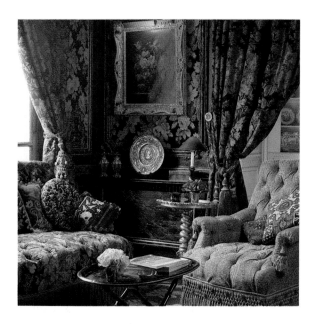

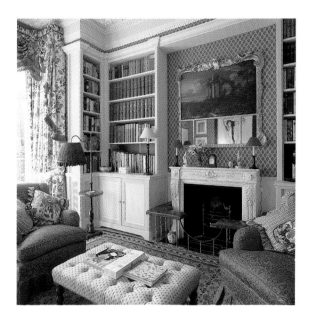

This room in Paris is a contemporary interpretation of French nineteenth-century Second Empire style, with masses of fabrics, tassels, fringes and *capitonné* seating. The accumulation of textiles, all-over patterns and over-stuffed upholstery is fundamental to the revivalist atmosphere. (See, too, pages 214–215.)

Deep-buttoned upholstery lends itself to rooms with books and open fires, where obvious signs of comfort seem especially relevant. Here, in a setting designed and decorated with advice from Christopher Smallwood and Jane Churchill, a buttoned stool and fender look more fitting than plain upholstery.

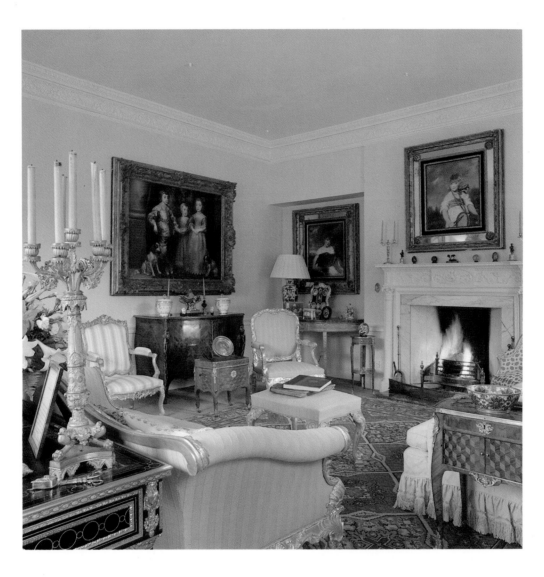

Gilded highlights: the drawing-room of a house in the West Country, shown on pages 90–91.